THE PRESS
AND THE
MODERN PRESIDENCY

THE PRESS
AND THE
MODERN PRESIDENCY

Myths and Mindsets
from Kennedy to Clinton

Louis W. Liebovich

PRAEGER

Westport, Connecticut
London

Library of Congress Cataloging-in-Publication Data

Liebovich, Louis.
    The press and the modern presidency : myths and mindsets from
Kennedy to Clinton / Louis W. Liebovich.
       p.   cm.
    Includes bibliographical references (p.) and index.
    ISBN 0–275–95926–0 (alk. paper)
    1. United States—Politics and government—1945–1989. 2. United
States—Politics and government—1989– 3. Presidents—United
States—History—20th century. 4. Press and politics—United
States—History—20th century. 5. Government and the press—United
States—History—20th century. I. Title.
E839.5.L495 1998
973.92—dc21   97–23010

British Library Cataloguing in Publication Data is available.

Library of Congress Catalog Card Number: 97–23010
ISBN: 0–275–95926–0

First published in 1998

Praeger Publishers, 88 Post Road West, Westport, CT 06881
An imprint of Greenwood Publishing Group, Inc.

Printed in the United States of America

The paper used in this book complies with the
Permanent Paper Standard issued by the National
Information Standards Organization (Z39.48–1984).

10 9 8 7 6 5 4 3 2 1

This book is dedicated to my wife, Shirley,
who is a fount of patience and understanding.

CONTENTS

IV. The 1990s: Starting Over

ACKNOWLEDGMENTS

I extend a special note of appreciation to Mitch Kazel, senior teaching associate in the Department of Journalism at the University of Illinois, for his Internet wizardry, and to Jennifer Simmons for her valuable research assistance. A note of thanks is offered also to Ellen Sutton, University of Illinois communications library director, for her invaluable help in finding research material.

PROLOGUE

GETTYSBURG, PA.—In an obvious attempt to polish his sagging image and quiet rumors about marital strife in the White House, President Lincoln traveled to this small town yesterday to offer words of comfort to grieving relatives.

As the war dragged into its third year and the Union suffered terrible losses here this week, the speech appeared to be as much a veiled attempt at an early re-election bid as a vehicle of consolation. Seeking to look presidential and to smooth over the latest verbal indiscretions by his wife, Mary Todd Lincoln, the somber president counseled his listeners to remember the sacrifices soldiers suffered on the nearby battlefield.

Polls just released yesterday show that Lincoln's war policies are quickly losing favor. Forty-eight percent of respondents indicated that the president was not prosecuting the war successfully, while only 15 percent found the president's war strategy acceptable.

Democratic leaders in Congress labeled Lincoln's Pennsylvania speech as "demagoguery."

Had Abraham Lincoln delivered his immortal Gettysburg Address in the second half of the twentieth century, it is likely that the above news story, or something quite similar, would have found its way into a major newspaper the next day. It is the way the presidency was covered 125 years after Lincoln's era.

That is not to say that Lincoln did not have his detractors or that newspapers did not attack him editorially while he was in office. They just did so in a different way. Politically and regionally partisan, the newspapers of the day were bent on unabashedly furthering their own ideological and political agendas. To them, the president represented his party and its philosophy. They either heartily agreed or violently disagreed.

But in the latter part of the twentieth century, media coverage had traveled through eras of objectivity and interpretation, and reporting on the presidency had become much more complex and quantified. Journalism was different, and media had changed. Journalists sought objectivity but often muddied this goal with personal observation and interpretation laced with innuendo and meaningless poll data.

Public visions of the White House became steady streams of instantaneous snippets intoned daily by photogenic television reporters instead of flowery dispatches written by vagabond literati, who graced the White House only infrequently during Lincoln's time. Much of what Americans learned about the presidency in the 1860s they read in low-circulation newspapers in scattered villages. In the late twentieth century, Americans gleaned their vision of the White House to a great extent from thirty-second packaged summaries: assessments of the entire day's activities boiled down to three paragraphs read from monitors and broadcast nationwide through a prodigious collection of equipment conveniently set up on the White House lawn, or through wire service or major newspaper reports.

The changing nature of communications in the United States has altered the role and perception of the presidency. This book explores how the media evolved from 1960—a hundred years after Lincoln and during the birth year of the television-dominated presidency—to the final years of the century, when a succession of failed administrations had soured voters on White House politics.

The bogus news item that begins this chapter embodies the prototype of reporting that surrounded the White House in the last three decades of the twentieth century after the Kennedy and Johnson administrations. By the time Bill Clinton assumed office in 1993, international or domestic initiatives and speeches by the president were often perceived in media reports as efforts to improve the president's standing with the public. Political motivations were seen hidden everywhere, and any attempt to bargain with foreign or domestic leaders was accompanied by a reference to the latest public opinion surveys. Coverage was often nauseatingly personal, and national events and issues were frequently submerged by a morass of commentary and personal observation. Thus, as is exemplified here, reference to the actual content of Lincoln's historic Gettysburg Address is withheld until the second half of the third paragraph. Journalists of the early 1990s likely would not recognize an historic speech because they would not be inclined to give credit to expressed wisdom. They would not want to be seen as shills for a public relations–minded president. Balance in reporting was largely replaced by antagonism and unstinting criticism. Prying into the personal affairs of the president and his family took precedent over analyses of issues and political initiatives.

How did this evolution come about? Why did the first transformation from political partisanship in reporting during Lincoln's time to objective and analytical reporting during John F. Kennedy's tenure ultimately transmute to a barrage of personal attacks on the president? Who is responsible? When did this alteration begin? Why did it start? What is its impact on public policy and the lives of mainstream Americans? Are presidents responsible for this trans-formation, or are the media? Or both? How has this affected voting patterns, elections, and public attitudes toward national policy? What has this meant to public knowledge of governmental issues? Are journalists aware of this trans-formation, and what do they intend to do about it? Will advancing information technology in the last few years of the twentieth century help to inform Americans better and dilute the skepticism that seems to have gripped not only journalists but the public generally? This book addresses these questions. It also re-visits some commonly heard historical arguments about how media affected elections and policy decisions after the Eisenhower Administration, probing to learn whether generally accepted historical explanations are accurate or placed in proper perspective.

In a broad-based examination of the presidency in the last four decades of the twentieth century, this study focuses not just on the White House but also on journalism, changing media patterns, and the White House press corps. I hope that a historical perspective will help to explain more completely the state of White House–based news reporting during a troubled generation of news gathering and dissemination.

I
THE 1960s
TRAGEDY AND TRANSITION

CHAPTER ONE

MYTHS OF THE 1960 ELECTION

The year 1960 was a beginning in American presidential politics, a starting point to a revised relationship between journalist and president. Not only did television become a consequential factor in the 1960 election, but it established itself as the primary vehicle of information in presidential politics—supplanting newspapers, magazines, and radio and quickly burying newsreels for all time. Yet radio, magazines, and newspapers and the presidency itself changed in the 1960s. As the decade opened, two candidates jousted in a gentlemanly manner in anticipation of one of the closest elections in history. Reporters asked respectful questions and reported the campaign in both metaphoric and, in most cases, courteously objective terms, leaving the opinionated prose to the editorial writers and the television commentators.

By the end of the decade, tolerance between correspondents and the president had begun to dissipate. Reporters interpreted as much as they observed, while probing more deeply and critically into the private life of the president. The 1960s brought transformations in the pressroom, the White House, and the public's perception of the role of the presidency.

Historical recollections of the 1960 election have been somewhat distorted. Much of what is believed to be true about the momentous campaign is either myth or misleading speculation. This is partly because of the Kennedy mystique and partly because of the wholehearted acceptance of the Pulitzer prize–winning book *The Making of the President 1960* by Theodore White. While a marvelous and groundbreaking piece of journalism, White's book is nonetheless highly speculative and, having been published in 1961, lacking in historical insight. Still, it has been accepted virtually on faith, and some of its assumptions are not accurate.

What is true is that the 1960 contest was one of eight pivotal presidential elections in American history—the others being 1800, 1828, 1860, 1896, 1912, 1932, and 1948—one that would linger in American politics for decades to come.

There were many precedents. Five candidates seriously seeking the presidency for the first time in 1960 would become either president or vice president in the next sixteen years. Never before in history had one election produced such a collection of new and influential candidates. Never before had the primary elections become so important. This signaled the destruction of the party system at the presidential level, a structure that had been in place since 1800. Rarely would Americans become as excited and enthused about an election. For the first time in over one hundred years, the vice president was considered seriously as a viable candidate for the presidency rather than as a political placeholder to be thrust unprepared into the Oval Office in the event of a tragedy. For only the second time in the century, a U.S. senator was elected. Never before had candidates debated before national audiences, relying nakedly on their powers of persuasion to influence millions of American voters directly. Rarely would a candidate and then president excite the passions of the electorate with his charm, good looks, and controversial private life. Never had television been the all-encompassing ritualistic seeing eye that brought the election to the American public so directly and with such impact.

But if the 1960 election was a beginning, just as with all other events in the continuum of history, it had to be an end too. This year initiated the end to the informal relationship between male reporters and president, where really important information was gathered over dinner or at some other social occasion. John F. Kennedy's popularity brought hundreds of reporters clamoring for that personal interview or tendered answer at an impersonal press conference. The disappointing revelations about his personal life that came to light in the years after his death shamed reporters into probing more deeply into the most private affairs of ensuing presidents and candidates, thus re-drawing the rules for White House reporting.

The 1960s also shattered the American public's confidence in the stability of the presidency, an equilibrium that had been built up over thirty years, a stability unknown prior to the New Deal. From 1933 to 1961, only three presidents held office. All retired with the respect of even their political adversaries. After that, Kennedy was assassinated, Lyndon Johnson was driven from office because of an unpopular war, Richard Nixon resigned during his second term, and Gerald Ford and Jimmy Carter were defeated in office. Only two other sitting presidents had been defeated in the previous eighty-eight years. Television-oriented primary elections, accompanied by brutal campaign schedules and rehearsed speeches, replaced party politics and convention bargaining as tools to nominations. The permanence of the office would change with Kennedy.

Newspapers transformed in the 1960s. Too many died because of years of neglect, outdated labor policies, aging print facilities, the rising cost of newsprint, and television. To compete with the timeliness of television, newspapers frequently interpreted events of the day, telling readers why the day's news occurred as much as who, what, when, where, and how. Many newspapers turned away from political news altogether, preferring to emphasize features and entertainment. Columnists, voices of individual opinion since the 1930s, lost much of their influence and power over the presidency. The greatest columnist of all time, Walter Lippmann, died shortly after Kennedy's assassination, and many other popular columnists gave up writing, opting for television commentary. News magazines became more influential, and their correspondents increasingly found the president available for interviews, just as often as the most important newspaper reporters. Finally, as the 1960s progressed, Americans grew uncomfortably aware of the power of the national media, fretting openly about abuses of the media and how such excesses might affect their lives. Conservatives openly claimed that a liberal bias had developed in the media subtly influencing the political complexion of the country, to the detriment of voters.

The powerful figures who had dominated American print journalism for a generation had begun to disappear. Robert R. McCormick, publisher and editor of the *Chicago Tribune* for nearly four decades, died in 1955. In 1960, the *Tribune*, the dominant newspaper in the second largest city in the nation, was seeking to re-define itself. William Randolph Hearst, creator of a vast newspaper, magazine, and wire service empire in the late nineteenth century, died four years before McCormick after more than sixty years as a commanding force in American journalism. By 1960, the Hearst empire was crumbling. Henry Luce, co-founder of *Time* magazine in 1924 and builder of the Time-Life-Fortune empire, was ending his reign as the personal force behind the nation's largest news magazine. He retired in 1964 and died in 1967, and Time-Life-Fortune became a corporate entity with vast holdings in all areas of mass communication. These brash media figures, who dictated policy and ideology, gave way to conglomerates—corporations whose leaders sought to entertain as much as inform and who saw presidential politics not as ideological struggles in which they must enmesh themselves but marketable commodities that demanded election-year packaging.

Television not only presented the candidates on the campaign trail and broadcast the first presidential debates ever, but also became a daily evening news ritual. Walter Cronkite at CBS and Chet Huntley and David Brinkley at NBC had developed into household names, more recognizable than the presidential candidates. By the time of Kennedy's assassination, evening network television news had expanded to thirty minutes from fifteen, and presidential strategy focused on influencing broadcast first, not print.

The year 1960 also marked a beginning of an end to the bitter memories of World War II. In May of that year, Adolf Eichmann, the Nazi overseer of the Final Solution—the systematic destruction of Jews and other minorities during World War II—was captured in Argentina and transported to Israel, where he was later tried, convicted, and hanged for crimes against humanity. Before the decade had ended, the word *Holocaust* would be attached to the inconceivable atrocities committed by Eichmann and his henchmen. The war had altered the face of the globe and continued to influence foreign and domestic policies in the United States, but its grip on the world was loosening. People were looking forward rather than backward. During the 1960 election, both Nixon and Kennedy touted their heroic service in the military during World War II, but their words and deeds in 1960 were directed to a postwar generation. In the 1960s a new era was taking shape; this one would comprise voters who knew about the horrors of World War II only from history classes. The 1960 election was one of the last dominated by the graduating class of Depression and War.

Who were the voters in 1960? The retirees had lived through four wars and the most serious depression in history, many having served in the war to end all wars. The public mood in 1960 suggested that they and others had seen enough tumult in their time. Younger adults were born just before the Great Depression, and already in their short lives they had experienced two fighting conflicts and the Cold War. They wanted homes in the suburbs, two cars, and the freedom to forget years of want and uncertainty. Teenagers, not yet able to vote, coveted new challenges and new ideas. Though they would not leave their marks until later in the decade, their youthful enthusiasm had an impact even as the decade opened. All Americans seemed ready for change in 1960, anxiously hoping to shed the power politics of the previous generation and to continue the policies of self-determination that had swept the world fifteen years earlier. They were eager to build something new from this most spirited election.

Transition from 1956

The listless 1956 campaign had left a void in presidential politics. The Democrats renominated Adlai Stevenson, former governor of Illinois, and the

Republicans the incumbent Dwight D. Eisenhower, former hero of the invasion of Normandy in June 1944. Occupied by the Suez and Hungarian crises and recovering from a heart attack a year earlier, Eisenhower hardly campaigned and easily overwhelmed Stevenson for the second time. It was scarcely an election—perhaps the most poorly contested election of the twentieth century.

It was clear from the time that Eisenhower won re-election that 1960 would be vastly different. All the nominees from both parties during the past seven elections were either no longer politically viable or were dead. New faces would appear, if not necessarily new ideas.

Democratic hopefuls included Missouri Senator Stuart Symington, popular in his home state but virtually unknown elsewhere; Minnesota Senator Hubert Humphrey, the liberal former mayor of Minneapolis; Lyndon Johnson, the rough-and-tumble Texan who had risen to be majority leader during his first term in the Senate; John F. Kennedy, the handsome and popular Massachusetts senator who had barely lost a convention fight to Tennessee's Estes Kefauver for the vice presidential nomination in 1956; and, of course, Stevenson, who refused to enter the primaries but waited hopelessly for the Democrats to draft him for a third consecutive time.

The Republican primaries were dominated by Vice President Richard Nixon, who had built a career as an aggressive anticommunist while a member of the House Un-American Activities Committee in the late 1940s, as senator from California, and later as vice president. Just months before the 1960 primary campaign, Nixon had re-established his credentials during a spirited debate with Soviet Premier Nikita Khrushchev, while the pair toured a kitchen exhibit in Moscow. Nixon's only challenger, New York Governor Nelson Rockefeller, was too tentative in his quest and too liberal for much of the party.

Nixon traveled frequently on Eisenhower's behalf, establishing foreign affairs credentials and supporting Republicans in local and regional races. Nixon had built a political power base, unlike any other vice president in modern history. Now, a sitting vice president wanted to be the first one in 124 years to succeed to the presidency without a death intervening. Though Nixon lost, the vice presidency would never be a dead-end post again.

For the first time in history, the primary elections proved to be key to the Democratic nomination. Even Franklin D. Roosevelt did not experience a smooth primary path in the 1932 campaign. He had to win the nomination at the convention. Al Smith had virtually no competition in 1928, and every other Democratic primary since 1920 had either produced the re-nomination of an incumbent or had been inconclusive. Kennedy changed all that. Thereafter, every primary struggle, Republican or Democratic, was hotly contested, except when an incumbent sought re-nomination—and sometimes then too. Party conventions, except for the hoopla and protests, became formalities.

Kennedy won every primary he entered, his narrow victory over Humphrey in Wisconsin and then his conquest in heavily Protestant West Virginia sealing the nomination. Johnson's last-minute maneuverings failed to dent the Kennedy bandwagon, and the Massachusetts senator won on the first ballot. This not only elevated the open primary to the principal vehicle to the nomination but placed a heavy responsibility on press coverage. Ballots, not convention dealing, would decide future party nominations. How the public perceived the candidates would in large part be determined by media coverage. When the primary system expanded greatly a decade later, it became clear that the media had replaced the party power structure.

The West Virginia primary victory spurred speculation later that Kennedy had bought the election through heavy personal campaign spending or had enlisted the help of the underworld in sweeping to victory. It is true that Kennedy's father, Joseph, had amassed a vast fortune and was willing to spend as much as was necessary to earn his son the presidency, but this explanation ignores the Kennedy campaign strategy. Rockefeller, too, was wealthy, but he bumbled to a losing effort against Nixon, who certainly had no personal financing. Unquestionably Kennedy's money helped, but more to the point, he was willing to take Humphrey on in a predominantly Protestant state and was willing to work for every vote in both Wisconsin and West Virginia. Americans like to think everyone can someday be president, but, in truth, any campaign takes money. Yet, time and again in the postwar presidential era, it has been shown that money does not ensure victory. Money helped Kennedy, but he won the nomination with his campaign strategy and style.

The charges of mafia aid seem more a product of the conspiratorial atmosphere that pervaded America after Kennedy's assassination and following conclusions by the House Select Committee on Assassinations in 1979 that decided there might have been a possible mafia connection to Kennedy's death. Kennedy's Hollywood pals included Frank Sinatra, whose biographers claimed later that he had acted as a go-between for Kennedy with mob boss Sam Giancana in an effort to secure labor union support in the West Virginia primary. Unfortunately, innuendo and gossip surrounded Kennedy. JFK's many short-term trysts and his affinity for Hollywood were mostly responsible for this. Speculation surrounded Joseph Kennedy, who reportedly ran illegal bootlegging operations with mob complicity during the 1920s. It was also learned in the 1970s that while president, Kennedy had liaisons with Judith Campbell, who was Giancana's girlfriend.

JFK certainly did not need the mafia's money. This presumes he needed mafia organization and influence. It also assumes that gossip can be accepted as historical fact. Naturally, there are no written or audiotaped records of any conversation that can confirm any of these claims. Hollywood is known for exaggeration and fabrication. Yet both Joseph and John Kennedy's shabby personal behaviors will not allow a total rejection of any rumors or allegations. The results of the West Virginia primary seem to indicate that West Virginians were unconcerned about JFK's Catholicism and impressed with his personal campaign presence, regardless of union influence or excessive spending. Did the mafia help Kennedy? There is no historical documentation of such a charge, but there is the Kennedy mystique. If West Virginians were truly anti-Catholic, it is unlikely Giancana would have been able to exert enough influence to overcome that prejudice, which suggests that Kennedy won despite his religion, but not because of mafia help.

What is clear is that Kennedy's victory in West Virginia helped to bury for all time the unpleasant legacy left from Al Smith's defeat in the 1928 election— the assumption that a Catholic could not win the presidency. Without documentation, the rest is speculative hearsay that will feed upon itself without foundation, until proved or disproved. Mob influence was not the key to the 1960 Democratic primary campaign. The mood of the country and the demand for a youthful, exciting new image were the deciding factors.

For his part, Nixon had virtually no opposition to the nomination until he reached the convention in Chicago in late July. Then Rockefeller, in exchange for his support, demanded concessions on the party platform. During a secret meeting, Nixon reluctantly agreed. The new planks were more liberal, and this rankled many of Nixon's regular party, conservative supporters. This was not a major blow to the Nixon campaign, however. The conservatives had nowhere else to go. Yet the Nixon candidacy had begun with secret negotiations away from the focus of reporters and with a rift in the party that would reverberate four years later.

The campaign started with the momentum in Kennedy's favor. On September 12, two months after his nomination, Kennedy successfully put the Catholic issue to rest with a speech in Houston in which he assured voters that he was just a person who happened to be Catholic, not a tool of the Vatican. Now the two candidates could turn away from bigotry and get on with the real campaign. Public opinion surveys indicated that the lead shifted back and forth throughout the campaign. Kennedy won by the narrowest of margins: 112,000 votes of 60 million cast.

What was the media's part in the campaign, and what has been written about that role? Theodore White is the perpetrator of much of the lore surrounding television and the general election. Four debates, all televised, highlighted the campaign. The first took place in Chicago on September 26. Most of the controversy and, indeed, the central focus in any discussion of the 1960 general election swirls around that first debate. White's speculation about its impact and his impressions as to who won or lost need re-examination.

In his book White contends: (1) Nixon lost the campaign because most Americans thought more highly of Kennedy's performance during this debate; (2) Nixon failed to make good use of makeup, causing him to look haggard with a slight beard, and he wore a light suit, so his image blended with the background scenery; (3) sample surveys indicated that a majority of those who watched on television thought Kennedy had won and a preponderance of those listening on radio contended Nixon was the victor, proving that the visual images had made a difference; and (4) 6 percent of those polled after the election said the TV debates had been a deciding factor in their minds and most of those 6 percent voted for Kennedy, thus deciding a close election in Kennedy's favor.[1] Don Hewitt, who produced the debate for the Columbia Broadcasting System, proclaimed years later that when Kennedy left that studio, he had the election won.

Are Hewitt and White correct? The black-and-white tape of the debate was examined over and over again. Kennedy's darker suit does provide a marked contrast with the set background, while Nixon's light gray suit does not. Nixon looks tired and less certain of himself than the confident Kennedy, but the contrast is not great, especially on a black-and-white television. Nixon looks like Nixon. Perhaps what voters reacted to was the real Richard M. Nixon and the real John F. Kennedy, untouched by television training techniques of later years. Did Kennedy succeed because he basically was a more honest and compassionate person, and that is what the television audience saw? Was Nixon unable to sway voters because he was Richard Nixon or because of the clothes he wore and the makeup he did not use? There are several explanations for the results of the first debate.

White contends that surveys by respected pollsters showed that radio audiences had a markedly different impression of the debate, proving the visual impact. Were these surveys accurate and reliable? After all, this was twelve years after the polling debacle of the 1948 Truman-Dewey election. Kennedy press secretary Pierre Salinger remembered that polling information during the Wisconsin primary that was provided by private pollster Lou Harris to Kennedy in March was completely inaccurate.[2] Can we really assume that a handful of listener and viewer surveys were adequate predictors of audience opinion? One of White's cited surveys was a sampling of 400 people, all from the New York metropolitan area.[3] What does that tell us about Winona,

Minnesota, or Terre Haute, Indiana? Are just New Yorkers, especially in 1960, a legitimate sampling of overall American sentiment? And if 100 million Americans were watching the debates, nearly as many persons as there were voters in the nation at the time, who was listening on the radio? Probably a few people who were at work or driving in their automobiles and could not concentrate as much as those at home watching television.

What about those who said they decided on Kennedy because of the debates? Is that really why they voted for him? Did they decide that was probably why they voted for Kennedy after the question was put to them and when a yes answer suddenly seemed to make sense? Was the real reason, deep down, because they had grown up in the Depression with President Roosevelt and simply could not vote for a Republican? Why didn't White cite any polls about the Democratic coalition? Did voters not trust a man who used Alger Hiss as a scapegoat and was accused of misusing campaign funds before the 1952 vice presidential campaign? Was the 1960 election a continuation of the 1958 congressional election trend when voters had swung heavily in favor of the Democrats? Did Kennedy and his young, attractive wife embody the spirit of renewal and change that was sweeping the country in 1960 more than Richard and Pat Nixon? Were Americans weary of the Cold War and inclined to feel that Kennedy, the Democrat, would pull them away from nuclear confrontation more effectively than Nixon? Did they see the Democrats as more likely to guarantee a strong economy? Did Kennedy outmaneuver and outcampaign Nixon, concentrating on strategic states instead of visiting every state in the union? Despite Nixon's foreign affairs experience and Kennedy's unimpressive record in the Senate, was Kennedy simply the better person for the job?

These rhetorical assumptions are just as logical as White's TV explanations. White is not wrong so much as his emphasis is out of balance. Certainly the first televised debate in the history of the country played out before an audience comprising much of the electorate was a momentous occurrence, but in such a close election a blend of factors combine to determine the result. White's implication is that in a pre-television era, Nixon would have won. However, that is speculation that ignores too many traditional political factors that came into play in 1960. White could easily be wrong, but his thesis has been readily accepted as fundamental truth. The reiteration of White's contentions over and over without challenge is a disservice to history.

And, of course, Hewitt's assertion that Kennedy left the studio a winner after the first debate is pure nonsense. Kennedy won by the slimmest of margins. After the election, 10,000 disputed votes in Cook County, Illinois, disappeared mysteriously, preserving Kennedy's victory there and perhaps nationwide. No one could have predicted the outcome of the election until the last votes were counted. If the debates had been so decisive, why didn't polls and the final results reflect that decisiveness? Kennedy and Nixon exchanged leads in the polls throughout the campaign. The normal percentage of error attributed to any polling made these presumed leads even more questionable. It could be that the lead never changed—just the percentage of error in the polls.

The emphasis on television also ignores the fact that except for the debates, television was not the dominant medium for news and information in 1960. The evening news was only fifteen minutes, and informational programming outside regular newscasts was decreasing significantly from the mid-1950s. The Columbia Broadcasting System, the undisputed leader in news telecasting, was replacing special hourly news shows with entertainment. Television producers faced problems with mobility. Cameras were not portable, and, except for staged events, it was difficult for technicians to follow the candidates closely. Print media still provided the bulk of the information that Americans absorbed during the campaign. What Americans read in their local newspapers after the debates, or at any other time during the campaign, and what they read in any news magazine may have been more decisive than television.

What role did reporters and newspapers play in the election? Newspapers overwhelmingly favored Nixon. Kennedy drew the editorial support of only 16 percent of the nation's dailies, so certainly it was not newspaper endorsements that boosted Kennedy. Nixon supporters and conservatives maintained that Kennedy mesmerized reporters, who were more inclined to write favorably about him because he was one of them—a Harvard graduate and a liberal. These arguments ignore some basic journalistic canons. Political reporters are more interested in stories than promoting candidates. The Kennedy people for the first time perfected the use of instantaneous transcripts of speeches and discussions, giving reporters on deadline written verbatim copies of Kennedy's words, so that their jobs were made easier. The Kennedy entourage also made a point of providing daily quotes for reporters and seeing to their travel needs. Nixon and his campaign staff did not like reporters and treated them as intruders. By and large, the coverage in the campaign was reasonably balanced, while editorial support from newspapers favored Nixon, because most of the nation's newspapers still had Republican leanings. If volume of coverage favored Kennedy, it was because Kennedy worked harder to get his ideas into print.

It is not possible to separate all these factors and single out television as the deciding component. It is folly to try. The election was a coin toss. Any variable cited—or all of them—could have provided Kennedy with that small edge. White's postulations made fascinating reading in 1961, but a case could be made more easily that television's role was decisive in the 1980 election than it could be made for the 1960 campaign.

The more significant precedents of the 1960 election are Kennedy's personal appeal, which undercut party allegiances in presidential politics, his election to the presidency from the Senate, and the selection of the more liberal candidate, setting the stage for change in the 1960s. These are interpretations emphasizing more traditional political themes and downplaying the impact of television, but they are more historically accurate.

White's theories did, however, alert Americans to the power of television at an early stage. Only a few years later, politicians, including the vice president of the United States, and other media critics contended that television had unfairly skewed candidate access to the voting public. Uncomfortable with this seen-but-hardly-understood medium, Americans fidgeted and nodded collectively when these charges were leveled. After White's book was published, Americans knew, or thought they knew, what television could do to a campaign. Whenever the power of television is debated, someone stands up and exclaims, "Yes, but television elected Kennedy in 1960!" In retrospect, it is almost irrelevant whether White is accurate or incorrect. His ideas have been accepted, and the shaky concept that television elected John F. Kennedy will be perpetuated for all eternity.

NOTES

1. Theodore H. White, *The Making of the President 1960* (New York: Atheneum, 1961), 286–95.
2. Pierre Salinger, *P.S. A Memoir* (New York: St. Martin's, 1995), 73.
3. White, *The Making of the President 1960*, 294.

CHAPTER TWO

KENNEDY AND THE RESURGENT PRESIDENCY

Despite the four televised debates, Nixon and Kennedy typically skirted the most crucial issues of the day. Both carefully avoided discussion of racial tensions in the South, spoke in generalities about détente with the Soviet Union, rarely discussed Laos and Southeast Asia, never offered specifics about education, and promised to balance the budget but without explaining how. In retrospect, if one examined the speeches and public statements of the candidates, one would hardly recognize the real issues of the 1960s. Kennedy's conservative campaign themes belied the steps taken during his administration, and Nixon had backed away from the confrontational rhetoric of the kitchen debate with Khrushchev the year before.

Seeking election to the presidency is not the same as holding office, however, and many of the ambiguities Kennedy employed in 1960 would not suffice in 1961. The new president needed public and congressional support, or he would face defeat of his first-term initiatives. He needed to convince the 50.3 percent of Americans who voted for Nixon and others that his election had not been a mistake, that he could address intelligently the complex issues of the day. Consequently, a new Kennedy appeared. In a historic inaugural speech, the president challenged Americans to "ask not what your country can do for you—ask what you can do for your country." He captured the mood of optimism and daring and established the concept of a New Frontier. Kennedy was one of those rare people who could sense the temperament of the public before the collective feeling was widely recognized.

Imagine telling Americans in the 1970s or 1980s that they needed to be less selfish and more devoted to the common good of the nation. Kennedy would have been excoriated editorially the next day and most likely booed off the podium at the inauguration. But in 1961, the speech was welcomed by press and public alike. The often repeated words of January 20, 1961, tell us much about America then, and more about the intuitiveness and insightfulness of Kennedy and his advisers. A bland inaugural speech, promising much and demanding little, would have set the Kennedy Administration on the wrong path.

The young president did not stop there. Six weeks later, he created the Peace Corps, a low-paying volunteer organization that sent Americans, mostly young people, overseas to work with the poor. He encouraged Americans to pursue physical fitness, initiating a fad of fifty-mile hikes. This not only delighted youthful Americans but set a style for the 1960s, the decade of communal sharing and personal improvement. Kennedy harnessed idealism as no other president had since FDR.

In so doing, he established a dichotomous trend. The public found him irresistible, but journalists, especially editors and editorial writers, were not so idealistic, nor were they inclined to give Kennedy the benefit of the doubt. The inaugural speech and the Peace Corps made a strong start, but winning over the press would not be that simple. Print reporters would be especially difficult.

Yet when he chose to hold his first presidential news conference live on network television five days after the inauguration, Kennedy illustrated his penchant for taking risks. The gesture also showed that television was a medium designed for him, just as radio fitted Franklin D. Roosevelt. Such a move did not endear him to newspaper and magazine journalists, however, and it could have backfired.

Much has been made of this initiative, and it was good one. Yet had television's influence developed more slowly, the decision could have hurt the president. Print reporters in 1961 voted against allowing television reporters to join the White House Correspondents Association because they did not consider broadcast correspondents to be legitimate journalists. Upon learning that Kennedy would hold live press conferences, the *Chicago Tribune* sneered that Kennedy was establishing "government by public relations."[1] The *Tribune* and most other newspapers and magazines did not recognize the shape of the future. Kennedy did. He not only visited with television reporters but agreed to submit to filmed and sometimes even live interviews for specials and occasionally even the regular evening news. The television emphasis was only one of a series of positive steps that Kennedy took to combat the notion that his presidency was a fluke, resulting from a close election. It may have been the most daring and important one, however.

Kennedy hoped to eradicate the notion that his administration would be politics as usual. His early decisions had little to do with policy, fiscal matters, world affairs, or important domestic issues. They concerned public relations and construction of a kinship with voters and the press. Could Kennedy have done this without television? Probably not as well, but, yes, he could have. He substituted personal popularity for a legislative agenda, instead of relying on both as FDR had a generation earlier. That is not to say that Kennedy had no agenda for Capitol Hill, but he and his staff realized that in the 1960s the president first had to capture the support of the constituency through the media. That would then translate to pressure on Congress. The difference between 1933 and 1961 was the emphasis upon influencing the public before Congress and on using television as the fulcrum, while still not neglecting newspapers and magazines. Television magnified Kennedy's personal appeal and brought him close to the voters more quickly, but it was his public relations savvy that set the positive tone for his early presidency.

Still, in the early months, despite his and Jackie Kennedy's personal popularity, the president was widely regarded as a superficial, playboy ex-senator who came to the White House by happenstance. His record in the Senate was mediocre, and, in some ways, the constant attention to his personal charm and good looks hurt his credibility among Washington insiders.

That is why the decision to appoint the unknown Pierre Salinger as press secretary was surprising and at first regarded as unwise. Salinger had been a reporter with the *San Francisco Chronicle* and then a contributing editor in the West Coast office of *Collier's* magazine. His career had been fashioned far away from Washington, but in 1957 he had served as an aide on the Senate Select Committee on Improper Activities in the Labor or Management Field, working closely with chief counsel Robert F. Kennedy, the future president's younger brother. John F. Kennedy was a member of the anti-racketeering committee, and it was chaired by Arkansas Senator John McClellan. Salinger's relationship with Bobby Kennedy provided him with opportunity. When *Collier's* folded in late 1956, Salinger accepted a position under Bobby Kennedy. This smoothed the path to becoming presidential press secretary.[2] Salinger's main asset was his intense loyalty, but his age in 1961 (thirty-five years old) only encouraged seasoned Washington reporters to conclude that the new administration was filled with neophytes. James Hagerty, the long-time professional who had served with perfection under Eisenhower throughout his two terms and New York Governor Thomas Dewey before that, was a stark contrast to Salinger. The first few months of the Kennedy Administration would be a trial for both the young president and Salinger, but Salinger was efficient and on good terms with reporters and he even instituted twice-a-day press briefings. Eventually Salinger justified Kennedy's confidence, proving to be a solid choice.

The first opportunity for Kennedy to erase the "inexperienced" tag came in April 1961. Upon taking office, the president learned that a plan had been hatched during the Eisenhower Administration for an invasion of Cuba. Communist insurgent leader Fidel Castro had seized power from dictator Fulgencio Batista on January 1, 1959, and had busily converted the tiny Caribbean island to a Marxist state right under Eisenhower's nose. Expatriate anticommunist Cubans had been training for several months in Florida, preparing to invade and repatriate Cuba with the understanding that the U.S. Central Intelligence Agency would help provide air cover.

Kennedy was torn. The plan was loosely held together and the invasion force undermanned, with only 1,500 soldiers. A failed attempt would bring about exactly what Kennedy hoped to avoid: apparent proof that he did not have the intellectual capabilities or leadership qualities to fight a Cold War. On the other hand, Cuba was an embarrassment and a security threat to the United States. It was difficult for Kennedy to ignore an opportunity to remove Castro.

The assault, known as the Bay of Pigs invasion, was crucial to the image of the new presidency. By the second week of April, media leaks had sprung up everywhere, and Kennedy realized he had to act or scrap the mission. Reluctantly, he gave his approval, and on April 16, the invasion began. Refusing to involve Americans directly, Kennedy ordered that no U.S. planes provide air cover. The invasion was a disaster. After three days, Castro's forces had wiped out or captured nearly all the intruders, while Kennedy watched helplessly.

He had failed his first international test, and editorial reaction was swift and disparaging. The president had lost face with all but the most sympathetic editors. The split in perceptions persisted. Journalists found Kennedy charming but of questionable talents for the Oval Office, while public support hardly wavered. The president's approval ratings in polls reached 87 percent. Americans were still enamored with the new president, but eventually Kennedy would need more, and the Bay of Pigs fiasco made that goal more difficult.

The press's role in covering the assault raised other questions. *The New York Times* learned of the invasion plans days before the launch but, at Kennedy's urging, had withheld most information. So had the Associated Press. Had full stories been published, it is unlikely the invasion would have occurred, and the disaster that followed would have been averted. Is it the role of a free press to withhold knowledge of military plans during peacetime when the U.S. government insists officially it is not involved? What are the responsibilities of newspapers, magazines, radio, and television in such instances?

In a speech to the American Newspaper Publishers Association in New York eleven days after the invasion, Kennedy called on journalists to exercise more restraint in writing and publishing articles in times of military action. Kennedy angered editors further by asking for voluntary censorship. The Bay of Pigs mistake was Kennedy's, not theirs, editors concluded. Reporters are trained and urged at every level to reveal fully to the public plans to involve the country in the affairs of other nations. Protection of the lives of Americans and the security of the nation are the only circumstances in which journalists hesitate. Ostensibly no Americans were involved. From a practical perspective, news organizations withholding this information reflected more a trust in Kennedy than a commitment to national security or the public's right to know. Yet there were only a few news organizations with advance knowledge of the invasion, and the decision lay with those editors and reporters. The trust that *The New York Times* placed in Kennedy is not necessarily indicative of Kennedy's relationship with the press generally. He was not held in as high regard with most newspapers as he was with the *Times*. In retrospect, the entire affair does represent errors in judgment by editors who should have known better and sends a signal that the relationship at times between some members of the press and Kennedy was not as adversarial as it should have been, but it would be a gross overgeneralization to say that these decisions tell us very much about the press generally. And, still, here was Kennedy lecturing editors and publishers collectively on using more restraint.

In retrospect, Kennedy benefited both from a positive relationship with *The New York Times* and the respect the nation still held for the office of the presidency. It was wrong for reporters to sit on the story, but this judgment is mitigated by historical perspective, because the United States was in the midst of the Cold War. What should reporters have done? Probably report what they knew. Yet the role of the responsible journalist in such an instance, when the nature of a military action and the extent of the involvement of U.S. soldiers is unclear, is more complex beforehand than in retrospect. No journalist wants to endanger American lives or the lives of friendly forces. And the presidency was still larger than the press in 1961. Reporters were not inclined to challenge someone in such a powerful office.

The point is that Kennedy's personal influence and the mood of the times, not security concerns, affected the judgment of at least *The New York Times* editors and probably other newspersons. Kennedy served in a different era. He was the last president who could pick up a telephone receiver and squelch a story about a military action, even one that ostensibly involved tangential U.S. involvement. And he was John F. Kennedy, not Richard M. Nixon, Lyndon B. Johnson, Gerald R. Ford, or James E. Carter. His personal allure and a perception by both press and public papered over many weaknesses. Within three weeks, the public had all but forgotten the Bay of Pigs invasion; few wanted to dwell on the negative. This also was a luxury that later presidents would not enjoy. In return, Kennedy tried to insinuate that newspeople were responsible and called on them to act with more restraint, when probably they had shown too much restraint in the first place. This compounded the impact of the sorry fiasco.

THE EARLY KENNEDY REIGN

The remainder of the spring and then the summer of 1961 provided more foreign relations headaches for Kennedy. In 1960 Khrushchev had abruptly canceled a summit conference with Eisenhower. The Soviet Union had shot down an American U-2 spy plane. Eisenhower claimed the aircraft had accidentally strayed into Soviet territory, but he was embarrassed a few days later when Khrushchev revealed that the pilot, Gary Powers, was still alive and had confessed to being a spy. Eisenhower took responsibility and conceded that spy planes were distasteful but necessary and were frequently used by both sides. Nevertheless, Khrushchev utilized the incident as a propaganda tool and an excuse to shut down the talks abruptly. He left Paris just before the summit was to begin.

A year later, Kennedy and Khrushchev met on June 3 and 4 in Vienna, Austria. Kennedy and State Department strategists were anxious to erase the lingering U-2 embarrassment and to ease tensions in a nuclear age. However, at the meetings, Khrushchev berated Kennedy and lectured him on the abuses of capitalism and what Khrushchev regarded as an underhanded U.S. foreign policy. Just after the summit, Kennedy confided to James R. "Scotty" Reston, *The New York Times* Washington bureau chief, that he had badly underestimated Khrushchev. Officially, the U.S. government issued optimistic statements, but reporters and even his own State Department knew that Kennedy had been shown up. Khrushchev left convinced that the Soviet Union now had the upper hand.

On August 13 the East German government closed access routes from East Berlin to West Berlin. East Berliners had been escaping to the West by the thousands, exiting through the gates that separated the two parts of the city. Berlin was located deep inside East Germany. The outflow had created a drain on skilled labor, damaging East German industry and national morale. West Berlin had been part of West Germany since the two nations had been formed after World War II, but it was an island inside East Germany, and now, through Khrushchev's maneuvering, it would be further isolated. Within days, the East Germans cleared the area near the city's dividing line. Later, a huge wall was built, dividing the city and, symbolically, the world.

Kennedy issued dire warnings to Khrushchev but could do little else. East-West tensions heightened. For his own part, Khrushchev gambled on Kennedy's inexperience, while attempting to hold off hard-liners within the Kremlin. Weeks later, Kennedy ordered the United States to begin resumption of underground nuclear tests.

The president was caught in the flow of history. He had assumed office at a dangerous time, when policies established under Harry S. Truman and then Eisenhower had made accommodation extremely difficult. The Truman Doctrine of 1947, which committed the United States to fighting communism wherever it sprang up in the world, had been replaced by brinkmanship under Eisenhower and his Secretary of State John Foster Dulles. During these years, the United States and the Soviet Union had developed nuclear arsenals with thousands of warheads pointed at each other. It was not so much that communism could not live alongside capitalism but that each side did not trust the motives of the other in the international community.

With Joseph Stalin's death in 1953 and Khrushchev's ascension to power, the mutual antagonism abated only slightly. No U.S. president during this era could be effective without demonstrating his anticommunist credentials and taking a hard Cold War stance. Kennedy had hoped his personal powers of persuasion would hurdle these historic antagonisms, but he could not have been more wrong. On the other hand, Khrushchev mistook Kennedy's uncertainty for weakness, and, in the end, it would be Khrushchev's miscalculation that would be most costly.

THE DESEGREGATION MOVEMENT RESUMES

In the spring of 1961, Negroes resumed their efforts to desegregate the South. On May 20, a group of freedom riders, as they called themselves, took a Greyhound bus from Birmingham to Montgomery, Alabama, to desegregate the bus waiting station there. Local whites waited, and when the bus arrived, they pummeled the freedom riders with baseball bats and lead pipes. More buses arrived in the ensuing days, and Kennedy reluctantly sent 550 federal marshals to protect them.

Horrified editorial writers in the North lambasted Kennedy for his reluctance and called on the nation to re-examine its commitment to democracy. Kennedy's liberalism was tempered by political reality. His razor-thin victory left him too weak politically to antagonize Southern congressmen. Though the Democrats held a large majority in both Houses, the Congress was split three ways: Republicans, Northern Democrats, and Southern Democrats. Without the support of the Southern contingency, Kennedy did not have a majority.

He was angry at the Rev. Martin Luther King Jr., leader of the civil rights protesters, for not having more patience in the civil rights struggle. Like Eisenhower before him, Kennedy acted only when forced to protect lives. In Alabama in 1961 and later in Mississippi, Kennedy, like Eisenhower in Little Rock, Arkansas, in 1957, wished it all would just go away.

White Northerners watched the beatings on television and read about them in newspapers and magazines, many learning for the first time about the oppression that came with segregation. Kennedy eventually cast aside his reluctance and wholeheartedly supported the fight for integration. But in 1961 he was still Kennedy the politician. Negroes and their commitment, and then the media and its portrayal of white brutality in the South, fueled the civil rights movement in 1961, not John F. Kennedy, or his brother, Attorney General Robert Kennedy.

The media and Northerners were just as culpable, however. Most newspapers, even in the North, employed no Negroes. Editors generally regarded the protesters as troublemakers, even if they were victims of brutality. Later, in the 1970s, many Northerners opposed desegregation as violently in their neighborhoods as whites did in the South. Most Americans in 1961 did not understand the implications of a racially divided society. The images on the television screen forced them to confront segregation. The real public relations errors in 1961 were committed by Southern whites, in both official and unofficial circles. Had Southerners substituted nonviolent resistance for brutality, Northerners would not have cared about the desegregation movement, and Kennedy would have ignored the issue. But Kennedy could not ignore what he and other Americans were seeing nightly on television.

In the fall of 1962, Ross Barnett, governor of Mississippi, physically blocked James Meredith from entering the administration building and enrolling as the first black to attend the University of Mississippi. Violence resulted, and Kennedy had no choice but to send troops. In the summer of 1963, when Alabama Governor George Wallace sought to prevent the enrollment of Vivian Malone and James Hood as the first two Negroes ever to attend the University of Alabama, Kennedy was forced to act once more. These dramatic confrontations established Kennedy in some circles as a leader of the early civil rights movement, but in truth he was not. Media depictions of the events and the persistence of Martin Luther King Jr. and his followers brought the first successes in the battle for civil rights.

There were other standoffs in 1962. In March, Kennedy finally earned his first public relations triumph. United States Steel and the United Steelworkers Union had reached tentative agreement on a contract that would avoid a strike and help to hold down inflation. The union had accepted a 2.5 percent wage hike, and the steel company, for its own part, had indicated it would avoid price increases. The deal had been brokered by Secretary of Labor Arthur Goldberg. Ten days later, U.S. Steel announced a 3.5 percent price hike, and most of the nation's other major steel companies followed suit. Kennedy was livid. Attorney General Bobby Kennedy sent agents to the homes of the steel company executives to harass them. The president denounced the steel magnates publicly in no uncertain terms. Within three days, the steel companies relented.[3]

Kennedy's tough stand was universally praised by commentators and editorial writers from around the country with the notable exception of conservative papers such as the *Chicago Tribune,* which sided with big business, as usual. The president had finally found an opportunity to demonstrate his dedication to the interests of the public. Never mind that the steel companies had never specifically agreed to withhold price hikes and that Bobby Kennedy had used probably illegal and certainly unethical methods to force the steel company executives to back down. The public heard nothing about the harassment and little about the specifics of the contract negotiations. Kennedy had triumphed over big business, and that was news.

But as the fall of 1962 approached and the off-year elections promised, as usual, a rollback of the majority party in Congress, Kennedy's approval rating dropped to 62 percent, the lowest since he had taken office, though still quite high for a sitting president.[4] Reston wrote in *The New York Times* in late September 1962 that Kennedy was more popular outside Washington than inside the capital. He had reached the public but not the Congress and, by implication, not the press either.[5] As the end of his first two years in office approached, Kennedy was still searching for that one issue or event that would legitimize his credentials with official Washington.

Despite the Washington skepticism, the Kennedys created a stir throughout the rest of the country and the world. No other president and first lady had ever prompted such personal adulation. Jacqueline Kennedy's tour of India and Pakistan in the spring of 1962 not only charmed the South Asian public, but also elevated the career of neophyte NBC journalist Barbara Walters. Only Walters was able to gain an interview with Jackie during the trip, and her career took off after that.

Jackie redecorated the White House and then led a television audience tour through the first family's home during a prime time program on Valentine's Day, 1962, that drew heady Nielsen ratings. Throughout the Kennedy presidency, millions of American women mimicked Jackie's hair styles, her clothing selections—including her pillbox hats—and her gentle manner. Mrs. Kennedy was among the youngest first ladies ever, and her doting attention to her young children, Caroline and John Jr., pleased Americans, who still believed in the importance of mothers staying home with their children. When her last child, Patrick Bouvier, died shortly after birth in 1963, the entire nation mourned.

Kennedy elegance fascinated readers and viewers. John F. Kennedy's delightful Boston accent, his taste in elegant clothing, and his debonair style all attracted incredible attention. Jackie's refined manners, stylish clothing, lilting voice, gracious good looks, and intelligent manner enraptured. She captured the hearts of foreign dignitaries and foreign audiences. During a visit to Mexico, Mexicans held up signs that read, "Jackie *si*, Kennedy no." In Vienna, Khrushchev asked anxiously to be introduced to Jackie. No other first lady ever fascinated the public as much. No other president ever attracted the adoration of the female public the way John F. Kennedy did. They seemed to be the perfect family couple, the husband and wife everyone in the country wanted to be.

And it was all a lie. John F. Kennedy was the most unfaithful man ever to occupy the White House. He cheated on his wife often and with great enthusiasm, and Jackie reportedly accepted a million dollars from John's father, Joseph Kennedy, for agreeing to remain married to John. Among Kennedy's consorts were actress Marilyn Monroe, who committed suicide in 1962; Judith Campbell, girlfriend of Chicago mob boss Sam Giancana; and Mary Meyer, sister-in-law to Ben Bradlee, Washington bureau chief of *Newsweek* magazine and one of Kennedy's closest friends in the media.

Kennedy spent much of his time and energy covering the evidence of his many conquests. So did his associates and underlings. Yet it was one of the worst-kept secrets in Washington. Almost any Washington reporter from the 1960s has a story or two to tell about Kennedy and his sexual escapades. Obviously Ben Bradlee knew.

Why did reporters keep the secret from the American public? Charges were made later that this was evidence that Kennedy had co-opted White House reporters. Why else would they not describe such indiscretions, when twenty years later even the most minute details of presidents' and presidential candidates' private lives were given complete coverage?

The answer lies in historical perspective, not Kennedy's special relationship with reporters. In the 1920s Warren Harding had a torrid affair with a young woman that was not revealed until after his death. Franklin Roosevelt had many paramours, including his wife's secretary, Lucy Mercer. Eisenhower was more than just a mentor to his chauffeur, Kay Summersby, in England during World War II. Reporters simply kept all these personal affairs of presidents to themselves. It was an unwritten rule.

The correspondents needed favorable relations with the president to be able to gather information for stories. Revealing an illicit personal presidential dalliance would take great courage. Beyond that, however, many of the reporters "understood." Nearly all were male, and some had affairs or were having affairs themselves. It was a male world, run by men. Perhaps the changing gender makeup of the White House press corps ended the kind of studied silence that existed during Kennedy's time.

Certainly reporters who knew of Kennedy's relationship with Judith Campbell had to be alarmed at this serious error in judgment. She could have been passing along the most sensitive information to underworld figures. The illicit relationship likely compromised any federal effort to clamp down on underworld crime. The relationship that existed with Marilyn Monroe brought Kennedy to the level of a Hollywood vagabond who finds solace in superficial relationships with famous, alluring women. Ben Bradlee's silence about a married president's sleeping with his own sister-in-law, assuming Bradlee knew, certainly suggests that at least Bradlee, among reporters, had crossed an important line. Generally, ignoring private affairs was the practice of the times. That convention dictated that Kennedy's secret be kept, but certainly this was not in the interest of the American public.

Kennedy was also not the virile, healthy man he pretended to be. Early in the Kennedy Administration, Bobby Kennedy had heatedly denied that his brother suffered from Addison's disease, an affliction that causes high blood pressure and then damage to the internal system. The denial was false. Kennedy also had constant back pain. That is why he sat in rocking chairs and why he had a special wading pool constructed in the White House basement. The public knew nothing of the details and, at one point, when Kennedy's pain was obvious, the White House issued a statement saying that the president had injured his back on some rocks while swimming off Cape Cod.

During the Kennedy years, personality was substituted for issues. Given the frailties of humans, this can be dangerous. Herbert Hoover was driven from office in 1933 because his philosophy and management tactics had failed. Hoover was widely believed to be uncaring and indifferent to suffering. Nothing could have been further from the truth, but it was his policies and ideology that failed him ultimately, and this traditionally was what presidents had to answer for.

In Kennedy's case and thereafter, style was substituted for substance, and when a decade later Americans learned the truth about Kennedy's personal lifestyle, there was a great disappointment and anger. Americans had been duped. Kennedy was not what he appeared to be. The Camelot that Theodore White referred to after Kennedy's death never existed in fact or in spirit. This news was disheartening and ultimately caused public resentment and disillusionment. In some circles, this disenchantment translated to a distrust of reporters, who had been in on the duplicity. It also vented a growing frustration with the presidency. Revelations in the 1970s about Kennedy's personal trifling damaged the image of the presidency at a time when world and national events already had caused enough harm. When the presidency becomes a public relations and image-making office more than a source of leadership and policy proposals, the presidency becomes quite fragile. Keeping Kennedy's secret may have been the way of the times, but Kennedy, those around him, and White House correspondents conspired unknowingly to strike a heavy blow to the presidency in the long run.

PRESS STRATEGY

Kennedy's strategy placed the highest importance on influencing reporters and the media. There is no question of that. But was he successful? In the end, yes, but his presidency basically was divided into two parts: the first twenty-one months and the last thirteen. The dividing line was the Cuban missile crisis.

During the thirty-four-month presidency, Kennedy and his staff monitored media reports closely. Kennedy himself read many newspapers and watched news broadcasts nightly whenever he could. He granted personal interviews frequently and allowed television interrogations live, an unprecedented step. He invited reporters to informal and official functions and consulted often with the most important journalists in Washington. By asking for input from opinion makers such as Walter Lippmann, the crafty Kennedy knew he was making it difficult for correspondents to criticize him later. But Kennedy did not like to be reproached, and much of the monitoring of the media was the result of the president's thin skin. He would remind reporters who criticized him that he had read their words and was not above going over their heads to the home office.

Yet Kennedy enjoyed being around reporters, and they liked him. He wanted to know everything about them, including how much money they earned. Author of the Pulitzer Prize–winning book *Profiles in Courage*, Kennedy rightly considered himself an accomplished writer. (Some historians claim Kennedy did not really write the book, but no tangible proof has been offered.) Most important, Kennedy understood, as did FDR, that reporters are valuable to their home offices only if they are generating stories. Daily, he saw to it that reporters had stories, either through detailed press releases or through press briefings with Salinger.

His frequent press conferences took on the air of good-natured bantering before the television cameras. It was JFK's affability and his genuine fondness for reporters that brought him close to them, not his Harvard background or his liberal philosophy. He was a public relations man at heart. Still, during the first twenty-one months of his presidency, Kennedy was not regarded by editors and reporters as a world and national leader. His early slips had remained with him, and the 1962 congressional elections appeared to be a toss-up in the first days of October.

At that time, U.S. reconnaissance discovered that the Soviet Union had taken steps to place missiles in Cuba. Kennedy ordered the U.S. Navy to prepare for a blockade and a possible invasion. On October 14, air photos showed decisively that the Soviet Union was constructing offensive missile launch pads in Cuba. A few days later, Salinger was told to lie to the press if there were inquiries about the large number of persons visiting the White House. Kennedy's advisors were split over whether to blockade Cuba or bomb the suspected missile sites. As word leaked, Kennedy issued statements denying any action was pending. While in Chicago, he faked a cold and returned to Washington, claiming he was too ill to deliver a speech in Milwaukee. He also contacted the publishers of *The New York Times*, the *Washington Post*, and *Time* magazine, asking them to withhold stories about Cuba.

On October 22, Kennedy told a national television audience that construction of offensive missile bases in Cuba had been detected. A blockade of Cuba would begin, Kennedy announced, and a quarantine against Soviet shipments of any military or nuclear weaponry would be established immediately. This meant that Soviet ships would be boarded and searched if they approached Cuba, a move that, by international maritime law, could be considered an act of war. He sent a letter to Khrushchev warning of a possible nuclear confrontation. Khrushchev replied that Kennedy had no right to take such action. On October 25, U.N. Ambassador Adlai Stevenson confronted his Soviet counterpart, Valerian Zorin, during a special U.N. session, asking Zorin if he denied there were Soviet missile sites in Cuba. Zorin refused to answer, but Stevenson would not allow the Soviet emissary to dodge the question. "I am prepared to wait for hell to freeze over, if that is your answer," Stevenson snapped back.

Kennedy and his top aides prepared to evacuate to underground quarters in Virginia in case of nuclear attack. In some parts of the country, people began to buy every food product and staple they could obtain in anticipation of fleeing to privately built bomb shelters.

As Khrushchev and Kennedy exchanged messages, the confrontation in the Caribbean came closer. Then the Soviet ships bound for Cuba turned around, and Khrushchev promised in an urgent message to Kennedy on October 28 to remove missiles from Cuba. Eventually an accord was worked out whereby the United States agreed never to invade Castro's Cuba. The Soviet Union removed its offensive nuclear weaponry from Cuba and never introduced them there again.

The U.S. public and media praised Kennedy uniformly. Khrushchev had been humbled, it had generally been concluded. But, in truth, Kennedy's inexperience had brought the world to the brink of nuclear disaster.[6] Emboldened after Vienna, Khrushchev had gambled that he could continue to bully the young president. Kennedy had acted with great restraint during the crisis, but agreeing never to invade Cuba meant that the island nation of 8 million would be a thorn in the side of U.S. presidents for the next forty years. More important, the nuclear holocaust that the world had sought to avoid for seventeen years nearly took place. Cold War policies and hostilities that Kennedy had failed to mitigate nearly destroyed the planet. This was no triumph for either Kennedy or America.

The press had played a crucial role in this confrontation. Agreeing to withhold stories seemed to be responsible gestures, but when the public learned later that print media had done so, ensuing presidents had difficulty convincing the public that they were leveling with the voters during times of crises. Yet certainly there was more at stake here than in the Bay of Pigs crisis. Panic could have easily gripped the country if the entire truth had been known. In this instance, withholding details from a panicky public seemed to be a responsible step.

During the exchange of messages between the United States and the Soviet Union, John Scali, the American Broadcasting Company's diplomatic correspondent, had acted as a courier by conveying an oral message from Alexander Fomin, a minor Russian official, directly to Kennedy. Scali had known more about what was occurring than did Salinger.

Scali probably thought he was helping the world peace process by transporting Fomin's message, but such actions by a journalist were unforgivable. Scali lost his objectivity, and the many charges the Soviet government had leveled about U.S. journalists' being government agents were confirmed to some extent. Journalistic ethics are important, especially in a crisis. Scali should have asked Fomin to contact someone else. He feared that time was running short, but aside from the ethics question, Scali's amateur diplomacy could have cost a great deal. If somehow he had blundered in his handling of the meeting or conveyance of the message, the world could have been destroyed. In such a grim situation, the world did not need journalists masquerading as diplomats.

In general, the press and the president acquitted themselves reasonably well during October 1962, but certainly the policies and Cold War attitudes that led up to that month were not admirable. The world should never have been brought to the edge of annihilation. There was no reason for celebration or for Kennedy to be regarded as a hero. The crisis was the result of an accumulation of wrongly formulated policies and attitudes over two decades.

Nevertheless, the public and press did laud the president. In the November elections, the Democrats lost only four seats in the House and gained four seats in the Senate, to maintain comfortable margins in both chambers. Within a few weeks, Kennedy's approval rating swelled to 76 percent. The tone of news coverage changed. Republican editorial writers were still critical, but the inflection had a respectful timbre. Even the *Chicago Tribune*, which used the harshest rhetoric imaginable during the Roosevelt and Truman Administrations, had muted its language in 1963. It is difficult for even the most outspoken news people to criticize the president uncharitably when he is popular with the public and has proved himself under fire. Besides, McCormick's ghost was beginning to recede at the *Tribune*, and editors were less certain of the path that newspaper was taking. The "World's Greatest Newspaper" was not ready to take on the popular John F. Kennedy in late 1962.

THE KENNEDY ASSASSINATION

The missile crisis having elevated his presidency, Kennedy turned to other details. The year 1963 was dominated by more involvement of Americans in Vietnam and by continued civil rights demonstrations in the South. Now, Kennedy seemed to be a media hero in these struggles. The public and the press accepted Kennedy's assurances. When a Buddhist monk doused himself with gasoline and lit a match, Madam Nhu, Vietnam president Ngo Dinh Diem's sister-in-law, who was visiting in the United States, said there should be "more barbecues." Madam Nhu became known as the Dragon Lady. The public forgave Kennedy for Vietnam. Diem's assassination in September brought only hopes that a less autocratic leader would assume power in South Vietnam.

On September 2, the Columbia Broadcasting System expanded its news from fifteen to thirty minutes, and the real beginning for television news took shape. Local news programs were forced to extend their programming to thirty minutes, and Americans now had double the usual evening local and national news. The other two networks soon followed suit.

Television came into being during an era of strong presidents. Because it is simple to grab a statement from one person, the president, and focus on his policy initiatives, television naturally tends to concentrate on the executive instead of the legislative branch in the first place. Television's coming into existence at a time when Congress had forfeited much of its power to the White House anyway tended to exaggerate the role of the presidency further. Because Kennedy was popular and came across well on television, his success in Washington seemed to be magnified. It was still Congress that made the laws and approved the budget, but it seemed that Washington was Kennedy's town. Now television would have more time to spotlight Kennedy daily. Had Warren Harding been president in 1963, the president and television would not have found such accommodation. But beginning with Kennedy, television developed an evening news format that survived largely on the president's whereabouts and daily activities. This would prove to be a difficult burden for future presidents.

In September 1963 television supplanted newspapers and magazines as the leading source of news about the presidency, and no president thereafter could escape the cameras. CBS's chosen symbol, the CBS eye, was especially appropriate. The constant public appetite for news about Kennedy speeded up television's reliance on the White House for news and set in motion a chain of events that would make occupying the Oval Office a nearly impossible task for mere mortals.

Other concerns occupied the attention of Americans in 1963, however. On November 21, Kennedy flew to San Antonio, Houston, and then Fort Worth, where he spent the night. Published reports on the morning of November 22 detailed the route the presidential motorcade would take through downtown Dallas. At approximately 12:30 P.M., two bullets fired from a rifle struck Kennedy in the head, and he died moments later.

Lee Harvey Oswald was arrested in a moving picture theater that afternoon. It was concluded by police and later an investigative body, the Warren Commission, that Oswald acted alone firing a rifle from a window of the Texas Book Depository, killing Kennedy and wounding Texas Governor John Connally. Oswald was shot to death at close range as he was being transported from jail two days later. His killer was identified as nightclub owner Jack Ruby. The shooting was seen live on national television. Ruby was tried and sentenced to life in prison, where he died of cancer a few years later.

That is about as much as is known accurately. Conspiracy theorists wonder how Oswald could have fired so many shots in such a short period of time. Some have pointed to a film taken at the time of the assassination, which they claim shows a shadowy figure in a police uniform with a rifle behind the grassy knoll along the motorcade route. Why was Oswald in Mexico just months before the shooting? Why had he spent so much time in the Soviet Union? What of his supposed connections to the Central Intelligence Agency? Was Ruby's obvious association with the underworld significant, especially in view of Bobby Kennedy's efforts to jail Teamster President Jimmy Hoffa and considering John F. Kennedy's relationship with Judith Campbell? Can anyone believe an FBI investigation conducted under the leadership of J. Edgar Hoover, who had been blackmailing Kennedy?[7] Did the Warren Commission, which interviewed thousands of witnesses under the direction of chair Earl Warren, former Supreme Court Chief Justice, really have access to the proper information given that the FBI did most of the investigating? Will we ever know the truth?

Only the last question seems to have an undisputed answer: no. In the 1960s, Americans tended to accept the verdict of the Warren Commission. In the 1970s and 1980s, conspiracy theories flourished, and a special House Committee on Assassinations concluded in 1979 that it was likely that Oswald had an accomplice. In the 1990s, there was a tendency to return to acceptance of the single-assassin theory. Too many questions remain unanswered for these suppositions to die peacefully, especially in view of the duplicity engendered by Kennedy's secretive sex life and by J. Edgar Hoover's outrageous use of the FBI to spy on a variety of powerful and not-so-powerful Americans.

It is curious, though, that none of the national media explored the inconsistencies in the single-assassin theory until years later and that the Warren Commission report was largely accepted without question after it was issued. Later, when the public became fascinated with conspiracy ideas, television and films exploited this infatuation with ridiculous and outlandish movies and programs, espousing every theory ever concocted.

All this is quite incidental to the fact that Kennedy is dead. Nothing will change that. The ensuing events in the three days after Kennedy's assassination, including his funeral, were captured on television. It was and still is the most poignant time in the history of American television. Four American presidents have been assassinated, two of them the most popular men ever to occupy the Oval Office (Abraham Lincoln being the other). Eight American presidents have died in office: four in the nineteenth century and four in the twentieth century. Kennedy's presidency became the seventh shortest in history; only Harding, Gerald R. Ford, James Garfield, William Henry Harrison, Zachary Taylor, and Millard Fillmore served fewer days in the White House. Only the most studious historians are familiar with any of those six, except Ford. In time, Ford's Administration too will be obscure.

But Kennedy and his legend will live on. Although most of his agenda was unfulfilled, he imbued the nation with a spirit of optimism, the likes of which have not been seen since. The presidency and the public's acceptance of the powers of that office may have been at an all-time high when Kennedy was assassinated. Kennedy, unlike the other six short-term presidents, is regarded as one of our most successful presidents. It was as much his image and the timing of his death as his deeds that contributed to this overall impression.

The deaths of Lincoln and Franklin Roosevelt were as traumatizing for Americans as Kennedy's passing, but the ensuing funerals and dramatic events were not seen on television. Kennedy's death came when he was still extremely popular and reminded the world just how influential television had become.

It was the assassination, and not the debates, that brought the power of television to a zenith.

Why did the media not investigate the assassination more aggressively? It is hard to offer an assessment of the activities of several thousand news-gathering organizations, but here are some possible explanations: One, it is not entirely true. Thousands of articles carrying speculation did appear after the assassination, but few solid facts were unearthed, and the suppositions were not given much credence. Maybe the facts just were not available. Second, J. Edgar Hoover was a powerful force, one that even the strongest newspaper or television network did not want to antagonize. Third, there was a certain feeling that the Warren Commission would find the truth, and the inclination was to wait for the commission report. Fourth, the shock blunted the desire of both media and public to dredge up the facts of the case in the weeks and months following the assassination.

Whatever the reasons, the lack of solid information after the president's death helped to fuel the conspiracy theories. Just as television's depiction of the funeral was one of the most dramatic moments in American history, lack of fundamental investigative reporting in those days brought about later uncertainty and distrust of both government and media, especially in the years when the actual details of Kennedy's private affairs were revealed. The fuss about television's images of the Kennedy assassination only partially obscures the lack of inquiry by the media as to the details of the shooting.

Interest in the Kennedy family remained high during the 1960s, especially with Bobby and Ted Kennedy still actively involved in national politics. Jackie Kennedy was hounded by reporters for the remainder of her life. Her marriage to shipping magnate Aristotle Onassis created as much stir as King Edward's abdication to marry a commoner in the 1930s. In fact, Queen Jackie had married a commoner in the eyes of Americans.

John F. Kennedy's greatest legacy is his contribution to the popularity of the presidency and his ability to substitute image for substance. No president after Kennedy would be able to occupy the White House without burnishing his image and relationship with the public through the media. Kennedy's term of office was the beginning of the modern presidency.

NOTES

1. "Live Press Conferences," *Chicago Tribune*, editorial, January 2, 1961.

2. Pierre Salinger, *P.S. A Memoir* (New York: St. Martin's, 1995), 43–54.

3. For a complete summary of the attempted steel price hikes, see Richard Reeves, *President Kennedy: Profile of Power* (New York: Simon & Schuster, 1993), 294–301.

4. "A Further Slash in Kennedy's Popularity," Gallup Poll in *San Francisco Chronicle*, October 11, 1962, p. 2.

5. James R. Reston column, *The New York Times*, September 24, 1962; also see Reston, "Kennedy Called More Popular in Country Than in Capital," *San Francisco Chronicle*, September 24, 1962, p. 1 (reprint of *Times* article).

6. For the most complete and accurate historical recollection of the events of October 1962, see Reeves, *President Kennedy*, 365–427.

7. For a complete summary of Hoover's attitudes and actions toward Kennedy, a summary of the FBI's relationship with the Kennedy Administration, and private Hoover memos detailing Hoover's covert activities, see Mark North, *Act of Treason: The Role of J. Edgar Hoover in the Assassination of President Kennedy* (New York: Carroll & Graf, 1991), 51–652. See also Reeves, *President Kennedy*, 66, 67, 288–93, 626–27.

CHAPTER THREE

LYNDON JOHNSON'S FRUSTRATIONS

After the Kennedy assassination, Secret Service agents rushed Lyndon Johnson to the airport in Dallas. On board the Air Force One flight to Washington, D.C., with Johnson were his wife Claudia (Lady Bird), Jackie Kennedy, and the body of John F. Kennedy. Just two hours after the fatal shots were fired, Johnson was sworn in on the plane. He moved into the Oval Office soon afterward, the unexpectedly hasty transfer angering the Kennedy family, especially Bobby Kennedy who detested Johnson. Bobby Kennedy himself and the Secret Service had asked Johnson to conduct the swearing-in ceremony quickly, but Kennedy had not expected the Oval Office invasion. Because of the threat of nuclear attack at any time, it was imperative that the vice president be sworn into office quickly so that the nation would not be without a president for even a few hours, but Johnson had not observed carefully the necessary social amenities at a delicate time. The antagonism between Johnson and the Kennedys survived until Johnson's retirement in 1969.

Kennedy's death brought both opportunity and sorrow. No person would wish to assume office under such circumstances, and Johnson knew he would be compared with Kennedy throughout his tenure. On the other hand, he had been so thoroughly ignored during the Kennedy years that he had considered removing himself from the ticket in 1964. Suddenly all had changed. He was president and held the sympathy of the country.

Johnson was a mirror opposite of the Kennedys. Born in the hill country of Texas, he had taught high school and served as a congressional aide before his election to Congress in 1937. He was a populist liberal devoted to the principles of the New Deal. He muscled his way to the Senate through an unprincipled campaign in 1948, stealing more votes than his opponent to gain the Democratic nomination by 87 votes.[1] A dynamo, who worked eighteeen hours a day, Johnson became majority leader in record time and shepherded a series of legislative packages through Congress during the Eisenhower Administration. He had accepted the vice presidential nomination only reluctantly in 1960 and chafed at the limitations of the largely ceremonial office.

Unlike Kennedy, Johnson had no polish. He bullied and steamrolled. Yet the new president was a serious politician with an impressive legislative track record. His political and lawmaking skills needed no validation. His first thirteen months in office were a breeze.

The Johnson family was unlike the Kennedy clan. Lady Bird had been as shrewd a political analyst as Johnson but was not enamored of the trappings of the official White House. She preferred to stay in the background, except when she supported her one pet project, beautification of America, an attempt to spruce up the highways and public areas of the nation so that traveling around the country would be a more pleasant experience for future generations. Billboards were removed in some places, and minor alterations took place in public parks. At Lady Bird's urging, many permanent flower beds were planted in Washington along the Potomac River. Congress balked at heavily funding the beautification program, however. A generation later, many states did adopt such programs, especially along expressways. Despite her pet project, Lady Bird was not Jackie Kennedy. Her acumen was lost on her stubborn and belligerent husband. She influenced him in the subtle ways that a wife did in those years, but she certainly attracted far less adulation than Jackie Kennedy.

Johnson treated his wife shamefully at times, seeking the favors of younger women around him on occasion and treating Lady Bird as a servant. It was not uncommon during his Senate days for Johnson to call the LBJ ranch and announce to Lady Bird that about a dozen guests would be piling in for dinner in the next hour. Dinner was always ready. At a presidential press conference, Johnson winked at reporters and told them he was tired because he had had a rough night. Lady Bird sat stone-faced on the podium.

Their two daughters, Lynda Bird and Luci Baines, were young adults when Johnson moved into the White House, and they married soon after. They were supportive of their father but were not the precocious youngsters of Kennedy fame or outspoken defenders of the family as was Julie Nixon Eisenhower in the next administration. The Johnson family was a supportive, traditional political family that remained largely out of the spotlight and was totally committed to the family interests. They were certainly not the pseudo-royalty that America had come to adore in the first years of the decade.

After assuming office, Johnson pledged to further Kennedy's domestic initiatives, renaming the New Frontier the Great Society, a term he first used at a speech at the University of Michigan in May 1964. To stimulate the economy, he employed a tactic that Kennedy had planned to use: he convinced Congress to enact a tax cut in early 1964. The crowning achievement of his liberal reform movement was the Civil Rights Act of 1964, which allowed federal authorities to become involved in desegregation efforts and to intercede when violence erupted against Negroes in the South if a person's civil rights had been violated. Also, the enactment of Medicare and Medicaid in 1965 was to have lasting implications for the nation's health care system. At the same time, Johnson continued to escalate the war in Vietnam but had to deal infrequently with Moscow, after hard-liners in the Kremlin forced Nikita Khrushchev into retirement, to be replaced by Leonid Brezhnev.

A clash between Panamanian and U.S. troops in the Canal Zone in January 1964 led to a brief diplomatic crisis that was resolved three months later, and when Fidel Castro cut off the water supply to Guantanamo Bay in Cuba in February, Johnson saw to it that the base developed its own supply.

On August 4, 1964, just before the kickoff of the general election campaign, the U.S. destroyers *Maddox* and *Turner Joy* in the Gulf of Tonkin off Vietnam reported that they had been fired on by North Vietnamese torpedo boats. The report was corrected later by the captain of the *Maddox*, who said there had been a mistaken sighting. But Johnson ignored the change in assessment and used the supposed attacks as a pretext for unlimited license to pursue the war. The Senate approved the Gulf of Tonkin resolution by a vote of 88 to 2, a declaration just short of war that allowed Johnson unlimited power to escalate the fighting. Johnson's approval rating in the polls soared from 42 to 72 percent overnight.

THE 1964 ELECTION

The 1964 election was a foregone conclusion. It seemed as if presidential candidate Barry Goldwater and the Republicans did all they could to aid the Johnson campaign. The party was split between Goldwater and Rockefeller. This time, however, conservatives made certain that for the first time in thirty-two years, the nominee would be a true conservative. Rockefeller, as usual, waffled and ran a poor primary campaign, dropping from contention early. The candidacy of Pennsylvania Governor William Scranton was too little, too late. As had been long anticipated, the general election pitted Johnson against Goldwater. At the Republican convention in San Francisco in July, Rockefeller denounced from the podium the extremists in the party, to a chorus of boos from the convention floor. Goldwater compounded the problem by declaring during his acceptance speech, "I would remind you that extremism in the defense of liberty is no vice. And let me remind you also that moderation in the pursuit of justice is no virtue!"[2]

Johnson received as many endorsements as Goldwater, including quite a few from Republican newspapers. *Life* magazine announced its support of Johnson in October, the first time any Time Inc. publication had endorsed a Democrat. The *Atlantic Monthly*, which had not endorsed a candidate in over 100 years, formally opposed Goldwater. Johnson received endorsements from the *Kansas City Star, Philadelphia Inquirer, Chicago Daily News, Chicago Sun-Times, Houston Post, San Francisco Chronicle, Cleveland Plain Dealer, New York Times,* and *Pittsburgh Post-Gazette*—most of them long-time GOP supporters. The Cowles, Scripps-Howard, and Hearst chains endorsed a Democratic presidential candidate for the first time in thirty years. On the other hand, many Deep South newspapers reflected shifting allegiances in Dixie because of Johnson's active civil rights stance, and they supported a Republican for the first time.

Johnson's campaign staff effectively used Goldwater's ineptness while trumpeting the robust state of the economy and downplaying the escalating war in Vietnam. A controversial television advertising spot, "The Daisy Girl," which appeared briefly on national television, focused clearly on Americans' fears of nuclear annihilation. While a young girl picked petals from a daisy in an idyllic setting, a voice in the background counted down to a nuclear launch. The spot ended with a horrifying visual of an atomic explosion and mushroom cloud. "These are the stakes . . . ," Johnson's voice intoned from one of his speeches. The ad implied that Goldwater could not be trusted with nuclear arms, although it never mentioned Goldwater by name. The commercial was pulled after a few airings, but Johnson knew how to play dirty, and nothing was off limits in one of his campaigns. Meanwhile, news coverage of the ad gave the Johnson campaign free publicity. The Arizona Senator, an honest and plain-talking conservative, was hopelessly outmatched as he challenged a sitting president, who came to office amid tragedy less than a year before the general election and who had a strong economy with which to entice voters. Newspapers fretted about the 5.4 percent unemployment rate and the $7.7 billion budget deficit, figures that future generations view as highly desirable. Inflation was around 1 to 2 percent annually. It was one of the most affluent times in American history.

"The Daisy Girl" advertisement and the successful depiction of Goldwater as a wild-eyed conservative only helped to pad Johnson's margin of victory. History was on Johnson's side. Goldwater's conservatism did not fit the mood of the country, especially with the robust economy. The only surprise on election day was Johnson's 61.3 percent share of the popular vote, the largest percentage in a contested election ever in American presidential politics. That translated to 486 of 532 electoral votes, also one of the greatest electoral landslides in history. The Democrats gained thirty-seven seats in the House for a three-to-two advantage and three in the Senate for a two-to-one majority there. One of the new senators was Robert F. Kennedy, of New York. Goldwater carried his home state of Arizona and five Deep South states—Alabama, Mississippi, Louisiana, South Carolina, and Georgia—completely breaking the Democratic hold on Dixie for the first time since Reconstruction.

Press coverage, newspaper endorsements, and television advertisements and coverage had little to do with the outcome. As with most other modern elections, the result was decided by near-term economic factors and long-term historical influences. The conservative element in the Republican Party was in a shambles. They had nominated one of their own for the first time in three decades, and the result was a disaster.

Goldwater supporters claimed later that their candidate had been undermined by the liberal national news media. This was one of the earliest claims that news media favored liberals in presidential politics, though Nixon had suggested that a media bias for Kennedy had been a factor in 1960 without specifically using the term "liberal." It was a theme that would be repeated in years to come. In 1964, as many newspapers endorsed Goldwater as supported Johnson, though numerous larger newspapers urged the election of the incumbent, and many fewer newspapers supported Goldwater than had supported Republicans in the past. Newspaper editorial boards had always favored Republicans, but in 1964 Goldwater was too conservative even for these editors. *The New York Times* editorial policies had been relatively conservative in the 1920s, before the Roosevelt era, but they had favored Democrats and liberals since FDR's tenure in office. Under Philip Graham and then his widow, Katherine (he died in 1963), the traditionally conservative *Washington Post* had become more influential and more liberal, as had the *Los Angeles Times*. The *Chicago Tribune* remained a Republican conservative newspaper but would soon modify its extreme ethnocentrism. The *Chicago Sun-Times*, a merged newspaper in the 1940s, had developed into a liberal voice in the nation's heartland, and the *Chicago Daily News*, always conservative, had come under *Chicago Sun-Times* ownership in the 1960s. The nation's news magazines had traditionally been conservative but moved to the left in the 1960s. *Time* would change completely after Henry Luce's death in 1967.

The national media, historically a bastion of conservative Republican support, had become more liberal; so had its readership and the nation, and by the 1960s the leanings of a newspaper editorially did not always translate into biased news coverage, as it had in the earlier part of the century. If conservatives were disappointed with a "liberal" media, it was probably because they had enjoyed mainstream editorial support for so many years or because newspapers and magazines were not diligent about challenging the false impressions the Johnson campaign had attached to Goldwater. At any rate, print media coverage of the 1964 election and any presidential election thereafter rarely influenced the ultimate outcome. Negative reporting on the Goldwater campaign was simply a result of Goldwater's disadvantaged historical position, the party split, and the mood of the electorate. He had no cogent issues popular with the majority of voters at the time, he was a conservative when the nation was swinging to the left, his party was divided, and he was painted by the Johnson camp as an extremist.

The impact of television coverage is harder to analyze. Television was more mobile and through improved technology was able to cover the campaign better in 1964 than in 1960. Viewers had settled into a routine by 1964, watching television during prime time religiously. The conventions were covered gavel to gavel by all the networks, and viewers had few, if any, options because the three networks commanded 90 percent of the audience. The conventions, then, had a captive viewership, but neither party took advantage of this. The proceedings were punctuated with all the folderol and haranguing that had always marked the quadrennial American political celebrations. Television was still a guest, not a director. Nevertheless, it is certain that the dissension on the podium at the Republican convention that was broadcast nationwide had to have affected voters to some extent. Television's presence, not its bias, seemed to have worked against Goldwater at the convention.

During the campaign, television news coverage nightly hammered home the assumption that the election was a foregone conclusion. Nearly every report contained some reference to Lyndon Johnson's huge lead in the polls and the futility of the Goldwater campaign. But it was the news, and not the newscasters, that affected the coverage. Chet Huntley, one of the co-anchors for the National Broadcasting Company, never liked Lyndon Johnson, he revealed later. The Columbia Broadcasting System's Walter Cronkite was scrupulously neutral. Eastern Establishment leanings in 1964 were not as much a factor as the quick assumption that Goldwater had no chance to win the election.

But this was not an incorrect theme. It raises the question of just how neutral television newscasters or other reporters should be in analyzing an election. Should they not have reported that voters seemed to prefer Lyndon Johnson? That would be dishonest. Yet in a television age, a candidate who is perceived as losing finds it twice as difficult to convince voters of his or her legitimate chance of winning. Although Goldwater really did have little hope of victory and it was a newsperson's obligation to report the facts as they appeared, this compounds the problem of fair play in media coverage. In a more modern television age, popular television reports are more carefully worded, with words such as "appears to be ahead," or "would seem to enjoy a comfortable lead," or "perhaps faces an uphill battle." In 1964, such balanced language was not as common, but how to cover a lopsided presidential race remained a problem for decades.

This and the residual effect of Theodore White's commentary on the 1960 election created discomfort among many Americans in their perception of television's role in presidential politics. Although they mostly voted for Johnson, Americans were sympathetic when Goldwaterites cried foul. Conservatives for at least another generation would see television, newspapers, and magazines as their ideological foes and would point to the Goldwater debacle as inimitable proof. Yet in 1964 and in presidential general elections that would follow, media played a very small role in the ultimate outcome. They influenced the primaries greatly but not the general elections, which tended to be referenda on the acceptability of the incumbent. The role of the media in the 1964 general election and since has traditionally been greatly exaggerated by media opponents and proponents.

As his second term began, Johnson's landslide offered the legislative muscle needed to push through nearly any bill he wanted, an enviable position. Fewer than 300 men had died in Vietnam. But as the casualties mounted and the public tired of Johnson's plans and promises, the course of the presidency would change forever. Within four years Johnson would be a beaten man. The first major turnaround in the modern presidency was about to take place. No one would have predicted it in November 1964.

LBJ's Domestic Agenda

Johnson devised a complete domestic agenda. In 1964 he had laid the groundwork for expanding the national social safety net. Under Franklin D. Roosevelt, government had become a friend, the protector against big business. Yet Roosevelt had generally only established work programs and a retirement system. Under Johnson, no American would be without a government program in time of need, and black Americans could look to the government for full support for the first time in history.

In 1965 and 1966 the Johnson Administration established fair housing and fair jury selection processes. The Department of Housing and Urban Development was created, and the first comprehensive health planning programs were established. Consumer protection programs were initiated, and unemployment benefits were augmented. Johnson himself visited rural, poor areas of the country and promised that his Great Society would provide a better future for the nation's poor. In all, ninety-seven bills passed Congress during 1965 and 1966, reforming and remodeling government and its relationship to society.

But by the end of 1966 public perception of the president had begun to change. Oil prices had risen sharply, and inflation fears plagued the business community. In August 1965 riots devastated Watts, an inner-city neighborhood in Los Angeles. After a routine traffic arrest on August 11, rumors spread that police had mistreated a pregnant woman, and some Negroes in the Watts community exploded with rage. Rioting and looting followed, leaving the entire area in a shambles.

During the summers of 1966 and 1967, other major cities—Los Angeles, Washington, Omaha, Cleveland, Des Moines, New York, Baltimore, Atlanta, Providence, Minneapolis, Dayton, San Francisco, St. Louis, Nashville, Louisville, Cincinnati, Chicago, Newark, Detroit, and Milwaukee—were torn by rioting. A militant organization in Oakland, California, the Black Panthers, began to gain a strong following among disenchanted young Negroes. Martin Luther King Jr.'s philosophy of nonviolent resistance was crumbling. Johnson's efforts at revitalizing the inner cities and establishing civil rights guidelines seemed ineffective to both whites and Negroes.

The Democratic Party lost seats in both the House and Senate in the 1966 off-year elections, not uncommon after a landslide in the previous election but an ominous sign for Johnson. More than 4,000 men died in Vietnam in 1966.

As Johnson's popularity with the public began to wane, his relations with reporters deteriorated even more drastically. He set a record for number of press secretaries. Pierre Salinger stayed on with Johnson for only a few months before leaving to run, unsuccessfully, in California for the Senate. He was succeeded by George Reedy, a former wire service reporter who had been on Johnson's staff for more than ten years. He lasted only about a year and a half. Bill Moyers, age twenty-nine, a long-time friend from Texas, held the position for a similar time before being replaced by Johnson's final press secretary, George Christians, who had been press secretary to two Texas governors. Johnson berated and bullied his aides and press secretaries in the same way he attempted to browbeat the press corps. He worked long hours and expected everyone around him to do the same. Few could keep up the pace.

Johnson held press conferences about once every two weeks in 1964 and then about every four weeks after that. Only a fourth of his press conferences were covered live by television. Half were off the record.[3] The conferences were not great television theater as they had been with Kennedy. Johnson was not comfortable before cameras. Rather, he was in his element wheeling and dealing, convincing legislators to support his programs. Television was an intruder in Washington, he felt. Johnson had been around the nation's capital much longer than the cameras had, but he was the president who followed Kennedy, and Americans had come to expect the drama of the president's dueling with the press before a national audience. Johnson disappointed them.

He disillusioned reporters too. Reporters were tools to be used to gain an end, Johnson believed. It had always been this way in Texas. He believed that friendly reporters would write whatever he suggested they write, and unfriendly ones were not worth his time. But Washington was not Texas, and the press corps—White House reporters particularly—had come to expect royal treatment. Johnson disliked the stodgy press conferences, and though he held a number of them, he sought to impress correspondents the most through one-on-one discussions. He would often pull a reporter aside and harangue him or her for as much as two hours at a time, making his case and pleading his points without allowing the journalist even so much as one question.

Women reporters caused the president great consternation because he was not used to dealing with women at the business level. He held a traditional view of a woman's role. NBC correspondent Nancy Dickerson, for instance, noted that Johnson had once tried to seduce her, but mostly he just flirted. She wrote that he had only one serious affair with an unidentified woman and that was before he became president, but that he also had a relationship with his biographer Doris Kearns.[4] Sex and women were not the problem; but his low regard for women as equals was. He once told an aide to have sex with a woman reporter who had been particularly critical so that she would report on his Administration more favorably. He often called reporters and pompously told them on the phone, "Now, listen, this is your president calling."

Johnson's manner provoked many in the press corps, and they began to regard him as something of a buffoon. Certainly his cowboy boots and occasional foray on horseback were alien to the many easterners who dominated the press corps. Part of Johnson's problem was this press snobbery, but much of it related to his domineering attitude. Kennedy had been just as heavy-handed when he had to be, but he controlled reporters with style and panache. Johnson used coarse tactics in crude and obvious ways. More important, his one-on-one discussions were not revealing or newsworthy. They were speeches filled with rhetoric and hyperbole.

Often after such discussions, correspondents and columnists wrote negatively about the president, and he felt stabbed in the back. He had given these correspondents much of his precious time, only to be criticized afterward. This had never happened with Kennedy. It must have been because the reporters were Ivy League like Kennedy and unlike Johnson, Johnson reasoned. There is some truth to that, but more to the point, they were not Texans who understood Johnson and accepted his bombast.

A few incidents during the Johnson years helped to establish a lasting impression with both public and press. One was during an informal press conference in 1965, when Johnson was asked about his health. He reported that he had a gallbladder operation and then pulled up his shirt to show the scar. This amused and appalled the correspondents, who found Johnson's manners disturbing, and quickly they reported the faux pas to the public. On a second occasion, Johnson was showing off his dogs, Him and Her, and picked both up by the ears. When offended animal rights activists complained, Johnson explained that he always picked the dogs up by their ears, and it did not hurt them.

These incidents were blown out of proportion, as often happens in the modern presidency, but they also illustrate Johnson's lack of understanding of public imagery. Perhaps he was correct—lifting the animals by their ears did not hurt them—but that is hard to explain to an American public enamored of their pets. The gallbladder scar incident gives us a clue as to how little Johnson understood the symbolic role of being president. In the 1960s most Americans looked upon the president as a role model. Since Franklin D. Roosevelt's Administration, the president had been the ultimate protector and guiding light for the common person. After he has consumed a few beers, Uncle Fred at a family picnic pulls up his shirt and shows his surgical scar; the president of the United States does not do so in view of the White House press corps. How could such a man be the symbol of the Free World?

These negative feelings became important when the Vietnam War dragged on. Through the urging of aides, particularly Defense Secretary Robert McNamara, Johnson continued to escalate troop commitments in Vietnam. The solution seemed within grasp: just a few more Americans in the war and just a few more successful skirmishes, and the end would come. Americans had expected to subdue the Vietcong and North Vietnamese regulars quickly, but the scattered bands of fighting guerrillas kept hanging on, and casualties mounted on both sides. Bombing of the North continued almost unabated after 1965, and the number of American soldiers in Vietnam reached almost 500,000 by 1967. Total casualties in the war up to that time exceeded 100,000, and deaths reached nearly 15,000.

During times of war, military and political leaders exaggerate enemy losses and minimize their own casualties. The Johnson Administration took this approach to a new art form, placing a positive spin on every skirmish and greatly distorting casualty figures. The result was a widely used euphemism, the "credibility gap." This simply meant that Johnson was widely believed to be a liar. In truth, he was no greater a fibber than were Roosevelt and Woodrow Wilson during the two world wars. Wilson campaigned in 1916 on a platform that extolled his having kept America out of World War I, all the while knowing that American involvement was inevitable. Roosevelt claimed neutrality in 1940 and 1941 but exaggerated the nature of skirmishes between U.S. and German sea forces, extended a lend-lease commitment to Great Britain, and cut off oil and scrap metal exports to Japan.

Both presidents had muzzled their real intentions while doing what they felt was in the best interest of the American public. Johnson was merely following their precedents, but the outcomes of the world wars vindicated Wilson and Roosevelt in the minds of the public, while Vietnam became "President Johnson's war." The credibility gap became a problem because the war developed into a dilemma, and Johnson's unpopularity magnified all his other public relations difficulties. All the success on domestic policy that Johnson enjoyed in his early administration was overshadowed by disenchantment with the progress of the war. Then his deteriorated image and bad press seemed beyond control.

It is a quirk of casual history that Americans refer to the 1960s as a time of protest and anti-establishment fervor. Except in the black community, this was not true until late 1966. The early 1960s more resemble the 1950s in both public attitude and feelings about government. By late 1966, this positive feeling and hard-line attitude toward fighting communism wherever it arose in the world had begun to dissolve. What is generally referred to as the "Sixties" is the time period between late 1966 and late 1970, a time of rebellion among some of the nation's youth and a few older adults. It is a time when many of the social mores of Americans changed, but surprisingly this was not really the catalyst for change in the presidency. It was disenchantment with the length and prosecution of the war. This will be personified in the next chapter, but this mood of disappointment needs some explanation for understanding the political events that led up to the tumultuous and sorrowful year of 1968.

By 1967, an unpopular draft system had begun to scoop up young men as soon as they were eighteen years old, except those wealthy enough and well educated enough to enroll at a college or university. Antiwar fever climbed steadily on the nation's campuses and among the young everywhere. Johnson's confidence was shaken, and he appeared tired and distracted in his few television appearances. The nation's domestic and international problems had begun to weigh heavily on him.

An offensive launched by the North Vietnamese during the lunar month of Tet in January 1968 brought Johnson's tenure as president to an end. The battle itself was actually a terrible strategic disaster for the communist forces, but during the fighting, North Vietnam sappers entered the compound of the U.S. embassy for a few hours, threatening those inside. They were eventually driven off, but Americans watching on television saw this standoff and were convinced that Johnson's assurances that victory was at hand were illusions. Support for the war remained at about 45 percent in national polls, but approval of Johnson's conduct of the war dropped from 40 to 26 percent.[5]

At the same time, the junior senator from Minnesota, Eugene McCarthy, was campaigning in New Hampshire. McCarthy said he would end U.S. participation in the war immediately if elected. Because he sought to unseat an incumbent president in his own party, few newspeople gave McCarthy much chance of winning and little attention, but on March 12 he stunned the country by nearly defeating Johnson in New Hampshire, winning 42.4 percent of the votes cast by Democrats to Johnson's 49.5 percent. Days later, Robert F. Kennedy entered the race. On March 31, Johnson announced on national television that he would not accept his party's nomination for president in 1968. He claimed later that he had intended for a long time not to seek re-election, but few believed him. Vietnam had ended his career.

THE 1968 ELECTION CAMPAIGN

The 1968 election campaign was perhaps the most tragic one in the history of the country. Only four days after Johnson's announcement, the Rev. Martin Luther King Jr. was shot and killed in Memphis by James Earl Ray. His death horrified the nation and set off riots in more than 100 major cities. King had been a calming influence during a time when young blacks had chafed at the slow progress of civil rights. His death left a terrible void in the integration movement and, coming so close to the assassination of John F. Kennedy, kept the nation wondering about the safety of its leaders.

Vice President Hubert Humphrey entered the race, thus offering a stand-in to Johnson supporters. Having set a political upheaval in motion, McCarthy was largely forgotten. Humphrey waged an aggressive battle against Kennedy but could not overcome the memory of Robert Kennedy's dead brother and the popularity of the Kennedy name. Bobby Kennedy rolled through the primaries, capping the campaign with an overwhelming victory in the final primary in California on June 4. After he spoke to a cheering throng in the lobby of the Ambassador Hotel in Los Angeles early on June 5, Kennedy and his coterie took a short cut through the hotel kitchen. There, Sirhan Sirhan, a Jordanian national living in the United States, was waiting with a gun. Upset by Kennedy's public support of sending aircraft to help arm Israel, Sirhan opened fire on the candidate. Kennedy died three days later.

The appalling murder sickened the nation. What had promised to be an exciting and revolutionary election year had become a nightmare. The Democrats were in disarray, having a choice between the vice president of a discredited and unpopular regime and a colorless, one-issue junior senator.

The Republicans were in a similar quandary. Shortly after Goldwater's defeat, Michigan Governor George Romney attracted national notice. Romney, a former auto executive who had rescued Michigan from near bankruptcy, represented a more moderate wing of the Republican Party, far away from the Goldwaterites. During 1965, Romney had toured South Vietnam and told reporters that a U.S. presence in Vietnam was morally correct. In September 1967 as the primary campaign approached, Romney informed a television interviewer that it had been unnecessary for the United States to get involved in Vietnam. He added that he had been "brainwashed" by generals and diplomats there in 1965. Romney, the front-runner, had terminated his campaign before it began. He limped into the primary season and dropped from the race two weeks before the New Hampshire contest to avoid an embarrassing defeat.

Nelson Rockefeller, the other moderate GOP hopeful, announced he would not be a candidate in March and then in April said he would. His now-legendary waffling once again took him out of the running. Senator Charles Percy of Illinois, Mayor John Lindsay of New York, and Governor Ronald Reagan of California were too new to the scene. The Republican candidate pool was empty. Only one candidate remained: Richard Nixon, whose career had seemed badly damaged after his loss to Kennedy in 1960. He compounded his woes by conducting an ill-advised campaign for governor of California in 1962. Nixon had been far away from California politics for over ten years. The incumbent, Pat Brown, trounced him, and at a tense press conference later, Nixon told reporters he was finished with politics, adding, "You won't have Nixon to kick around anymore—because, gentlemen, this is my last press conference."

Nixon took a position with a law firm in New York City, but could not stay out of politics. He constantly stumped for local GOP candidates throughout the years leading up to the 1968 primary, setting the stage for his amazing comeback. Quietly Nixon rolled up an impressive array of victories in the Republican primaries and had a lock on the nomination before GOP moderates knew what had occurred. Although Johnson had buried Goldwater in a landslide just four years before and although the Democrats dominated local and national politics at almost every level in the 1960s, Nixon's stunning comeback placed the Democratic Party in an unenviable position as the conventions approached.

Humphrey was a likable, talkative liberal who had earned a respected record on civil rights as mayor of Minneapolis in the late 1940s. But despite a liberal record, Johnson had been pummeled by the New Left, or young anti–Vietnam War movement, and was despised by the conservative right. As vice president, Humphrey was closely identified with the Johnson regime.

When the Republicans gathered in Miami in early August, there was a harmonious, festive environment. Rockefeller hoped to prevent a first-ballot Nixon victory and to create a deadlock, but Nixon's organizers were too clever for that. In a well-planned and -executed convention maneuver, they offered perks such as free meals and airport shuttles to nearly every delegate who arrived. The purchased goodwill, the weak field of opponents, and Nixon's strong showing in the primaries were more than enough to guarantee a first-ballot victory with little controversy.

The Democratic convention in the last week of August was another matter. To begin with, only last-minute negotiations coerced by Mayor Richard J. Daley had avoided a telephone strike that would have affected the convention and crippled convention communications. A taxi strike also complicated matters. But the real problem was security.

For months prior to the convention, the Youth International Party (YIPPIES) had been passing out flyers on campuses all over the Midwest, inviting college students to come to Chicago and disrupt the convention. They planned to roast a pig in Lyndon Johnson's honor and heckle Humphrey and his supporters. Police had plenty of advance warning, and it did not take much foresight to anticipate that this would be a tumultuous convention. Yet no one in the media or in the party anticipated what transpired those four days in Chicago.

Chicago of the 1960s was nearly insulated from the growing antiwar unrest that had gripped campuses and many large cities. It was a tough, blue-collar, no-nonsense industrial city, where 1920s values still flourished. Daley was the last of the big city bosses, and his word in Chicago carried the weight of ten presidents. Nothing of any worth was accomplished in Chicago without Daley's approval and without some more-than-token payment to city hall and the Democratic Party. The police force was one of the most corrupt in the country. After a stop for a traffic violation, a Chicagoan routinely handed over his driver's license with a $20 bill enclosed. The license would always be returned with a warning against endangering lives—but no ticket and no $20 bill.

Sending thousands of long-haired, ill-mannered protesters into such a climate is akin to pouring fuel into a smouldering bonfire. Clashes with police occurred in Grant Park, in Lincoln Park, and near the Conrad Hilton Hotel, where McCarthy supporters were staying. Protesters chanted phrases laced with foul language, threw rocks and bags of urine and feces at the police, and refused to evacuate public places after curfew. Police waded in with billy clubs and tear gas. Bloody confrontations marked the entire convention week, and by the time Humphrey was nominated, the Democratic Party was in a shambles. Thousands had been arrested or injured. Worse, the entire world watched on television as the leading nation of the free world conducted its political business amid violence and conflict in the streets. Later, the Walker Commission, headed by reformer Daniel Walker, labeled the confrontation a "police riot." Walker, however, was an anti-Daley candidate for governor four years later, and his political sympathies may well have colored the conclusions of the commission.

Democratic Party regulars claimed later that television was largely responsible for the confrontation; the demonstrators would have given up and gone home if they had not gained desired television exposure. But this is to ignore the temper of the times. Antiwar sentiments among a segment of the under-thirty generation had started to redirect the lives of these youths in the summer of 1968. The violence that had claimed the lives of two leaders of the left earlier in the year (King and Kennedy) had reaffirmed the injustice that many felt had come to represent the established party system.

The police, on the other hand, represented an older generation, who valued order and respect for established standards above abstracts. The confrontation in the streets was not about party politics and publicity per se. It was a microcosm of a division between a segment of one generation and a larger segment of another. It was about doing business as usual versus sweeping away an entire, entrenched system of values.

The city of Chicago and the Democratic Party barely survived this confrontation. The conflict would have occurred regardless of the presence of media, but this was the first year that the national convention coverage was broadcast in full color, and the color most prevalent was blood-red. Television certainly had an impact, but by its very nature it could not do otherwise. Police slamming nightsticks into the skulls of young, middle-class protesters is news—perhaps more important than the mundane matters on the convention floor, and certainly more dramatic. The coverage was not necessarily objective, however. In their zeal, the police had turned their anger on anyone in the vicinity, including reporters, camerapersons, and McCarthy delegates. Anyone not wearing riot gear was subject to a beating.

This turned some news organizations against the police, though by and large, as had been the case throughout the tumultuous late 1960s, newspaper editorial writers largely blamed violence on the protesters. Still, the police were roundly criticized for their excesses, especially their pummeling of newspersons. Police claimed that in such a chaotic climate, it was not a simple matter to identify who was a protester and who was a bystander. In an editorial commentary, Frank Reynolds, ABC news anchor, labeled such explanations as "baloney." Certainly there was an element of revenge in the coverage, but the undisciplined reactions of the police and planned provocations by the demonstrators created the tragedy and the concurrent press coverage. Reporters were anxious to focus cameras on the violence, because that is what is expected of them. If police beatings of newspersons entered into the slant of the coverage, then there may have been some culpability for the later violence, but certainly news executives' share of the blame was tiny compared to that borne by the police and some protesters.

The images of Chicago dogged the entire general election campaign and changed forever the way Americans viewed national politics. Conventions would no longer be simply gathering places for old-line politicians to flex their muscles. There would be changes in the makeup of the delegates, and never again would convention political maneuvering overshadow the primaries.

Ironically, the liberal Humphrey, Nixon's opponent, complained about negative press coverage and the attention that television paid to demonstrators and hecklers at Humphrey rallies later in the fall. Nixon met with far less harassment.

Having learned his lesson in 1960, Nixon refused to debate. Instead, he appeared in discussions in the round, where carefully selected audiences asked nonthreatening, simplistic questions. Humphrey allowed that he would stop bombing North Vietnam as an acceptable risk for peace negotiations, trying to put some distance between himself and Johnson while attempting not to appear to be abandoning the soldiers in Vietnam. Nixon, on the other hand, promised to pursue "a peace with honor." Though Johnson always considered Humphrey's campaign statement about the bombing to be a mistake, a few days before the election, the president announced a halt to the bombing of North Vietnam and a concurrent peace talk initiative.

Because of Humphrey's moves to separate himself from Johnson, because of Johnson's halt to the bombing, or because of an innate public dislike for Nixon, the gap between Nixon and Humphrey narrowed in the polls as election day approached. Nixon's 15 percentage point lead early in the campaign had dissipated. The predictability of the outcome was complicated by the third-party candidacy of former Alabama governor George Wallace, who had stood in the doorway of the University of Alabama five years earlier to bar the enrollment of the two Negro students, James Hood and Vivian Malone. Wallace claimed the allegiance of the white-dominant electorate throughout Dixie and in some parts of the North. Would Wallace torpedo Humphrey's chances by draining Democratic voters, or had these voters so abandoned the National Democratic Party that their support of Wallace would really hurt Nixon? It was unclear.

Humphrey was bitterly disappointed by the many newspapers that grudgingly endorsed Nixon. The biggest setback came just a week before the election when the liberal *Chicago Sun-Times* endorsed Nixon.

The election remained a toss-up as the long evening dragged into the morning. As dawn broke in the East, votes were still being counted, but by rush hour, it was certain Nixon had won by the slimmest of margins—just over 400,000 votes among 60 million cast. His percentage was 43.4 to Humphrey's 42.7 and Wallace's 13.5. Nixon received 301 electoral votes, Humphrey 191, and Wallace 46. Nixon had perpetrated the most dramatic comeback in American political history, but the country was torn apart by war and assassinations and weary and wary of politics. Nixon recalled a sign held up during the campaign by a young girl. It read, "Bring us together." A tremendous task lay ahead of him. He had won a pyrrhic victory.

SIXTIES IMAGERY

Many Americans do not remember who won the 1968 election but recall grainy newsfilm scenes of police wading into a crowd of demonstrators in Grant Park during the Democratic National Convention. They hardly recall that a man who had won one of the most convincing victories in American presidential history removed himself from a bid for re-election, that the National Democratic Party had lost the South forever, that the country had been split along generational lines, and that Americans would remain in Vietnam for four more years. That is so much history. They do know of a mistrust of politics, the presidency, and the media. That is the legacy.

The 1968 election proved to be the dividing line for presidential politics. It was the last time when a political convention would matter to the public or the party. Liberals charged that the 1968 convention was controlled by party hacks. In 1972 the number of primary elections would increase, and there would be a concerted effort to bring in delegates with varying racial, ethnic, and financial backgrounds.

The election was also something of a contradiction to what was perceived as the popular mood of the times. Wallace and Nixon had emerged from the bowels of the American right, anathema to the long-haired peaceniks who dominated the television screens and the front pages. The liberal Humphrey was the representative of the administration that had mired the nation in an interminable Asian war. None of these three candidates mirrored in the least the popular image of the late 1960s. Wallace represented the last dying gasp of a segregated South; the rock-solid, small-town Cold Warrior Nixon, the continuing, stubborn allegiance to libertarian values and U.S. world hegemony; and Humphrey, old-line blue-collar and New Deal liberalism. None of these philosophies fit the antiwar, New Left image supposedly popular among youthful baby boomers. Why was that?

The simple answer, of course, was that their candidate, Robert Kennedy, had been murdered, and the alternative, Eugene McCarthy, was not dynamic enough to win the nomination. But that is too rudimentary and ignores the great, subtle truth of the 1960s. The political values of the mainstream had not changed as much as has been depicted. There was still a large element in the nation who had accepted civil rights and the financial responsibilities of a social safety net only reluctantly. The majority of even the younger generation still clung to traditional classical liberal American values. The New Left was a passing phenomenon, whose rallying cry was tied to Vietnam and whose values would change, in most cases, once that war had passed from the American scene. In that sense, Nixon, Humphrey, and Wallace represented more of what Americans believed in 1968 than did Eugene McCarthy.

And reporters, editors, and television executives were much more comfortable with Nixon and Humphrey than with McCarthy or even Robert Kennedy. It was clear what Nixon and Humphrey, and for that matter even Wallace, stood for. Except for his "peace now" plank, it was unclear what McCarthy advocated. Robert Kennedy himself had held elective office for fewer than four years. He had been the most powerful advisor in his brother's administration, but his personal stand on many issues had never been tested or clearly defined. Nixon, Humphrey, and Wallace were a trio that editorial writers could sink their teeth into. The year 1968 was sullied with violence but ended with politics as usual. The late 1960s were years of transition from one set of social and governmental norms to another, but in between was politics as usual.

The year's events had been captured by color television cameras and sent around the world by Telstar. The real difference was that technology had made the campaign indelible in the minds of people around the world. The United States had stood naked and embarrassed by its own television cameras. There was no way to sweep the shootings, violence, and conflict under the rug, but the results were not terribly different from any other standard U.S. presidential election. Traditional candidates with conventional liberal and conservative values clashed in a politics-as-usual general election. Now, however, much of the South was lost to the Democratic Party for the rest of the century, and American politics had become world politics, thanks to television.

The ultimate change in the role of the federal government and in social relations in the country had been settled in the early years of the Johnson Administration. The confrontations and violence of 1968 revealed deep divisions within the country, but the most vocal voices would die down, and what would be left as Richard Nixon moved through his first term would be a deep distrust of the media and the presidency and a heavy financial commitment that would stagger the country. The emotions and rhetoric would die quickly— surprisingly so—and what would be left would be an undercurrent of doubt that would turn into a torrent in the decades to come.

During 1969, Nixon opened his quest for a "peace with honor" in Vietnam while demonstrations on college campuses expanded and grew louder. During the summer of 1969, more than a half-million young people gathered in a field in upstate New York near the town of Woodstock, listening to live rock bands and smoking marijuana openly. Woodstock and all its youthful excesses and enthusiasm seemed to be a microcosm of the anti-establishment sentiment among young adults in the 1960s. It seemed to be the essence of the 1960s. It was not, of course, but it, along with the Democratic convention, are what has been remembered. In July 1969, astronaut Neil Armstrong became the first person to walk on the moon. These are the images that remain with us from the 1960s, and television is the main reason. The 1960s had been a time of transition, but also a time of questioning and searching, and it was all presented live for anyone who cared to watch. The media and the presidency would never be the same again.

For his own part, Johnson withdrew to his ranch in Texas and hardly spoke in public. He grew long hair, a strange parallel to those who had most despised him, and turned somber and reflective. He lived only four more years. He is generally regarded as a successful president, but that evaluation comes with a mental asterisk: *Except for Vietnam.

The Johnson Administration influenced Congress to pass more historic and revolutionary legislation than any other presidency except FDR's. Yet Johnson could not control or influence reporters, and he could not find an honorable solution in Vietnam. His Administration had not only tangled the nation inextricably in Southeast Asia, but he had lied about casualties and the progress of the war. This would also be a legacy that Americans would not soon forget. A volatile and distrustful public came to view the presidency with skepticism, just a few years after the presidency had perhaps reached its height under John F. Kennedy. Johnson could not control the anticommunist fixation that had gripped the country for twenty years, and his stubborn commitment to Southeast Asia caused his undoing. The presidency and Vietnam would be intertwined for seven more years.

NOTES

1. For details on Johnson's election fraud, see Paul K. Conkin, *Big Daddy from the Pedernales: Lyndon Baines Johnson* (Boston: Twayne, 1986), 117–18. See also Robert

Dallek, *Lone Star Rising: Lyndon Johnson and His Times 1908–1960* (New York: Oxford University Press, 1991), 329–48.

2. Barry Goldwater, "The Republican National Convention Address," delivered in San Francisco, California, July 16, 1964, *Vital Speeches of the Day*, August 15, 1964, pp. 642–44.

3. For a complete text of all Johnson's press conferences through 1966, see George W. Johnson (ed.), *The Johnson Presidential Press Conferences* (New York: Earl M. Coleman Enterprises, 1978), vol. 1.

4. Nancy Dickerson, *Among Those Present: A Reporter's Viewpoint of Twenty-Five Years in Washington* (New York: Random House, 1976), 138–39.

5. George C. Herring, *America's Longest War: The United States and Vietnam, 1950–1975* (New York: Alfred A. Knopf, 1986).

CHAPTER FOUR

THE PRESS, THE PRESIDENCY, AND VIETNAM

Why was the United States involved in a civil war in Vietnam, and how did opinion makers and reporters for newspapers, magazines, television, and radio react to our lingering presence there? What did this mean to the presidents of the 1960s and even the 1970s? The answers to these questions are complicated and sometimes confusing. It is best to examine the war in Southeast Asia comprehensively, cutting across six presidencies. In this way the conflict presents itself in the overall context of continuing U.S. foreign policy.

The strife in Vietnam began long before the United States committed its military forces to the conflict, and U.S. participation unfolded slowly over more than a decade. After World War II, the Vietnam communists in the northern provinces sought to oust the colonial French, who controlled Laos, Cambodia, and Vietnam in Southeast Asia. The struggle persisted until 1954, when, after a military defeat at Dienbienphu in Vietnam, the French unilaterally withdrew. Through a treaty negotiated in Geneva, Switzerland, that year, Vietnam was divided at the 17th parallel into two countries.

In the post–World War II era, U.S. foreign policy was designed to combat communism wherever it appeared to be taking hold in the world. This position was first clearly enunciated in March 1947 when President Harry S. Truman urged Congress to provide financial support to Greece and Turkey to help in their struggles against communist insurgencies. The Truman Doctrine, followed by the Korean conflict and the unchecked excesses of McCarthyism in the early 1950s, reinforced American concern about communist domination of the world. In the midst of this Cold War frenzy in 1954 a corrupt, nominally democratic government was established in South Vietnam under the leadership of the French-educated Ngo Dinh Diem. Communists under Ho Chi Minh controlled the north. At this point, Vietnam drew almost no interest in the United States, newspapers and magazines barely reporting on events there.

Through a tumultuous seven years, the Eisenhower Administration supported the unpopular Diem, though dissent in South Vietnam was suppressed. Fostered by widespread peasant dissatisfaction, North Vietnamese regulars and communist Vietcong in the south infiltrated outlying areas of South Vietnam. The United States stepped up its economic aid and heightened its presence in South Vietnam.

In December 1961, President Kennedy opted to commit 2,000 military advisors. They were not to become involved in combat but were to accompany South Vietnamese regulars into the jungles to offer advice on military tactics. When the first American soldier died in the jungles of Vietnam on December 22, 1961, Americans hardly noticed. Concern at that time was focused on Laos, where a communist takeover seemed imminent and, of course, on Berlin and Cuba. Protecting Vietnam with a few military consultants seemed a natural and required step at the height of the Cold War, when the CIA was active in many unstable Third World countries. Not only did U.S. opinion makers not oppose such a step, they hardly noticed. American involvement in Vietnam began slowly and quietly.

Within three years, the U.S. commitment in Vietnam had swollen to more than 23,000 soldiers. Public Vietnamese dissent against Diem increased. In the fall of 1963 Buddhist priests demonstrated daily against the government. A coup and the assassination of Diem and his brother on November 1, 1963, caused civil chaos. After five changes in government, General Nguyen Van Thieu, a similarly corrupt and ineffective leader, came to power in 1965.[1]

The phantom attack on the U.S. destroyers in August 1964 in the Gulf of Tonkin (chapter 3) was the turning point for the United States. Once Lyndon Johnson had unrestricted license to wage warfare, thousands of ground troops were sent. This policy led the United States into deeper and deeper financial and military obligations, until Lyndon Johnson faced two choices: write off the lives of the several thousand soldiers who had died (24,000 by 1968) by pulling out of the country, or continue to escalate the fighting on behalf of an unpopular leader against an invisible guerrilla army that largely commanded the sympathies of the rural population. These options never became clear to Johnson or his key advisors, and for nearly six years they were not obvious to leading opinion makers.

In the fall of 1964, Johnson added a dimension to the war by authorizing the systematic bombing of North Vietnam by U.S. pilots. This incessant strafing of civilian and military targets alike served only to reinforce the determination of the North Vietnamese, who built underground storage and living quarters to survive the aerial pounding. From that time until 1968, the bombing of North Vietnam and the escalation of American troop commitments continued almost unabated. The United States dropped more bombs on Vietnam during that time than had been used in all theaters during World War II and spent $2 billion a month by 1967, according to historian George C. Herring.[2]

Johnson, the inveterate Texas warrior, could never back down from a fight, but he was too intelligent not to understand what was likely to lie ahead. Between 1964 and 1966, a critical, hard-nosed look at Vietnam by the nation's elite media would have had much impact, but it was missing. It is an irony of history that many still hold that the media, particularly television, drove Johnson from office by depicting the war in Vietnam negatively.

By the early 1960s Washington reporting had divided clearly into two camps: smaller media, mostly newspapers, which had one or two correspondents in Washington and concerned themselves with Washington issues affecting only their regions of the country, and the national media—wire services, networks, large newspapers, and national magazines—which reported mostly on national policy. The president concentrated his attention on the second group. In the 1960s reporters for these news organizations were mostly men who had lived through the Great Depression and a patriotic world war. They and their editors were inclined to back the U.S. position on foreign affairs. Few newspapers had stood up to Joseph McCarthy during his most influential years. Earlier, immediately after World War II, nearly all the nation's mainstream newspapers and magazines had supported the government's role as world policeman against communism. Because reporters rely heavily on government sources for information on foreign affairs and because most reporters and editors were sympathetic to virulent anticommunist ideology in the years after World War II—even one that committed the United States militarily—the questioning of Vietnam policy in the early 1960s was superficial. It took years for the nation's largest media organizations to understand fully the U.S. dilemma in Vietnam. During the early years of the war, it was difficult for correspondents such as David Halberstam, of *The New York Times*, to obtain space, let alone front-page treatment, for unfavorable stories. Some correspondents who did manage to file critical stories were asked by the Saigon government to leave the country. If George Romney was "brainwashed," so were a lot of other Americans. Had Johnson faced stronger criticism in those early years, he might have been saved from destroying himself. Media were guilty of too little criticism, not too much.

This is not to say that news, particularly television news, did not have a contrary influence. Not by any planned conspiracy but by virtue of its own technology, television tended to challenge the Johnson Administration's claims about Vietnam. The assertions that the war was going well were undercut by the nightly pictures of bloodied soldiers on stretchers being evacuated by helicopters, other scenes of carnage, and reports from the battlefield that the enemy was proving elusive. In 1965, CBS correspondent Morley Safer broadcast an on-the-spot report in the village of Cam Ne of American soldiers burning the thatched huts of peasants suspected of supporting the Vietcong. For many Americans, naive about the savagery of war, the graphic pictures were horrifying. As the war progressed into the Nixon Administration, the pictures became more explicit: Nick Ut's 1972 wirephoto of a nine-year-old girl, Phan Ti Kim Phuc, burned by napalm and running naked down the street screaming in pain, and television images of South Vietnamese army regulars executing a suspected Vietcong sympathizer by a pistol shot to the head.

No other war had been reported this way. Pictures of dead soldiers were not even seen by Americans during the first eighteen months of American involvement in World War II. But in Vietnam, reporters followed soldiers on patrol and filed reports that reached the United States within hours. Television film still had to be sent by airplane back to the United States for processing, but the film was usually seen the same day.

An optimistic report from the Johnson Administration was easily overshadowed by a thirty-second spot on the evening news showing the wounded returning from the jungles. Johnson made matters worse by ordering that casualty figures be juggled and negative assessments of the fighting be concealed.

He also refused to allow his military officers to make unfettered strategic warfare decisions. Often he would visit the war room at the Pentagon, looking over the shoulders of generals and personally intervening in military matters. His heavy-handed tactics led to public disenchantment and consternation within the military. Stories leaked that Johnson refused to leave strategic planning to the generals, and his military planning was directionless and amateurish.

By February 1968, Walter Cronkite candidly told his audience on the CBS evening news that the United States had involved itself in a stalemate in Vietnam. Other national media followed suit in the ensuing months, reversing a trend of support that had existed for more than five years. The Tet offensive, described in chapter 3, had sealed Johnson's fate.

Had the media turned on Johnson? Actually, reporters had begun to reflect a changing mood in the country. This explanation requires some lengthy examination of war and the American character, because this is where events too often have been oversimplified. War is rarely popular among the rank and file. Gaining popular support for armed hostilities is probably the greatest challenge a leader can face. Many people will die, most likely the young, who have the most to live for. Even the Germans, under the spell of Adolf Hitler, dreaded war when Poland was invaded in 1939. Only after a quick and nearly painless conquest in Poland did they express their overwhelming support.

Americans, who have not fought a battle on mainland U.S. soil for over 130 years, are particularly reluctant to become involved in wars, especially prolonged ones. Dwight D. Eisenhower campaigned successfully in 1952 in part on a promise to end the Korean War, little more than two years old at that time. Three and a half years has been the length of Americans' patience. The Civil War lasted four. There were draft riots and calls for Lincoln's ouster. Had Lincoln lost the election of 1864, the Northern resolve to fight the war to its end would likely have disappeared. During the eight years of the Revolutionary War, the patriots faced down desertion and general discontent. Impatience in England contributed to the British decision to negotiate peace.

Dissatisfaction with a lingering war, then, is not tied to the television age. No matter what the media reported, dissent would have complicated a long, apparently unending struggle thousands of miles away in a small Third World country on behalf of an abstract cause. Instantaneous reporting in newspapers, in magazines, on the radio, and particularly on television abetted this process. Media reinforced feelings of malaise. "Unpopular War?" Only after it had cost American lives and drained the U.S. treasury. Did the media create U.S. dissent? It enhanced it in the late 1960s by bringing home the uncomfortable truth and airing opposition points of view. Should a free press do anything else?

In fact, as has been pointed out, it took years for opinion makers to become disenchanted. At the same time, television and the cinema throughout the 1960s glorified war with its many television series and movies deifying the soldiers who fought in World War II. Those Americans who lived to see the Imperial Japanese Empire and Nazi Germany defeated relived those days in their living rooms and at their local theaters, reminding us that war has its purposes, even if its goals are not always apparent.

Could Kennedy, through his charm and positive press relations, have avoided the self-destruction inherent in the Johnson regime? Unlikely. Perhaps he would have delayed the inevitable, but by the time his second term had expired in 1969, Kennedy's popular image would have been badly tarnished had he pursued the same policies of escalation. We do not know that Kennedy would have continued to heighten the U.S. presence in Vietnam, however. Even in 1963, he was having second thoughts about U.S. policies there. That is not to say that Johnson's already strained press relations did not have a collaborative impact on public perception of his Vietnam policies. More to the point, though, is that negative press in this case was a concoction of several modern and historical factors.

What about the youthful demonstrators who began protesting en masse by the end of 1966 and whose legions disrupted the 1968 Democratic National Convention in Chicago? Perhaps they had overly influenced the nation's news organizations. The facts suggest otherwise. Demonstrations, even peaceful protests, were criticized editorially, except in so-called alternative newspapers and magazines. Americans who had lived through World War II were ingrained with the feeling that it was unpatriotic to oppose a country's commitment to war. Influential ABC commentator Howard K. Smith was particularly uncomplimentary toward the antiwar activists. Many younger Americans found little comfort in such an attitude and rallied around the ideal of "peace," assuming naively that anyone over age thirty inherently thirsted for war and bloodshed. Still, few influential reporters, editors, or news executives were of the baby boom generation in the 1960s and so the view that prevailed was that of the older generation. Demonstrators were often lumped together as lazy, pot-smoking, self-centered, coddled brats who knew nothing of the real world. Of course, merely reporting or covering a peace demonstration offered an antiwar point of view, and there were so many by the late 1960s that readers, listeners, and viewers felt that media were biased. "You do an awful lot to encourage that," Hubert Humphrey lectured television reporters and camerapersons, as he was heckled during a 1968 campaign speech. Coverage also led to a distorted sense of how many Americans actually opposed U.S. policies in Vietnam and a generalization about younger Americans and their feelings about the war.

Of course, the really tragic figures in the Vietnam conflict were the American soldiers, drafted and sent to fight, often against their wishes. Boosted by low tuition costs and a strong economy in the late 1960s, more young people were attending U.S. colleges and universities than at any other time in history. Full-time enrollment in an institution of higher learning entitled a young man to a deferment until graduation or until four years had passed since matriculation. This created an army mostly of the poor or the less academically endowed. Soldiers were asked to enter battle in a skirmish they did not understand and that made villains of them to their peers back home. They sensed the confusion, and morale dropped precipitously. Particularly devastating was a visit by film actress Jane Fonda to Hanoi, during which she expressed her support for the North Vietnamese. At that time, thousands of American soldiers had died or had been wounded, and thousands of others were being held in prisoner-of-war camps under unspeakable conditions. Even uncomplimentary coverage of Fonda's visit enraged many Americans.

Referring to long-term press coverage of the Vietnam War, Richard Nixon in a press conference in October 1973 told reporters:

> I have never heard or seen such outrageous, vicious, distorted reporting in 27 years of public life. I am not blaming anybody for that. Perhaps what happened is that what we did brought it about, and therefore, the media decided that they would have to take that particular line. But when people are pounded night after night with that kind of frantic, hysterical reporting, it naturally shakes their confidence.[3]

But it was not a media-fostered perception that Americans should pull out of Vietnam that spelled Lyndon Johnson's doom in early 1968. Polls after Tet indicated that nearly half the country still supported the war. Rather, it was the perception that the war was not being fought wisely that turned the public against the administration. Polls indicated that favorable reaction to Johnson's prosecution of the war had deteriorated.

NIXON AND VIETNAM

Richard Nixon felt no obligation to end the war in Vietnam quickly when he took office in January 1969. He had campaigned on a promise to seek peace with honor but had not defined what that meant. With 500,000 troops in Vietnam and a war on his hands that he could attribute to the opposition party, Nixon was in the enviable position of pursuing the same policies as Johnson largely without having to answer for them.

During his March 31, 1968, speech in which he announced he would not seek re-election, Johnson invited the North Vietnamese to negotiate. Hanoi accepted, but talks in Paris bogged down, and incessant bombing of the North resumed.

Upon taking office, Nixon chose foreign policy advisor Henry Kissinger to lead the negotiations. Kissinger, a refugee from Nazi Germany during his boyhood and a Harvard professor, combined just the right amount of panache and intelligence. He was a showman and unlike most of the other Nixon people enjoyed bantering with reporters. However, he was in the unenviable position of negotiating with an enemy that knew time was on its side. From the beginning, Nixon accepted the concept of inevitable withdrawal, but he never clearly enunciated this publicly. "Vietnamization" became a frequently employed buzzword, a euphemism for American withdrawal and substitution of South Vietnamese forces, handily financed by the United States. It cost more than 30,000 American lives and four years of strife to bring that perception to reality under Nixon.

The original rationalization for entry into the war was the domino theory: communism would spread across Asia, Africa, and Europe if it were not held in check in remote corners of the world such as Vietnam. U.S. foreign policy during the Cold War emphasized both protection of U.S. democracy against world communism and the role of world policeman as guardian over countries too weak to resist communist insurgency. Implanted within this concept is the notion that communism is a monolithic threat that knows no national boundaries and links together at every turn. In fact, the People's Republic of China and the Soviet Union were at odds in the 1960s, and Ho Chi Minh was suspicious of both.

But even that theory of protecting the weak and policing the world became confused. An incident in a small village in South Vietnam in March 1968 illustrated how U.S. policy had somehow lost its coherence. A U.S. army patrol unit led by Lieutenant William Calley was sent to the tiny village of My Lai because of reports that the village was harboring Vietcong sympathizers. Before the patrol unit had left, more than 500 villagers, including women and children, were shot, their bodies dumped into a mass grave.

The Army covered up the incident until it became public a year later. Calley was put on trial and found guilty of mass murder in 1971. He was sentenced to life imprisonment. Nixon commuted his sentence and placed him under "house arrest" in a comfortable apartment. He reasoned that Calley had only followed orders, and it was impossible for American soldiers to determine who was or was not Vietcong. On similar evidence, Nazis had been hanged after convictions at Nuremberg, Germany, in 1945 and 1946.

The My Lai incident seemed to be a microcosm of the chasm that existed in America. One officer explained after a village had been destroyed that "we had to destroy it to save it." Most Americans felt that the war needed to be fought more vigorously with less restraint on the U.S. military. Others believed the conflict was unwinnable and unjustified and that complete, immediate withdrawal was the only logical and humanitarian step.

Media steadily came to a more dovish position as the war dragged into the 1970s, though most opinion makers were reluctant to call for immediate withdrawal. That would be conceding that lives already lost had been wasted. In this way, Nixon actually mirrored the media position in private but assumed a more hawkish stance publicly.

The hawk position enraged antiwar activists, and in the fall of 1969 nightly demonstrations took place on many of the nation's college campuses. Some students refused to attend classes and instead gathered in groups to discuss the war and what steps could be taken to change U.S. policy. Most students, however, went about their business, and dissent outside campus was less frequent.

Meanwhile, Nixon strategists advised that the North was obviating both the bombing and ground troop resistance by infiltrating the South through the jungles in Cambodia. After taking office, Nixon ordered the secret bombing of Cambodia. The expansion of the war into Cambodia became public knowledge fifteen months later, and Nixon spoke live on television on April 30, 1970, to explain his reasoning. This led to the most vociferous and violent demonstrations against the war in its nine-year history. National Guard troops had to be sent to several campuses to quell disturbances, which had become increasingly violent.

On May 4, 1970, students on the campus of Kent State University in Kent, Ohio, confronted National Guardsmen sent to protect property. Students hurled objects at the young guardsmen, some of whom opened fire. Four protestors died. A wirephoto appeared on front pages the next day showing a runaway fifteen-year-old girl kneeling and crying over the dead bodies. Students rampaged on campuses throughout the nation, and some universities and colleges ended the semester early, sending students home with weeks still left in the term.

Americans could not comprehend what was happening. Calls for withdrawal from Vietnam had been building throughout the nation and in the media for three years, but Nixon held fast to his policy of bombing and negotiating. A group of dovish senators, including George McGovern, Democrat of South Dakota, introduced a resolution calling for complete withdrawal by the end of 1971. The resolution never reached a vote.

Just a month before his speech on Cambodia, Nixon announced the first withdrawal of American troops from Vietnam. After nine years of troop buildups, he opted for de-escalation while still pursuing a failed bomb-and-negotiate policy. By the end of 1971 troop strength had dropped from a high of 500,000 to 175,000. American public resolve to continue the war had all but dissipated. In December 1969 Nixon instituted a draft lottery system whereby young men were assigned draft numbers drawn at random, according to date of birth, similar to a system instituted in 1942 during World War II. In 1970, young men of draft age who had high lottery numbers could begin to plan their futures, a luxury few young American males had enjoyed for seven years.

Sensing the mood of defeatism, Hanoi launched a major offensive in the spring of 1972, renewing fighting that served only to increase the death toll. A final Christmas bombing of the North in late 1972 brought a chorus of angry responses from public and media against Nixon, but by this time Nixon was impervious to the outrage. He had won a second term and was beyond the clutches of his critics, he thought. Still, the American participation wound down to its final stages, and a peace settlement was reached in Paris a month later. The North Vietnamese agreed to return U.S. prisoners of war, and the United States consented to withdraw all its forces. Vietnamese troops on both sides remained in place, and Thieu, who continued as president of South Vietnam, signed the pact reluctantly.

Five years after the first calls by major newspapers and television commentators, the country and U.S. media resigned themselves to a nominal peace with honor. The country thus extricated itself from the longest and most frustrating conflict in its history, an eleven-year undeclared war in which more than 56,000 Americans died. The withdrawal also reversed a twenty-eight-year policy of unrelenting Cold War logic. Americans had had enough, and they hardly needed convincing from newspapers, magazines, television, and radio.

THE FINAL STAGES

As it turned out, the United States did not continue its billions in economic aid to South Vietnam. In the midst of an oil shortage and rampant inflation, Congress cut allocations to the Thieu government to $300 million. With little popular support, no U.S. military backing, and decreased U.S. funding, South Vietnam's demise was foreordained.

An aggravating complication was Nixon's Watergate troubles, which emboldened Congress. Demands were made in late 1973 that the United States refrain from any re-entry into the fighting. An aggressive military campaign by the North Vietnamese against the South began in early 1975. In less than four months, the North Vietnamese routed a disorganized and demoralized South Vietnamese Army and took Saigon on May 1, 1975. Americans fled the U.S. embassy at the last minute. The most enduring image of that last day was a wirephoto of U.S. Marines striking Vietnamese embassy employees with rifle butts to prevent them from boarding a helicopter departing the embassy. The Vietnamese who remained loyal to the South and to the Americans there paid a heavy price. The invading communists renamed Saigon Ho Chi Minh City and either killed all those loyal to the Thieu regime or sent them to "re-education camps," where they died or suffered physical and mental abuse for years.

The end also came in the middle of the Gerald R. Ford Administration. The images of the humiliating communist victory that served only to remind Americans of an unpleasant past transferred to Ford himself, who had had little or nothing to do with the conduct of the war. The United States sustained debilitating economic difficulties during the Ford Administration and Ford's pardon of Nixon for Watergate-related offenses had already put the president on the defensive. The Vietnam debacle heightened his woes.

Surprisingly, U.S. commentators had little more than wistful epitaphs to offer after the defeat of South Vietnam. Some mused about the ill-advised nature of involving the United States in an Asian land war, and others speculated that the war could have been won, except for a series of poor political decisions.

And then Vietnam simply vanished from the American psyche and from the pages and broadcasts of U.S. media. Rarely did any stories originate from Vietnam, and hardly was there an inquiry about conditions there. Ex-soldiers who had fought and, in many cases, sustained either psychological or physical wounds wondered what it had all been about. Americans generally had moved on to other worries and concerns. The Khmer Rouge communist regime rampaged through Cambodia, dispossessing nearly the entire country and killing more than a million of its own citizens. Hardly anyone in the United States took notice until a popular movie, *The Killing Fields*, recounted the horrible tragedy a decade later.

Vietnam was more than a humiliating defeat. It was the result of a foreign policy and an ideology gone wrong and a lack of aggressiveness on the part of news organizations. Overall media criticism of the war was late in coming and then focused on the Johnson Administration instead of the overall policies that had pervaded the country since the end of World War II. The domino theory was found wanting. The unification of Vietnam brought to an end more than thirty years of nearly continuous conflict there, and even under a communist regime, the country's economy improved. Yet communism as a world force not only remained static, but deteriorated in the 1980s. The theory of a monolithic communist threat in Asia was blunted in 1978 when communist Vietnam invaded communist Cambodia to drive out the brutal Khmer Rouge government.

The failure in Vietnam redirected foreign policy in the 1970s and 1980s. American leaders continued to intervene in the squabbles of other countries, but always with reluctance and at great peril to their popularity. Any military activity met with the media question, "Is this another Vietnam?"

Yet, this was barely the surface of the legacy of the longest war in U.S. history. Most important, hundreds of thousands of Vietnamese and more than 56,000 Americans died. Hundreds of thousands were wounded. It took chagrined Americans more than two decades to erect a monument in Washington, D.C.: a wall inscribed with the names of all Americans who died in the war.

Soldiers who suffered debilitating injuries were referred to veterans' hospitals, where they often received indifferent and borderline medical care. A defoliant, Agent Orange, used by the U.S. military in the jungles, sometimes caused nervous system damage to soldiers, but acknowledgment of U.S. culpability in these cases was long in coming.

U.S. voters now saw the presidency in a new light. Since the inception of the New Deal in 1933, the federal government and the president had been the friends of the people, the protectors of individuals' interests in the struggle against predator businesses. Now the government had become a boondoggling bureaucracy that led the nation into mystifying wars, only to turn its back on the unfortunate young men who were asked to risk their lives on behalf of their country.

The president had become not a kindly, understanding leader, but a scheming politician, who lied at every turn and whose sole motivation was to strengthen his political power. Or worse, he was a bumbling incompetent, who gained office because he was the grudging choice from a field of losers. From its zenith in the last year of the Kennedy era, the presidency had sunk to a new twentieth-century low. The repudiation of Lyndon Johnson, followed closely by the Watergate scandal that brought down both Richard Nixon and Gerald Ford, damaged the presidency for a generation to come. The juxtaposition of the two tragedies was as important as the distaste that followed each debacle. Public revelations about Kennedy's liaisons and the excesses of the FBI under J. Edgar Hoover at about the same time added to the disenchantment with official Washington.

Years later, many young Americans fail to understand the complexities of the Vietnam conflict. The divisiveness of the era and the bitterness that followed also tend to cloud memories. Lucid accounts of that period are difficult to come by. Everyone who lived through the era has an opinion, but rarely is it based on fact.

Part of the cloudiness of Vietnam is the role of the national media. The perception persists that raging student activists combined with a liberal media to undercut a serious effort in Vietnam. History suggests that the United States spent billions but executed the war poorly because of politics and an infatuation with aerial bombing. It also points to a media that collectively opposed the war quite late, and then mostly on the argument that military and political tactics were ill advised, not on the basis that the war was unwinnable or unjustified. Broadcast and print journalists generally recoiled from the tactics of antiwar protesters and frequently labeled activists broadly as violent crazies or disloyal draft dodgers.

For its own part, the youthful New Left dropped from the political scene, their last hurrah being George McGovern's ignominious defeat in the 1972 election. Eventually most of the protesters put on business suits and entered the establishment. Their politics even became more conservative generally.

Some were Reaganites in the 1980s. The core of their anger against the establishment had been the war in Vietnam. Its inglorious conclusion brought an end to the liberal raison d'être, but the disappearance of the New Left as a political force also suggests that their numbers and influence had been exaggerated in the first place.

The Vietnam era brought in its wake a diminished presidency, a deepened public distrust of the U.S. news media, a distrust of foreign entanglements, ballooning inflation, and a confused foreign policy. All those elements helped to frame the politics of the 1970s, 1980s, and 1990s.

Just as with the 1960 presidential debates, the perception in retrospect of what had occurred in the 1960s—the Vietnam era—was just as important to the politics of the future as were the events that actually occurred. The media with its criticism, Americans reasoned, had helped to destroy the heroic efforts of the U.S. soldiers in Vietnam, but nothing is further from the truth. Media criticism could have helped prevent the disaster that was Vietnam, but it was too late in coming. Yet the perception of media's role would affect negatively the attitudes of Americans in the years to come.

NOTES

1. For a complete history of the conflict in Vietnam see George C. Herring, *America's Longest War: The United States and Vietnam, 1950–1975* (New York: Knopf, 1986), vol. 2.

2. Ibid., 146.

3. "The President's News Conference of Oct. 26, 1973," in George W. Johnson (ed.), *The Nixon Presidential Press Conferences* (New York: Earl M. Coleman Enterprises, 1978), 369.

II

THE 1970s
THE DEATH OF PAX AMERICANA

CHAPTER FIVE

WATERGATE AS A MEDIA BAROMETER

In his estimation, Richard Nixon had too many enemies who would do him political harm. Since the tense farewell speech to reporters after his loss to Pat Brown in 1962, Nixon had regarded most journalists as a cadre of well-organized antagonists. Finally in the White House in 1969, he saw an opportunity not only to strike back but to turn the public against those newspapers and television journalists who had plagued his career. Perhaps no other presidency in U.S. history was more intertwined with press relations and the news media. There was never any chance for cordial or even civil relations between Nixon and the White House press corps because Nixon rejected that idea immediately. Reporters wondering how a Nixon White House would handle press relations did not have to wait long. His staff and his early decisions made his position quite clear.

Nixon surrounded himself with acquaintances from Southern California who had served in his campaign. His chief of staff, H. R. Haldeman, had been an advertising executive with J. Walter Thompson, as had press secretary Ronald Ziegler and other aides, such as Dwight Chapin, Larry Higby, and Kenneth Cole. Legal Counsel John Ehrlichman was a West Coast lawyer, who later moved into the powerful advisory position of assistant to the president for domestic affairs. All had shared political experiences with Nixon, giving him their loyalty.

When he entered politics as a young congressman from Southern California in 1947, Nixon was quick to capitalize on the power of the media. At the same time, he was deeply suspicious of that power. His relentless pursuit of State Department aide Alger Hiss in 1948 and 1949 and the subsequent headlines that brought him national attention had taught Nixon about publicity. At the outset of the 1952 general election campaign, when he was accused of using $18,000 in contributions illegally while a senator, Nixon addressed voters directly on television. The only thing he had ever accepted was a little dog named Checkers, he said, and the kids loved the dog, so they were going to keep it. Nixon had gone around the press corps and Congress and taken his appeal directly to the American audience through a paid political program. The Checkers speech was largely responsible for Dwight Eisenhower's leaving Nixon on the ticket.

When he entered the White House, Nixon continued his vendetta by rewarding those few newspeople who wrote and broadcast favorable stories and by punishing those who were critical, thus creating anger and suspicion. Despite the loyalty of the ever-present collection of White House advisors, Nixon trusted no one, not even his inner circle. Consequently, the Nixon years were marked both within and without by suspicion, misinformation, strained press relations, backbiting, and eventually shameful scandal.

Yet the deluge of brackish Watergate sewage that swept away the entire White House in 1973 and 1974 has concealed a forgotten historical fact: the first term of Nixon's administration was marked by some reasonably credible accomplishments. Nixon was a long-time Washington player who brought a rare expertise to foreign and domestic affairs. He acted carefully and astutely in foreign affairs and dealt credibly, though less effectively, with domestic issues. His undoing was his inability to recognize his own natural aptitude for policymaking and his constant scheming against critics and opponents. Convinced that he could hold the White House only by a series of illegal and underhanded operations, he was forced to resign less than two years after one of the most successful re-election campaigns in history.

Nixon was raised in Whittier, California, where his father operated a service station and grocery store. He worked his way through college and law school, entered private practice briefly, served in World War II, returned home, and then won election to Congress in 1946. As a member of the House Un-American Activities Committee (HUAC), Nixon investigated suspected communists in government, especially advisors in the State Department. His HUAC endeavors brought him the undying animosity of the nation's liberals and charges that he had helped to railroad the unfortunate Hiss, whose case became a cause célèbre among leftist sympathizers. It also propelled Nixon's career. After only two terms in the House, he won election to the Senate in 1950 and then was placed on the ticket with Eisenhower in 1952.

From there, the Nixon epic took the most astonishing twists and turns in presidential history: from the renaissance of the vice presidency, to the heart-breaking 1960 defeat, to the ill-advised 1962 California gubernatorial campaign, to the staggering comeback and narrow 1968 election victory. During his tumultuous career, Nixon developed into a composite of all his boyhood and political experiences, but one thing never changed: he never forgot or forgave.

More than any other modern president, Nixon integrated his family into his political life with great difficulty. Wife Pat shied away from the limelight. She campaigned for Nixon during his twenty-eight years in public office but came to dislike each campaign more intensely. She was seen at all the right rallies and meetings, answered her White House mail faithfully, and spoke glowingly of her husband in public, but she never advised him on governmental decisions and only occasionally involved herself in political matters.

Neither Julie nor Tricia, Nixon's two daughters, created lasting impressions on voters. Tricia resented living in the White House and in the early months refused to leave her room. Both daughters were grown, and both were married during the Nixon White House years. Julie wed David Eisenhower, Mamie Eisenhower's favorite grandson (for whom Camp David was named), but the marriage did not bring Richard Nixon closer to the Eisenhowers. Julie was an ardent supporter of her father and chastised those who would criticize him. David Eisenhower, later a respected historian in his own right, spoke out in support of Nixon frequently but is believed to have been a key source of information for Bob Woodward, who wrote negative books about the Nixon presidency and who, along with co–*Washington Post* reporter Carl Bernstein, helped to expose the Watergate scandal. Tricia married Edward Cox in 1971 and rarely spoke in public after that. The Nixon family was a political family that remained largely in the background, drawing little attention and hardly any controversy.

A key domestic question the nation's leaders were asking in 1969 was: Would Richard Nixon dismantle the social welfare programs that Lyndon Johnson and John F. Kennedy had erected in the 1960s? Certainly he knew that any such move would meet with stiff resistance from the heavily Democratic Congress. Whether because he was preoccupied with Vietnam or because he knew that he could not reverse a decade of legislation, Nixon hardly touched the Kennedy-Johnson agenda. In fact, he addressed the problem of crumbling inner cities by continuing the Model Cities program. Observers began to refer to the ultimate Cold Warrior Nixon as a "moderate."

But the early 1970s was a time of transition. It was one thing for Kennedy and Johnson to plan programs for social reform and for Congress to approve them, and quite another for the country to accommodate itself to such measures. The Medicare, Medicaid, and direct aid programs placed an enormous burden on taxpayers. Long-time entitlement programs such as social security broadened. This came at a time when the cost of the Vietnam War was already draining the treasury and causing inflation. Nixon responded with a short-lived wage and price freeze in 1971. The 1970s thereafter were marked by unchecked inflation, fanned by a brief Arab oil embargo in October 1973 that caused oil prices to soar.

School busing orders from federal courts and efforts to integrate housing caused clashes in the North. Blacks learned that northerners could be just as segregationist as whites in the South. While not enthusiastic about integration, Nixon did nothing to deter efforts that had begun in the 1960s.

The preoccupation with Vietnam did not prevent Nixon from addressing other foreign issues. The United States served as a neutral arbiter in the Indian-Pakistani war, and, during his second term, the United States in 1973 brokered a cease-fire in the Middle East after the Yom Kippur War between Israel and its Arab neighbors. A Strategic Arms Limitation Treaty agreement in 1972 was the first serious diplomatic effort to check the nuclear arms race since the Limited Test Ban Treaty of 1963.

The most astounding and successful event in the Nixon era was a visit to the People's Republic of China in February 1972, where the president paved the way for normalized relations with the world's most populous nation. Nixon, whose anticommunist credentials were above reproach, won public acceptance for the surprise trip, where others would have had difficulty. This initiative had a lasting impact on American foreign relations and helped to ease international tensions at a crucial moment in world history.

PRESS STRATEGY

All of these policies and programs, along with the winding down of U.S. participation in the Vietnam War, on the surface added up to a reasonably successful Administration record on domestic and foreign issues. Beneath the surface, ideological hysteria and paranoia were driving the White House toward disaster. The greatest abuse of the Nixon White House was its blatant violations of law in the pursuit of re-election. At the same time, Nixon hoped to cow reporters and news organizations into reporting less aggressively.

In pursuing this end, Nixon used three press strategies: (1) verbally attack news institutions and reporters to keep them on the defensive, (2) largely ignore the White House press corps, and (3) influence the electorate directly by using television while avoiding questions from journalists.

Vice President Spiro Agnew gladly helped to institute the first scheme. Within nine months of taking office, Agnew launched a series of attacks on the nation's elite media. He suggested that the nation's leading newspapers were operated by liberals, who were out to get the president. He alleged that network news was controlled by a small clique of self-interested individuals who hated Nixon and tended to favor liberal policies.

In a nationwide television address in November 1969, Agnew charged that network commentators were reckless in offering instantaneous commentary on Nixon speeches. In subsequent admonitions, Agnew sought to link news media with antiwar demonstrators. He labeled the demonstrators as "effete, impudent snobs" and on a separate occasion described network newspersons as "nattering nabobs of negativism."

The Agnewisms became legendary phrases that comedians repeated and liberals muttered, but the criticism had a serious side. Despite the indignant protest from the Fourth Estate, condemnation of the news media struck a chord of response from the public. Television's power had been growing throughout the 1960s, and many readers of Theodore White's ruminations had concluded that television was manipulating presidential politics, to the detriment of the country.

The Agnew-led criticism of the news media, especially television, played well outside Washington. It seemed to give voice to a fear harbored by many Americans in a time of turmoil. Many believed that the protests and violence of the 1960s had been choreographed by television camerapersons. The fear of television's power was not the only factor playing in the Nixon Administration's favor in the 1970s. Generally Americans desperately wanted Nixon to succeed. The turmoil and change was becoming too much. Vietnam had been around too long. Economic conditions were deteriorating. Prices were skyrocketing. The streets were becoming battlegrounds. What Nixon promised and what his long career in Washington indicated was a return to a calmer, more normal existence. He promised a peace with honor and to bring the nation together. It seemed that the constantly whining and negative news media were trying to prevent such a healing process.

In truth, Agnew's charges were largely unfounded bluster. Reporters naturally were not elected. Why should they be? The entire philosophy of the founding fathers militated against such a notion. The press was supposed to be free and INDEPENDENT. Correct or incorrect, reporters are expected to observe and report. The concept of interpretation that became popular in the 1960s allowed readers and viewers to hear more than just the facts. Done well, interpretive reporting provides the essence of informed communication. Done poorly, it slips into editorial commentary and blurs the accuracy of reporting. Agnew's charges, however, reflected the Nixon White House's predisposition to disagree with any interpretation that was not favorable. Nearly all the commentary offered in the early months of the Nixon administration was reasonable and fair, if not necessarily favorable.

Did network executives have too much power? Potentially, but that implies that they were abusing that power. Television in the 1960s and early 1970s was most cautious in its coverage and nearly bereft of hard-hitting documentary content. It was the most timid of the media generally. Certainly the daily reports from Vietnam were disturbing and carried much impact, but the intensity of the coverage was less than one would expect from an ongoing conflict that had split the nation. In fact, the power of the networks would be greatly diluted in the next two decades as cable television stations and networks claimed larger and larger audience shares. The 90 percent network audience share in 1970 provided an opportunity for abuse of the airwaves, but such had not occurred.

Were network commentators too quick to offer instant commentary after Nixon's addresses to the nation? Here there is disagreement. Often presidential addresses stretch on for twenty to thirty minutes. Prepared texts are handed to reporters about an hour before the speech, but not always. It would seem a difficult task to listen to a presidential speech and then, after a two-minute commercial break, comment at length on the contents. There is an obvious tendency in the news business to be first—with both the news and the interpretation. Commentary soon after a speech is certainly timely, but is it fair and accurate? This suggests haste can affect accuracy.

In truth, it depends on the complexity of the issues analyzed, the specific expertise of the commentator, the degree to which the president's remarks present new concepts, the scope of the problems addressed, and the amount of unsubstantiated information the president presents (commentary might require some fact finding to verify accuracy). Whether instantaneous analysis is fair, then, depends on a wide collection of variables, and a flat argument about whether it is or is not is just political invective.

The initial impetus for Agnew's attack was a speech delivered to the nation on television in October 1969. Nixon said that he would continue to press for an honorable solution to the Vietnam War. Reporters had expected a more earth-shaking announcement and observed that there had been nothing new in the speech. Agnew charged that they had no right to expect anything more than the president chose to or could provide and that television news executives were trying to usurp the power of the presidency.[1] In fact, reporters were correct. There *was* nothing new to report, but it is not certain that they could have deduced that in the short time they had copies of the text of the speech.

If the instant analysis was sometimes unwarranted, it was not the prime motivation for the criticism. Noticeably, the networks did cut back on their instant commentary in ensuing months, but they returned to the quick analysis after only a brief hiatus. It was also clear during the early Nixon years that network reporters and the rest of the Washington press corps, with a few exceptions, steered clear of confrontations with the White House. During Nixon's first term, public approval of Nixon was at first quite high, and criticism of the administration placed reporters in double jeopardy: possible disapproval from an aggressive White House and anger and resentment from the public. Most bowed to the pressure.

The second Nixon press strategy involved the White House reporters themselves. The Washington press corps, being closest in proximity to the Nixon White House, bore the brunt of the Nixon Administration paranoia. It was the Nixon strategy to keep them off balance and defensive. Early in the administration, the swimming pool in the White House where John F. Kennedy a decade earlier had soothed his aching back was paved over. New, more spacious press quarters were created, replacing the existing ones in the West Lobby. This moved reporters far away from the Oval Office and the White House entrance, where visitors came and went.

Press Secretary Ronald Ziegler briefed reporters twice a day, but often the synopses were filled with trivia and obfuscations. Ziegler refused to admit he might not have an answer to a question, and sometimes his answers were ludicrous. When Ziegler was asked about the European Council of Ten (an economic council), it became obvious that he did not know what the council was. Instead of conceding his ignorance, Ziegler simply responded that "we're not committed to any particular number."

Although he tried to please as much as aggravate, Ziegler drew mixed reviews from reporters. He answered directly to Haldeman, and so his independence, unlike most other press secretaries, was largely co-opted. He often reflected the arrogance of the Nixon White House, and his frequently condescending or roundabout responses at press briefings counterbalanced whatever news or information he managed to pass along. There was the feeling among reporters that the White House "news releases" were intended more to keep them busy with incidentals and away from the real news than they were to provide legitimate information.

More than the atmosphere in the pressroom, however, the Ziegler appointment and the press structure in the White House were indicative of the Nixon press strategy. Ziegler's advertising background was unique. Press secretaries had always had some training and experience as journalists. Ziegler's experience was in manipulating media for commercial reasons. Placing his office under Haldeman, another former advertising executive and the White House ax man, heightened reporters' suspicions of Ziegler and the press office.

To complicate matters, Nixon and Haldeman created for the first time a split White House communications apparatus. Ziegler was assigned to deal with reporters, and the job of generating public information about the White House was left to the communications office, nominally directed by Herbert Klein but in fact overseen by Haldeman and by Jeb Magruder, who was Klein's deputy director. Klein's office was in charge of churning out White House propaganda for editors and news directors around the country, in effect usurping the traditional role of the White House press corps.

This circumvention was part of the third strategy of simply outflanking the White House correspondents. Nixon rarely held press conferences. The thirty-nine that he conducted during nearly six years in office was a record low number for the modern presidency. Even those were often fruitless or punctuated by combative rhetoric, especially in the months after the Watergate break-in. Nixon, for instance, in response to a question from CBS's Robert Pierpont on October 26, 1973, said, "Don't get the impression that you arouse my anger." Pierpont responded, "I'm afraid, sir, that I have that impression," to which Nixon answered, "You see, one can only be angry with those he respects."[2] Ehrlichman told reporters in Los Angeles in June 1972 that the president saw little need for press conferences: "He doesn't get very good questions at a press conference, frankly. He goes in there for a half hour and gets a lot of flabby and fairly dumb questions and it doesn't really elucidate much." Nixon later disagreed with Ehrlichman, but Ehrlichman's contention seemed to be a more accurate reflection of the White House attitude. In fact Ehrlichman wrote later that Nixon told him privately, "Kicking the press is an art. Your flabby-and-dumb crack was good. You let them have it without rancor. That's what you have to do."[3] By meeting with reporters in a press conference setting only infrequently, Nixon avoided having to answer pointed questions and partially succeeded in controlling what the public learned about the Nixon White House and national policy.

That is not to say that Nixon did not give careful attention to television. More than any other president or presidential candidate up to that time, Nixon had learned that control of television could be a most effective tool. Nixon aides plotted strategies to influence the evening news, releasing information at opportune moments and writing texts that would almost certainly result in on-air sound bites. Visits to other parts of the world and the nation were carefully staged for maximum television exposure. Advance people were sent days ahead of time to round up supporters, who cheered lustily during Nixon speeches. Balloons, banners, streamers, and local Republicans were all in place for maximum television exposure.

For the first time, a sitting president visited comedy or talk shows to chat and look folksy. Nixon also answered questions on lengthy quasi-news programs with ABC's Howard K. Smith and NBC's Barbara Walters, discussions that produced little information but a maximum of positive Nixon TV exposure. Television became Nixon's friend, if TV reporters did not.

This strategy left correspondents, especially print reporters, struggling for legitimate White House sources of information. Left to their own means, many accepted material covertly, turning such intelligence into unattributed stories, sometimes just a step away from innuendo and gossip, further straining already tense White House press relations. The Nixon White House changed the relationship between the media and the president. It was now a struggle of image versus news interpretation with television as the central stage. The White House idea of press relations was not so much to inform but to guide and sometimes misinform.

The most heinous development was the Nixon White House policy of covert and illegal surveillance of reporters, political opponents, civil rights leaders, and antiwar activists. Anyone in a role of leadership or authority who spoke openly against Nixon was monitored by White House operatives, the Secret Service, the Central Intelligence Agency, or FBI agents under the direction of Nixon's friend, FBI director J. Edgar Hoover. Reporters were shadowed so agents could learn who was leaking information to them. Members of the White House even bugged each other. Secret Service agents were assigned to follow around and bug Donald Nixon, the president's brother who was conducting some worrisome business dealings with billionaire Howard Hughes.

The lawless atmosphere led to break-ins, burglaries, covert payments, disinformation campaigns against political opponents, illegal campaign contributions, bribery, and perjury. Watergate was not so much a scandal as it was a public revelation of a mind-set that governed the Nixon White House. Watergate was not a result but a symptom of what had gone wrong inside the Nixon inner circle. That attitude established itself long before the break-in at the Democratic National Headquarters. Other presidents may have used similar tactics on occasion (FDR planted a secret tape recorder in his desk in 1940), but none was as expansive, arrogant, and careless about it. Nixon's angry obsession with revenge had turned the White House into a seething camp of miscreants, possessed by the notion that White House enemies had to be eliminated, one way or another.

The downfall of the Nixon administration began with two highly publicized clashes with the press and with a secretive break-in at the psychiatrist's office of a former Vietnam policy advisor, all of which occurred in one year's time.

On June 13, 1971, *The New York Times* published the first installment of a series entitled "The Pentagon Papers," which tracked the history of U.S. involvement in the war in Vietnam. It was based on documents that had been stamped "top secret." Nothing in the Pentagon Papers was new; all the information had been made public at one time or another, but the documents on which the series was based had been classified as secret, and Nixon felt that publication of the information placed government security in jeopardy. After the third installment, the attorney general's office obtained a temporary restraining order to prevent further publication. It was the first instance in U.S. history of government-initiated prior restraint on a news medium. In the ensuing days, other newspapers and the Associated Press carried some of the details of the information from the Pentagon Papers anyway, and weeks later, the restraint order against *The Times* was lifted.

In response to the Supreme Court decision, Nixon ordered a break-in at the Brookings Institution. In a meeting in his office on June 30, little more than two weeks after the first installment of the Pentagon Papers, Nixon directed Haldeman to enter illegally the liberal, Washington-based institute and rifle the files there, according to a tape recording of the meeting that was released to the public in November 1996. Present at the meeting were Nixon, Haldeman, National Security Advisor Henry Kissinger, Secretary of Defense Melvin Laird, and Attorney General John Mitchell. Apparently the order to search the Brookings Institute was never carried out. According to information culled from the tapes in 1997, Nixon also discussed a break-in at the Republican National Committee headquarters to cast suspicion on the Democrats.

Nixon regarded the publication of the information about Vietnam activities as a slap in the face and told his staff to find the source of the Pentagon Papers leak. A "team of plumbers," led by ex-FBI agent G. Gordon Liddy, spent months tracking the leak to ex-Pentagon aide Daniel Ellsberg. In September 1971, in an effort to discredit Ellsberg, the plumbers broke into the office of Los Angeles psychiatrist Lewis Fielding, Ellsberg's former analyst, to steal Ellsberg's psychiatric records. The break-in gained the Nixon circle very little information, but when White House culpability in the incident was made public a few years later, it helped to clarify the pattern of illegal behavior that had dominated the White House.

In the spring of 1972, CBS aired a documentary, "The Selling of the Pentagon," in which it traced how the Nixon administration was spending millions of taxpayer dollars on jet plane flying shows, military exhibits, and other public relations gambits. The administration hoped to convince the public of the military's value—partly as an answer to the unpopularity of the Vietnam War and partly to avoid cuts in appropriations proposed by the

Democratic Congress. The CBS documentary angered not only Nixon but also congressmen who had been depicted as shills for the military. The show so vexed Nixon's people that the network and all its correspondents were put at the top of the enemies list.

THE 1972 ELECTION

In this atmosphere, Nixon launched a bid for re-election in 1972. His staff sought to ensure that their man was not only elected but also that he received an emphatic mandate. This they sought to accomplish by whatever method was necessary. The Committee to Reelect the President (CREEP) was headed by John N. Mitchell, who resigned as attorney general to devote his full energies to the campaign.

Policy matters were ignored so Nixon's highest level of advisors could spend nearly all their time organizing the campaign. They paid operatives to disrupt campaign rallies of Democratic candidates or to embarrass them by making it seem that they had engaged in unethical practices. In 1971, Nixon's people covertly used phoney stationery from the Edmund Muskie campaign containing polling results that appeared to try to discredit Ted Kennedy. This made the Muskie campaign organization seem to be using dirty tactics against Kennedy. Months later, food and flowers were sent COD to a Muskie rally in Washington; no one in the Muskie camp had ordered them. A bogus letter was sent to a newspaper in New Hampshire in February 1972 containing derogatory comments about French Canadians and blacks. The "Canuck" letter was attributed to Muskie. Memos were stolen, spies were planted, harassing phone calls purportedly made by Democratic candidates' supporters were placed to voters, and rallies were sabotaged throughout the primary campaign—all clandestinely by operatives hired by Nixon strategists.

The most significant Nixon White House blunder was the June 16, 1972, break-in at the Democratic National Headquarters in the Watergate apartment-office-hotel complex in Washington. Operatives had planted secret listening devices in the offices two weeks earlier but had returned to plant more. They were four Cuban-American men from Miami and a former CIA agent, James W. McCord Jr. The break-in was so clumsy and poorly planned that the burglars were caught, though at least twice a security guard had walked right by the office and ignored telltale indications that a break-in was in progress. The next morning Bob Woodward, a young reporter with the *Washington Post*, was assigned to cover the preliminary hearing, where the five men were charged. Woodward learned of McCord's CIA connections, and he and fellow reporter Carl Bernstein began to dig into the most famous investigative story in U.S. history.

Ironically, none of the dirty tricks was necessary. The Democrats were able to destroy themselves without any help. After the assassinations of his two older brothers, support for Ted Kennedy in 1969 was growing nationwide. The popularity of the Kennedy name and national sorrow over the deaths of John and Robert had provided Ted Kennedy with front-runner support from all over the nation. Particularly since most Democrats were either also-rans or not well known, it appeared that the 1972 nomination was Kennedy's. In July 1969 while returning from a late-night party on the Chappaquiddick Island off the coast of Massachusetts, Kennedy took a wrong turn and his automobile plunged off a bridge into the bay. A young staff aide with him, Mary Jo Kopechne, drowned. Kennedy claimed later that he had escaped the sinking automobile and then tried desperately to save Miss Kopechne.

But questions remained unanswered. What was an attractive young staff aide doing with Kennedy in his car after a late-night party? Was Kennedy drunk? Why else would he have taken a wrong turn on a familiar road? Shouldn't he have been prosecuted for reckless homicide? Most damaging, why didn't Kennedy report the incident to the police until nearly a day later? Massachusetts is Kennedy country, and there was little doubt that Kennedy would not be accused of anything more than a minor offense, but the general public was not so forgiving.

Kennedy eventually pursued the White House in 1980, but his viability as a presidential candidate was destroyed forever. Just two years after George Romney had incinerated his 1968 campaign with his "brainwashed" remark and just a year after Robert Kennedy was eliminated by an assassin's bullet, another front-runner in the next campaign had been voided. There would be more.

George Wallace's independent campaign created enmity among regular Democrats and he was shot in an assassination attempt during the primaries. Confined to a wheelchair, he was never an effective campaigner again. Consequently, as the primary campaign began, Senator Edmund Muskie of Maine appeared to be the new front-runner. In the 1968 campaign, Muskie, the vice presidential candidate, had shown himself to be a thoughtful and convincing orator. His voter appeal had been a campaign surprise and an effective asset to Humphrey, particularly in the light of Agnew's obvious weaknesses. Other contenders included Senator Henry Jackson of Washington; John Lindsay, mayor of New York, who had switched allegiance to the Democratic Party; former standard-bearer Hubert Humphrey of Minnesota; and Senator George McGovern of South Dakota. Though he still sought the nomination, Senator

Meanwhile, McGovern's problems were unending. Nixon's popularity had decreased in 1971 with the worsening economy and the interminable war. Polls indicated he was behind, but that had been in head-to-head samplings with Humphrey, Muskie, or Kennedy. Few had anticipated a McGovern candidacy. By 1972 with a better economic climate, decreasing troop levels in Vietnam, and the Nixon trip to China, the voter mood had changed. Besides, McGovern was pretty much an unknown. To make matters worse, his acceptance speech was delivered at 3 A.M. because of delays in the convention agenda, and most voters had already gone to bed. Many regular Democrats were excluded from the convention, under new rules adopted after the 1968 conclave. The delegate makeup had to contain gender and race diversity, reflective of the composition of the general populace. The regular Illinois delegation, including Chicago Mayor Richard Daley, stayed home. They sat on their hands for the general election too.

Then, just days after his nomination, McGovern strategists learned that Senator Thomas Eagleton, the vice presidential candidate, was in trouble. Newspapers had begun to investigate reports that Eagleton had mental problems. In fact, he had been hospitalized for mental illness three times during his career, but he had long before put those problems behind him. Still, Americans knew little about mental illness in 1972 and worried about a man who might be in charge of a nuclear arsenal and not be able to think clearly. McGovern called a press conference and told reporters of Eagleton's past medical history, taking Eagleton's secret past into the public arena for the first time. He expressed his support and confidence in Eagleton, but to no avail. Stories dominated the media for days, and finally Eagleton was asked to resign. After offering the campaign position to four or five candidates, who promptly said no, McGovern finally found Sargent Shriver, a Kennedy in-law and former director of the Peace Corps under John F. Kennedy. Shriver accepted.

The campaign was a disaster for McGovern. Nixon television ads depicted McGovern as a wild liberal who would put half the nation on aid of some kind. McGovern appeared weak and indecisive in the Eagleton affair, and his antiwar liberalism seemed out of place in 1972. The type of candidate idealistic young liberals had wanted in 1968 came to be the party standard-bearer in 1972, but the timing was not right. Nixon once again refused to debate, and instead held televised discussions with friendly audiences, where he answered softball questions. His supporters choreographed huge Nixon rallies, complete with young ladies in bathing suits and straw hats. The "Nixon girls" idea was about as innovative as the campaign got. The first campaign featuring many primaries over a long period ended with quite predictable results: much rhetoric, little discussion of issues, and a landslide Nixon victory. McGovern carried only

Eugene McCarthy's support had waned drastically in the light (
ished U.S. role in the Vietnam War.

The tumultuous Democratic convention of 1968 and the
nomination had engendered charges of too much party control. C(
the number of primaries was expanded by a third to twenty-two i1
first one, in New Hampshire, still remained the most importan
contents of the phoney "Canuck" letter, circulated by Nixon
appeared in the Manchester *Union Leader* in February 1972, c(
newspaper publisher William Loeb initiated a campaign agains
outspoken wife, Jane. Muskie responded by standing on the back o
truck in front of the newspaper building and denouncing Loeb as
coward." He then broke down into tears.

Voters admired Muskie's defense of his wife but worried about
tional candidate who cried when criticism came his way. What woul(
to him under the pressure of a nuclear confrontation? Muskie w
Hampshire with 46 percent of the vote to McGovern's 37 percent
campaign sagged badly after that, and he withdrew in early May,
victim of front-runneritis.

Humphrey's loss in 1968 hindered his perceived electability among
cratic voters, and the conservative but stodgy Henry Jackson could not (
the imagination of the electorate. New York City's financial and socia
reflected badly on John Lindsay, whose switch from the Republican Pa1
generated suspicion among party regulars anyway. McGovern, the le1
antiwar liberal from 1968, was the only candidate remaining. He
through the primaries, winning the nomination on the first ballot, alm(
default. Nixon had no real opposition and hardly campaigned durin;
primary season.

The expanded number of elections had not really influenced the outc
of the primaries but had certainly affected presidential politics. After mo.
of informal stumping, the Democrats campaigned in January and Februar
anticipation of the March 7 New Hampshire voting. They continued throu
out the spring until the June 20 primary in New York. Then came
conventions and the general election campaign. In all, McGovern was for(
to canvass for votes for more than a year, nonstop. So would candidates of t
future. Voters would grow tired of the interminable election process a1
reporters would become weary of trying to formulate stories for eleven mont1
about the same candidates who mouthed the same platitudes. The selection (
candidates had been removed from the backrooms, but the open primar
system plunged presidential politics into chaos and turned campaigns int(
endurance contests.

Massachusetts and the newly enfranchised District of Columbia. He even lost his home state, South Dakota. Democrats remained in control of both Houses, but it appeared that their hold on the presidency, dating back to Roosevelt's victory over Hoover in 1932, had been shattered.

Reporters, especially television correspondents, were overly cautious about favoring either candidate, fearing more charges of bias. Although Woodward and Bernstein had been working on the Watergate series of stories for nearly five months by election time, almost no other news organization had picked up on the scandal, except to publish or broadcast White House denials in response to *Post* stories. Polls indicated that more than half the country had never heard of Watergate. The historical facts about the press in the 1972 election concern not so much what was reported but what was not. As in 1964, the huge early deficit in the polls had placed the challenger's candidacy on the ho-hum story list. McGovern's elite leftist image turned off union supporters, and his rallies in blue-collar communities lacked enthusiasm. Traditional Democratic newspapers, especially in the South, overwhelmingly endorsed Nixon.

As is normal, though, neither news stories nor television advertising had affected the outcome of the election, only the margin of victory. Nixon had won four more years in the White House because U.S. participation in the war was ending, the economy had rebounded, and McGovern was not equal to the task. Nixon would never have to run for election again, and now he, Haldeman, Ehrlichman, and the others would settle matters with those on the enemies list. An inventory had been drawn up in September 1972 detailing those persons who had been particularly critical of the Nixon administration, including many journalists.

WATERGATE

Between October 5, 1972, and August 21, 1973, Nixon held only two press conferences, literally ignoring the White House press corps. His staff set about challenging the broadcast licenses of two television stations owned by the *Washington Post*. Reporters' telephones were bugged, and some journalists were covertly followed to determine from whom they were acquiring information.[4] If the Nixon White House gained satisfaction from such activities, it was short-lived.

Although the *Post's* Watergate investigation had been ignored by most news organizations in its early stages, the story was gathering momentum by the time of Nixon's inaugural in January 1973. In November 1972, a grand jury began hearing about Watergate-related offenses from witness testimony under the direction of Federal Judge John J. Sirica. Archibald Cox, a Harvard Law

School professor, was appointed by then-Attorney General Elliot Richardson as special prosecutor on May 18, 1973. Just days before the inauguration, the Senate Judiciary Committee, dubbed the Watergate Committee, decided to investigate government abuse stemming from Watergate-related matters. The committee opened hearings on May 17, 1973. The *Post* investigation was accompanied by an official grand jury probe and a Senate investigation. By the time the grand jury and the Senate Watergate Committee had finished their work, more than forty persons were in jail, including some of the most powerful people in Washington, a House committee had approved articles of impeachment against Nixon, and in August 1974 the president had resigned.

The entire Watergate series of events paralyzed Washington for eighteen months. Normal legislative business came to a standstill. Only a third Arab-Israeli War in October 1973 and an Arab oil boycott that caused massive gasoline shortages in the United States interrupted the paralysis that clutched official Washington.

In March 1973 James McCord, who helped plan the Watergate break-in, wrote a letter to Judge Sirica informing him that he and his co-defendants had been pressured to keep silent during their trials and that perjury had been committed. He then testified before the Senate Watergate Committee in private. Jeb Magruder, deputy director of White House communications, told the Senate Watergate Committee in May 1973 that the Watergate burglary had been authorized by Attorney General John Mitchell. Days later White House counsel John Dean informed the committee that Nixon himself learned about the break-in during conversations at White House meetings on September 15, 1972, and March 21, 1973. Nixon had authorized a cover-up, Dean testified. On July 16, 1973, Alexander Butterfield, an aide to Haldeman, told the committee that Nixon had secret, voice-activated taping devices installed in his offices and in the Cabinet Room in February 1971 that recorded all conversations in those rooms.

From that point, the Senate committee and the Sirica grand jury focused on obtaining copies of the tapes, which Nixon refused to give up. Cox pressed hard for release of the tapes, and on October 20, the White House ordered Attorney General Elliot Richardson to fire Cox. Richardson informed Nixon that he was resigning rather than carry out such an order. Deputy Attorney General William Ruckelshaus also refused, and he was fired. Solicitor General Robert Bork, third in line, then carried out Nixon's instructions and dismissed Cox, completing the "Saturday Night Massacre."

The nation and the rest of the world drew back in disgust. Nixon was in deep trouble. Until the massacre, many had assumed that Watergate was nothing more than a political vendetta dreamed up by the Democrats and the "liberal media." The presence of the tapes and Nixon's refusal to release them, coupled with the resignation and then the firings of Ruckelshaus and Cox, alarmed the nation and the news media as no other event had in years. The anger and revulsion took the White House by surprise. Newspapers nationwide demanded Nixon's resignation.

The firing did not work. Leon Jaworski was appointed to replace Cox and proved to be just as dogged as his predecessor. By this time, most of Nixon's staff had resigned and eventually served prison terms, including Chief of Staff H. R. Haldeman and domestic advisor John Ehrlichman. Alexander Haig was appointed the new chief of staff.

To complicate matters, Vice President Spiro Agnew, under investigation himself on unrelated charges of accepting kickbacks on construction contracts while governor of Maryland, resigned on October 10 after pleading "no contest" in a federal court to a charge of evading taxes in 1967. Nixon, while dodging the Watergate investigation, suddenly had to find a new vice president. In the middle of the Middle East crisis and the controversy over the tapes, he nominated House Minority Leader Gerald R. Ford, who was confirmed months later by the Senate.

In the spring of 1974, the House Judiciary Committee met to consider articles of impeachment against Nixon. On April 29, Nixon finally relented and released more than 1,000 pages of transcripts of tapes to that committee. On July 27, the House committee recommended, 27 to 11, that articles of impeachment be brought to the full House. Nixon released more tapes on August 5, hoping that this would show his innocence. Dubbed the "smoking gun" tapes, they indicated quite the opposite. Demands for Nixon's resignation reached a peak, and during a live televised address the evening of August 8, 1974, Nixon told the nation that he would resign the next day at noon, the first U.S. president ever to be forced from the White House in the middle of a term of office. Gerald Ford became the thirty-eighth president of the United States on August 9, 1974, the first person ever to reach the Oval Office without having been elected vice president or president.

THE MEANING OF THE NIXON YEARS

Years later, after Nixon had carefully attempted to revive his image through a series of public speeches and television appearances (Nixon died in April 1994), supporters argued that he had been railroaded from office. Had not a vindictive opposition press been out to undo the wishes of the electorate, Nixon would have served out his term and taken his place as one of the greatest presidents in history, they argued. In truth, Nixon had no one to blame for his demise but himself and his advisors.

Not only had they violated the nation's laws at will, but they had done so with great haughtiness and imprudence. Why, for instance, had the Democratic National Headquarters been burglarized in the first place? What in the world were Nixon operatives going to find among the junk mailings and posters? What would the electronic listening devices they were trying to plant actually tell them? What would party staffers say in an open office where dozens of people were milling about? Why tape private conversations in the Oval Office and then why not destroy those tapes immediately after it became apparent that their contents could ruin the White House? During the early days of World War II, Franklin Roosevelt had taped the conversations that took place in his office, wanting a record of what transpired during a period of American neutrality. Lyndon Johnson similarly recorded Oval Office conversations, stipulating later that the tapes not be released for public review until the mid-1990s. The question was not so much why there were tapes but why so many and why they had not been destroyed immediately when the Watergate investigation began. Tapes released in 1997 indicate that White House aides had considered destroying the tapes while Nixon was ill in the hospital, but they did not. Paranoia and arrogance. Everyone was out to get Nixon and his men, and they had to fight back with whatever means necessary, they reasoned. And Nixon wanted those tapes for history—that is, he wanted documented conversations to support his later recollections of his glorious years in the White House. He wanted to record and "prove" that many who visited him in the Oval Office had been duplicitous or underhanded. None of the Nixon people thought that the Watergate investigation would threaten them.

As to the press role in Watergate, it is true that the *Washington Post* management, supporters of the Kennedys and disdainful of Nixon, was less than objective. The facts of the Watergate investigation speak for themselves, however. The persistence of the two young reporters, Woodward and Bernstein, transcended politics.

Watergate in many ways was more about the Washington press corps than it was about White House corruption. It was, in essence, a media barometer. Many of the dirty tricks emerged from the White House perception that media were all-powerful and only a no-holds-barred approach to the 1972 election could save Nixon from press antagonism and resultant defeat. The Nixon concept of media as almost too overwhelming for the presidency caused much of the turmoil and national embarrassment of the early 1970s.

In fact, what had been evolving since 1960 and was almost in place in 1972 was indeed a diminished relationship between press and president, with the press having the upper hand. It was only a part of the press, however: television. It was not Woodward and Bernstein who brought down Nixon. It was Alexander

Butterfield's revealing on national television the existence of tapes of Oval Office conversations. Without those tapes, Nixon probably would have finished his second term, wounded but intact. The televised testimony before the Senate Watergate Committee and the impeachment hearings before the House Judiciary Committee led to Nixon's resignation. Both had attracted large television audiences and made Pennsylvania Avenue popular on Main Street. The average American found some steadfast interest in Washington politics.

Yet none of that would have occurred had not the *Washington Post* persevered under the most demanding circumstances, while no other newspaper, magazine, radio station, or television network picked up the story. Why was it that two young reporters who hardly knew the names of White House staffers when they began their investigation were able to steal the story of the century right out from under the noses of the most talented group of journalists in the world? Because White House press relations had reached a managed and formalized stage in 1972 that had changed Washington news gathering. Influential reporters did not have off-the-record dinners with the president as they had during Eisenhower's time. They did not get to share thoughts and ideas with the chief executive on a fishing trip, as they had during the Truman years. They were shut out, given press releases at carefully choreographed press briefings, and herded into more spacious but isolated offices. Meanwhile, television had come to dominate White House media objectives. It is ironic that the *Post* had so heartily revived print investigative journalism in Washington, because the influence of that genre of serious reporting was actually dying—to be replaced by gossip, innuendo, and tidbits about private lives of candidates and presidents.

The *Post's* persistence may have salvaged the role of the nation's press as watchdog over the presidency. In 1908, the *New York World* under Joseph Pulitzer persevered when President Theodore Roosevelt sought legal recourse in New York, after a damaging series appeared in the newspaper. The *World* had unmasked Roosevelt's unethical maneuvering to allow the United States to begin construction of the Panama Canal. Had the *World* not been able to combat the power of the presidency, an influence much superior to that of the Washington press corps in those days, the power of the media in this country might have been seriously damaged. Similarly, had Nixon succeeded in his efforts to destroy the *Post* financially and to suppress the Pentagon Papers' stories, the Washington press corps would have been badly compromised. Both the *World* and the *Post* had editorial policies opposed to the political leanings of the presidents in those instances, but in both cases had they not been determined to back their rights to investigate the president's malfeasance, the independence of all media would have been sabotaged.

While television ultimately brought an end to the Nixon Administration through its broadcasts of congressional hearings, broadcast news reporters usually were not interested in more than thirty-second summaries of White House events, hardly conducive to exploring an unfolding scandal. Only after the Saturday Night Massacre did television begin to bore in on Watergate. Besides, when an investigative story breaks, the target always has the advantage of using the other media. A journalist naturally shies away from following up on someone else's investigation, the story another reporter unearthed. The innate tendency is to downgrade the other's investigation and quote only the target's comments that there is nothing there, only a vindictive hatchet job.

All this added up to a shameful lack of aggressiveness in the early months of the Watergate investigation. Later, unfolding scandals in the Reagan and Clinton administrations would also be marked by a curious lack of determination to get at the facts. Nixon was not hounded from office by a malevolent press corps; he was allowed to stay in office too long by a reluctant press brigade.

Reporters on the scene during the Nixon years knew all this. Many realized that they had been kept busy with Nixon-orchestrated press releases and public relations gambits. Coupled with the press management present during the Vietnam-dominated Johnson Administration, Watergate brought a new aura to the White House pressroom. Antagonism toward and mistrust of every president who succeeded Nixon dogged press-president relations. Yet reporter aggressiveness was generally limited to hostile questions at press conferences and a penchant for reporting innuendo and gossip. Good, solid investigative reporting of government malfeasance was not enhanced in the next twenty years by Watergate. Reporters had become too accustomed to the pack journalism and press conference mentality to look outside the Capitol–White House grounds for major stories, as had Woodward and Bernstein.

As for the two young reporters-turned-celebrities, a movie and two Pulitzer awards made them national heroes. Bernstein was a little bitter about the outcast role that he and Woodward had played in the days after the break-in. A few years after Nixon resigned, Bernstein visited Milwaukee to address a state teachers' convention. He refused to talk with local reporters. When cornered behind stage just before the speech, he finally held an impromptu press conference, but was largely unresponsive to questions. He lectured two dozen Wisconsin reporters, many of whom had never been to Washington, about the general lack of responsible reporting in America. They all nodded and studied their shoes. Bernstein appeared to be more disgusted with the profession than with the presidency.

Later he left the *Post* for a series of independent writing assignments, the speech circuit, and a brief but unspectacular stint with ABC News. Woodward continued as an editor with the *Post*, taking time off occasionally to write more tell-all books about official Washington, until all in the nation's capital, from the president on down, learned to speak freely with Woodward or find themselves as targets in the books.

Watergate's greatest disfigurement was its damage to the American psyche. Since Franklin Roosevelt's New Deal, Americans had looked to government for protection. In the years after Watergate, the federal bureaucracy was seen as a detached group of insulated politicians in Washington who cared nothing for the American public or the American way of life. Popular movies in the next two decades depicted presidents as scheming liars, whose sole purposes were self-aggrandizement and self-enrichment. In these popular characterizations, the CIA plots illegal foreign invasions, the FBI is controlled by a bigoted tyrant, the White House inner circle is a group of power-hungry miscreants, American foreign relations are tainted by outrageously self-centered concerns, and the notion of fairness is all but exterminated.

Watergate had shattered the innocent public naiveté that had marked the Kennedy years. Promises and assurances would not be accepted with unskeptical enthusiasm in the post-Watergate era. The common question formulated for the president in the hinterlands would not be, "Why should I doubt the president?" but, "Why should I think the president is not lying?" This was not only because Nixon was forced to resign and nearly all his inner circle was sent to prison, but because large numbers of Americans had watched it all with careful interest on television. Never before or since had the public so avidly immersed itself in Washington's affairs. They would not remember the Washington of other eras, but they would recall Watergate Washington. That would be the Washington they would envision as they went to the ballot box and listened to pleas for patience and understanding from other presidents.

Consequently, if reporters were rancorous toward presidents and intent on revealing their personal foibles, the public in the 1970s and 1980s was only too ready to read and hear about these shortcomings and believe them. This then had the circular impact of a serpent swallowing its tail. The more negative the reporting, the less the president said publicly and the more carefully he chose his words. The more prying into personal backgrounds, the more reluctant were politicians to seek the presidency. Still, in an increasingly complex world, serious, substantive stories about troubling world and domestic issues were losing currency, partly because of the disgust with Watergate but also because of the changing role of journalism generally.

If the image of the presidency suffered because of Watergate, so did that of the Washington press corps—not for the reasons cited here, but because a public already fearful of the power of the press watched as a newspaper investigation forced the resignation of the most powerful person in the world. After the heady days immediately following the resignation and the popular movie *All the President's Men*, doubts set in. Was this not proof that the press was too omnipotent? What was it that Richard Nixon did that was so terrible? He bent a few rules to get reelected. "They" all do that. But Nixon's real mistake, it was reasoned, was that he did not kowtow to the all-mighty reporters and news managers. Well, good for him! Maybe he went a little too far, but it's the press that Americans have to fear.

This theme played out over and over again in the next several years. Reporters explain what they do and why they do it. The public, arms folded, listens in disbelief. The next several presidents hold out their hands in wide-eyed innocence and plead, "Why do we have to be victimized?" The press and what reporters do with their time became as much an explored theme as the presidency itself. Reporters, who had always been in the background, asking questions and reporting stories, were now in the foreground. What the press was thinking and reporting became as much a source of interest to the public as the presidency itself. No aspect of the press and presidency emerged unchallenged after the events of 1971 to 1974.

NOTES

1. For a complete account of these incidents see Joseph C. Spear, *Presidents and the Press: The Nixon Legacy* (Cambridge, Mass.: MIT Press, 1984), 114–15.

2. George W. Johnson (ed.), *The Nixon Presidential Press Conferences* (New York: Earl M. Coleman Enterprises, 1978), 373.

3. See John Ehrlichman, *Witness to Power* (New York: Simon & Schuster, 1982), 285–87.

4. See Spear, *Presidents and the Press*, 111–76.

CHAPTER SIX

MR. FORD'S DOUBLE-EDGED SWORD

Gerald Ford took office under most trying circumstances. His one blessing was that both press and public were ready for a period of tranquility, but through his own miscalculation he quickly surrendered that advantage. Only a month after Nixon's resignation, Ford made a politically fatal mistake that would extend the painful influence of Watergate and cost the new president the White House.

The House Minority Leader for eighteeen years at the time of the Agnew resignation, Ford had represented the congressional district in and around Grand Rapids, Michigan, since 1949. The son of a small paint company owner, Ford was a highly rated center on the University of Michigan football team in the early 1930s. Later he was graduated from Yale Law School. Despite his lengthy Capitol Hill experience, he appeared to be an unusual choice for vice president in 1973, because he was not close to the Nixon White House. Many Nixon people looked upon Ford contemptuously, concluding among themselves that he was ineffective and unimaginative. Still, Ford possessed a needed quality: a reputation for honesty and sincerity, something sorely lacking on Pennsylvania Avenue. Those qualities gave Americans hope when Ford took office in 1974. Just twelve years after reaching its apex, the presidency was at its lowest point since the Teapot Dome scandal in 1923. In September 1974, however, the public believed that an honest person was in control and that a new era was beginning.

The business of the country badly needed the president's attention. Paralyzed by Watergate, neither the executive nor the legislative branches had time for the federal government's daily needs, many of which had become more urgent during the Watergate stalemate. Inflation heightened the cost of fuel, housing, food, consumer staples, automobiles, clothing, and just about anything else Americans needed. Shortages of some basic needs, including fuel and even meat, appeared periodically. Homes and automobiles were particularly unaffordable to consumers used to having two cars and at least a three-bedroom home. The Vietnam War dragged on, though U.S. troop commitments had been eliminated. Court-ordered school integration angered some whites and turned many local school districts into legal battlegrounds. Japan and Germany had begun to cut into U.S. domination of world markets of consumer goods. The Middle East remained tense (a civil war would break out in Lebanon in 1975), creating a real danger of a fifth Arab-Israeli war. Despite the thaw in relations with China, the Cold War continued unabated with the accompanying threat of nuclear holocaust ever present.

Ford and Congress needed to act decisively, but the new president realized that the imperial White House of the 1970s had created skepticism. He needed to patch White House relations with the media first if he wished to build a positive image and win public confidence. Once secured, this acceptance, he hoped, would translate into rapid resolution of pressing issues.

This needed publicity blitz would require a careful choice of press secretary. Ford decided not to pull someone from his old congressional staff. Instead, he chose the type of press secretary that had been popular in the early years of the century during the Wilson, Hoover, Roosevelt, Truman, and Eisenhower Administrations: an experienced working journalist. Jerald terHorst, Washington bureau chief for the *Detroit News*, accepted the position with the understanding that he would be honest and upfront with reporters. Ford agreed. What made terHorst nearly unique was his selection from among the active White House correspondents. Only *Baltimore Sun* reporter Joseph Short, Truman's second press secretary in 1950, had made such an abrupt transition. The distinguished and well-regarded terHorst seemed to be the perfect choice after the undignified and disrespected Ronald Ziegler. Reporters could be certain that terHorst would be upright and forthcoming.

Shortly after taking office, photographers requested candid pictures of Ford, photos that illustrated the lifestyle of the new president. "Was there anything that Ford did that was unusual and might create an insightful photo opportunity?" terHorst was asked. The four Ford children were nearly grown. The youngest, Susan, seventeen, was a student at a private school in Bethesda, Maryland. No cute kiddy pictures there. Betty Ford, who later would become as well known and perhaps more admired than her husband, provided only modest photo fodder. There was one possibility. Yes, terHorst told reporters, the president liked to toast his own English muffins in the morning, a task usually assigned to a White House steward. Muffins. Fantastic. Photographers snapped pictures one morning and, within hours, Ford was seen nationwide heating and buttering. He was a regular guy, not someone who planted secret tapes or plotted against opponents.

This nonevent seemed to warm the public. For the first time in the 1970s, the nation had a president free of an unpopular war and unfettered by a growing scandal who also toasted his own breakfast food. Ford aides luxuriated in the sympathy and enthusiasm from the nation's news media and the public. This was the time to put Watergate completely behind, Ford reasoned. Nixon was no longer president, but now a private citizen and, shocked by Watergate revelations that summer, many wanted Nixon to answer for his alleged crimes. Most of Nixon's close associates had been sentenced to prison. Why not Nixon, the one in charge? Ford and his advisors sought to avoid a court spectacle and possible incarceration of a former president, thus humiliating the GOP and the nation. Before any charges were even filed against Nixon, Ford decided on September 7, 1974, to offer Nixon a full pardon for any crimes he might have committed while in office, the president's constitutional prerogative. It was unprecedented to offer a pardon to a former president. Only days before, during his first press conference, Ford had evaded a question about such clemency.

TerHorst was aghast. Such a decision, consummated without consulting him, would undercut his credibility and leave him in an untenable position, he told Ford. If the pardon was issued, he continued, he would have to resign. The president was adamant and announced the decision the next day, a Sunday. TerHorst resigned.

The press secretary had gauged the mood of the public more accurately than had Ford. Both journalists and voters saw the pardon as the same backroom dealing that had marked the Nixon years. Had Nixon cut a deal with Ford when he resigned? How come the common criminal goes to prison for robbing a gas station and the biggest crook in the country is pardoned? How can the president ever say again that he stands for justice? The president explained that there had been no deal before the Nixon resignation, but the furor would not die. Everything Ford undertook for the rest of his administration was viewed with skepticism. In the days after the pardon, polls recorded a dramatic dip in his popularity from 70 percent approval to 50 percent. Gone now was the one advantage that Ford had possessed during the troubled seventies: his reputation for honesty and integrity.

The impact of the decision was deadly. While stirring up the Watergate debate again, it brought questions about Ford's shrewdness and political intuitiveness. What seasoned politician would commit such a horrendous mistake? Were all those accusations about Ford's being a dolt actually true

(Lyndon Johnson had said that Ford could not "walk and chew gum at the same time")? What other kind of person would rouse such unwanted passion just weeks after the wrenching resignation of the previous president?

Not surprisingly, the national media portrayed terHorst as a fallen hero, a person of principle who would not bend to politics. Ford appointed as terHorst's replacement another working journalist: Ronald Nessen, White House correspondent for NBC. TerHorst returned to the *Detroit News* as a columnist, and his first opinion piece dealt with his decision to resign. But was the terHorst decision proper? What is the role of a press secretary? To weigh his judgment against that of the president and take issue if the interpretations differ? TerHorst said that this particular decision was so momentous that he could not live with its consequences, but did he not realize that being a press secretary had its risks? All press agents must somehow put the best face on bad decisions from time to time. TerHorst, of course, did not see himself as just a press agent, but as a journalist in a different setting, whose loyalties were divided between the president and an obligation to the public. This may have been right and honorable, but it served as a warning to other presidents. It appears that the dilemma will not be repeated soon. No president for the remainder of the century appointed a working journalist as chief press officer. Ensuing chief executives made certain that their press secretaries had no divided allegiances.

LIVE FROM NEW YORK

Nothing Ford did after that first month in office seemed to be given a fair examination by the public or press. The pardon in 1974 became THE PARDON in 1975 and 1976. Reporters picked up on Lyndon Johnson's unkind remark about Ford's intelligence and repeated it frequently. Photo opportunities became nightmares. An avid golfer, Ford participated in a golf tournament and shanked a tee shot, striking a young woman standing in the gallery. Not injured seriously, the woman accepted Ford's apology later, but in the post-pardon environment, a passing event that would normally have been the third or fourth story for one day on the evening news received days of attention. Ford stumbled on the steps disembarking from Air Force One in Salzburg, Austria, and THE STUMBLE was played over and over again. During a dinner address, while Egyptian President Anwar Sadat sat nearby, Ford misidentified him as the president of Israel. Reporters nodded knowingly.

During the Nixon Administration, NBC had experimented with a late-evening comedy show, "Saturday Night Live." That time slot had traditionally been an unwanted one, most viewers preferring to party or enjoy themselves away from the home, rather than watch television in the last hours of a Saturday evening. The program, unusual in that it was live and the entertainers were poorly paid unknowns from comedy clubs in New York, was an instant hit. Americans, especially the young anti-establishment sixties generation, reoriented Saturday routines so they could be home by 11:30 P.M. One of the program's standard weekly skits was a parody of Nixon and his family or Nixon and his White House underlings. Actor Dan Aykroyd seemed to capture the Nixon stodginess, insecurity, and penchant for self-indulgence. Comics had mimicked presidents as far back as Theodore Roosevelt's time, but the popularity of a late-night television program brought the mockery to a new level.

After the successful Nixon parodies, audiences expected presidential lampooning, and actor Chevy Chase delivered, spoofing Ford's supposed clumsiness during the two and a half years of the Ford presidency. Imagery can be a double-edged sword. What is the meaning of a president's stumbling on a runway stair ramp? The same as a president toasting his own English muffins, perhaps—meaningless unless somehow more is attached. To show what a good sport he was, Ford during the 1976 campaign allowed Nessen to participate in a "Saturday Night Live" skit with Chase. Ford even made three taped appearances, in which he introduced the opening of the show, a serious mistake. Amid a tough election campaign, international tension, post-Watergate suspicion, and crippling inflation, it was not good judgment to allow Nessen to legitimize the lampooning. More Americans watched "Saturday Night Live" than watched the NBC evening news. The impression left with too many otherwise uninformed viewers was that even the press secretary thought the president was a klutz.

Apparently White House advisors, particularly Nessen, did not realize how deeply alienated Americans had become and how skeptical and unaccepting of the power of the presidency they were. Now, Americans wanted to make fun of the president and to believe that they were just as competent as he, but possessing even more moral scruples. The president was not a world leader and a revered figure, but a duplicitous conniver at best and a bumbling fool at worst. Ford never shook that image. Even respected historians writing in the late 1970s and the 1980s referred to Ford as an unintelligent bungler, as if this were an accepted fact. John F. Kennedy or Pierre Salinger could have appeared on "Saturday Night Live" without repercussions, because Kennedy was a revered figure who could afford self-deprecation. Ford was not.

If this double-edged imagery was unfair and subjective, it was also a creation of Ford's tactical errors. After all, it was he who issued the pardon and he who authorized Nessen's visit to "Saturday Night Live." It was he who agreed to create the muffin toasting image and he who ignored the advice of his first press secretary.

For the next two years, Ford's initial errors seemed to hound him. Visits to the Soviet Union and China were labeled by editorial writers as unnecessary politicking. Why would he undertake such travels so soon after Nixon had visited those countries, except to enhance his image? The president could not be trusted to look after the nation's interests anymore. Ulterior motives were always at work, Americans believed. The kind of underlying cynicism that marked the bogus news item about Lincoln in the introduction to this book had begun to punctuate coverage of the presidency.

As inflation mounted, Ford recalled FDR's efforts to galvanize the public during depression and war. Patriotic slogans had energized Americans. So, too, would a campaign to reduce inflation. During a speech in October 1974 Ford introduced WIN buttons—Whip Inflation Now—that he hoped Americans would wear to create inflation awareness. Columnists and other opinion writers derided WIN, and Americans ignored the buttons. This was not the Great Depression and Gerald Ford was not Franklin Delano Roosevelt. Watergate-savvy voters would not be manipulated with slogans—certainly not from a president who had just pardoned Richard Nixon.

In November 1974, the Republicans and Ford paid for Watergate and the pardon. Democrats gained seats in both Houses for a nearly two-to-one advantage in both chambers. Shortly after, Ford's nominee for vice president was confirmed by the Senate. After fourteen years of dabbling in presidential politics, Nelson Rockefeller finally became an official part of Washington. Rockefeller's impressive influence on Wall Street and his moderate record helped to prop the sagging Ford Administration, but to the conservative wing of the party, the devil had just been given a contract for the party's soul. Ford not only ran into image problems as 1976 approached, but he also was staggered by a conservative backlash.

Meanwhile, reporters were allowed to return to the West Wing of the White House en masse, no longer banished to their basement quarters where the pool had once soothed Kennedy's aching back. Ford held frequent press conferences and answered questions freely. If Nessen was somewhat condescending and devious, Ford was not. There was an underlying mistrust after the pardon, but when Ford was directly involved, reporters had little about which to complain. Had he risen to the presidency at another time under other circumstances, Ford might have been re-elected, his place in history greatly enhanced.

Not only did Ford misstep on his own, but history too worked against him. The cost of the Vietnam War and the 1960s social safety net not only fanned inflation but created unemployment. Usually inflation is accompanied by nearly full employment, but such was not the case with the stagflation of the 1970s. The United States' grip on international markets was loosening. World competitors cut into American industrial profits, and workers, used to years of steady employment, suddenly faced the threat of economic insecurity.

There were other public miseries. The oil shortage had brought about changes in federal highway policies, and speed limits on interstates were lowered to 55 miles per hour, angering busy commuters and truck drivers, particularly motorists in the West. Under the threat of loss of federal funding, states—many reluctantly—also lowered speed limits. On May 1, 1975, Saigon fell to the communists, and though Ford had nothing to do with the defeat, Americans quickly associated the failure with the incumbent. A general malaise fell over the country.

Still, there was interest in the new occupants of the White House, if only because they were new curiosities. To voters, the Ford family seemed more interesting than the Nixons. Oldest son Mike was a theology student in Massachusetts; Jack, a forest ranger in Washington; Steven, a high school student in Alexandria, Virginia; and Susan, the youngest, a student at a private girls' school in Bethesda, Maryland. Most of the Ford children avoided the press, Jack being the exception. In May 1975 he told reporters he and his Secret Service agents had pot parties, a claim that the Secret Service immediately and vigorously denied.

It was the First Lady, however, who left her mark on America during the brief Ford presidency. A divorcee and a former model and professional dancer, Betty married Gerald Ford in Grand Rapids in 1948. She raised all her children while living in the Washington, D.C., political milieu, a highly unusual family circumstance even for a president's wife. But the suffocating Washington political atmosphere did not seem to hold back the Fords. They all seemed to be well adjusted.

Reaction to Betty Ford tells much about the changing environment in the country. First, there was almost no discussion anywhere in the media of her having been divorced. Nelson Rockefeller's remarriage only a decade earlier had drawn much controversy, perhaps damaging his presidential hopes. True, the Fords were married long before he became president, but the complete disinterest in the topic illustrates how social mores had quickly changed. Just as Eugene McCarthy's Catholicism was of no particular media or public interest in 1968 eight years after the Kennedy breakthrough, Betty Ford's divorce was of no consequence in 1974.

On the surface, she seemed to be content as a mother and White House hostess, but she unexpectedly spoke out on issues that alternately embarrassed and pleased her husband. She chatted with truck drivers on the citizens' band radio and told Morley Safer on CBS's "60 Minutes" in 1975 that she assumed her children had experimented with marijuana. If Susan had an affair, she would talk to her about it but would not be surprised, Mrs. Ford told Safer. She supported a woman's right to an abortion and spoke in favor of the proposed Equal Rights Amendment to the Constitution, a sensitive subject for conservatives. The amendment, which never gained ratification, would have constitutionally prohibited any form of discrimination against women. Conservatives claimed that this would destroy the family and force unwanted public accommodations such as unisex public lavatories, charges that supporters scoffed at.

Ford and his strategists, who had their hands full battling the surging conservative wing of the Republican Party, found Betty Ford's public remarks unfortunate. However, reporters appreciated her candor and the public, just fifteen years removed from the staid 1950s, accepted her social views with surprising calm. The women's movement had been gaining momentum since 1970; more important, Betty Ford came across as a mother and independent person forced to deal forthrightly with issues that plagued any concerned parent.

However, it was not her remarks about social issues but a near personal tragedy in September 1974 that endeared the First Lady to the nation. Malignant lumps discovered in the right breast forced an operation. Up until this time, women did not talk about radical mastectomies. Many died of cancer rather than undergo such disfiguring operations; still others who accepted the surgery refused later to venture into their usual social circles out of embarrassment. Betty Ford's courageous public discussion of her operation and her personal campaign as an advocate for breast self-examination later probably saved thousands of American women's lives.

She spoke out on politically sensitive issues when her views differed from those of her husband, establishing herself as an individual rather than just an extension of her husband's personality. This seemed to capture the mood of women voters in the 1970s. She did not sit in on strategy meetings, advise Ford openly on domestic and foreign policy, or chair committees, but Betty Ford made it clear that she had her own ideas. This broke ground for First Ladies such as Rosalynn Carter, Nancy Reagan, and Hillary Rodham Clinton, who were even more active in their roles as presidential advisors. Betty Ford, more than Jacqueline Kennedy, set the tone for changes in the role of the president's spouse. In 1978, a year after her husband left office, the former First Lady revealed that she was suffering from alcoholism and drug dependency but was seeking counseling. Once again, her public and personal revelations gave others courage to meet similar problems. Later, a clinic was established in her name. If the 1976 election had been a referendum on the First Lady, Ford would have won hands down. Unfortunately for the president, he, not his wife, had to win election.

THE RISE OF JIMMY CARTER

In many ways the 1976 campaign represented a break with the past even more so than the 1960 election. No one in the 1960 field was a serious candidate in 1976. Humphrey did not enter, and Ford, feeling pressure from the right, asked Nelson Rockefeller to step aside, a request to which Rockefeller agreed and announced on November 3, 1975. Ironically, the new era in presidential politics would be led in part by Rockefeller's replacement on the ticket, Kansas Senator Bob Dole. Dole would be a quadrennial candidate for the GOP nomination thereafter, finally representing his party as the nominee for the presidency in the 1996 election. Just before the primaries, Ford fired William Colby as director of the CIA and replaced him with George Bush, the ambassador to the People's Republic of China and a former congressman. With Bush back in Washington and Dole on the Ford ticket, the Republican presidential cast of characters was almost set for the next six elections.

But before the Ford-Dole ticket was nominated, a wide-open Democratic field had to be winnowed, and Ford had to turn back a challenge from the other of the last successful participants in Republican presidential politics in the twentieth century: former governor of California Ronald Reagan. Being the first president who had been elected to neither the presidency nor vice presidency, Ford was at a distinct disadvantage. Ronald Reagan decided not to wait until 1980 but to press his candidacy immediately. Many political epitaphs have been written for men who attempted to unseat an incumbent president, but in 1976 voters were still fuming over the pardon, and a deteriorating economy was setting a decidedly conservative national tone. Voicing a theme that would become familiar in the 1980s, Reagan billed himself as an outsider free of Washington political entanglements. Not only did Ford have the pardon to answer for, but he had to address the perception that the nation was beginning to drop to second-class status both economically and politically in the world.

Until 1960, primaries largely had been showplaces where candidates demonstrated to party regulars their vote-getting abilities, so that the delegates would turn to them at the convention. John F. Kennedy had shown that the primaries could be an end unto themselves, but even then he had to fight Lyndon Johnson to gain a surprise victory on the first ballot at the convention. What with a verbal gaffe, an assassination, an untimely automobile accident off the coast of Massachusetts, and a tearful speech in New Hampshire, being front-runner had not proved to be terribly fruitful in 1968 and 1972. Only one candidate per party seemed to survive the various front-runner mishaps. Primary competition had not been terribly influential in the selections of the nominees, but 1976 was different. Not only was the field filled with newcomers, but there were even more primaries, and they would largely decide who would be the next president.

The primaries changed presidential elections forever. Party support and allegiance were not so important as media imagery. Candidates in contested races won not on their influence within the ranks but by virtue of their direct sway, state by state, with the voters, mostly through the media.

Also in 1976, Congress enacted campaign financing laws stipulating that the taxpayers would provide matching funds for parties ($13.3 million each) and financing for the two general election major party candidates ($21.8 million each), limiting the amount of money individuals or corporations could donate. Nevertheless, loopholes allowed unlimited party donations, obviating the intent of the election financing reform movement and creating political action committees and other funding vehicles that made a mockery of the revisions. Initially, though, the shift to large numbers of primaries and public funding of campaigns pleased populists, who wanted wider fields of candidates. The 1976 campaign was the first test, and, sure enough, someone came from nowhere.

The governor of Georgia, Jimmy Carter, had appeared as a guest on the popular CBS quiz program "What's My Line?" in 1975. No panelist could guess his occupation or his identity. Outside Georgia, he was unknown. Carter realized that his anonymity in a post-Watergate campaign could be an asset. In the early months of the campaign he shook hands with puzzled voters and toured newspaper city rooms amid whispers of "Who's that?" But voters wanted someone who was from somewhere other than Washington.

Reporters who had covered the monotonous 1964 and 1972 campaigns and the violent and tumultuous 1968 contest hoped the 1976 race would be a wide-open newsworthy brawl with interesting new faces. The Democratic contenders included the indomitable George Wallace, now in a wheelchair after a would-be assassin's bullet had paralyzed him. Others were Arizona congressman Mo Udall, Indiana Senator Birch Bayh, Oklahoma Senator Fred Harris, Washington Senator Henry Jackson, George McGovern's 1972 running mate, Sargent Shriver, and Jimmy Carter. Idaho Senator Frank Church and California Governor Jerry Brown entered late in a stop-Carter effort. Udall and Harris were liberals of the McGovern ilk, and Wallace and Jackson were conservatives. McGovern, Edmund Muskie, and Hubert Humphrey declined to run again.

Carter, a moderate and a desegregationist from the small community of Plains, Georgia, embodied a strange hybrid of old South charm and 1970s realpolitik: a Deep South Democrat with a liberal social message. A born-again Christian whose father was an ardent segregationist, Carter was a career Naval officer with a degree in nuclear engineering. After returning home to operate the family peanut farm outside Plains, Carter had earned four years in the governor's mansion with a gritty, hard-fought, populist campaign that featured a new South desegregationist, anti–big money message. He was a cross between the pugnacious, segregationist Wallace and the sixties-style liberals, Udall and Harris.

One new feature of the high-volume primary season was the Iowa caucuses, gatherings of small numbers of party faithful where straw votes were taken. So few persons participated that normally the caucuses would not mean anything, but they took place on January 19, a month before the New Hampshire primary. From the moment the primary season began, the Carter organization pushed hard, with volunteers from Georgia fanning out across Iowa and New Hampshire to ring doorbells and charm New England Yankees and Midwesterners with their lilting accents. Reporters marveled at the innocence of the Carter workers and the grass-roots nature of the campaign, but few of them accompanied the ex-Georgia governor or gave him any chance at the nomination. The candidate with the broad, toothy smile promised voters, "I will never lie to you." Carter outpolled Bayh and Harris, 27 to 13 to 10 percent in Iowa. Then on February 24 in New Hampshire, he edged Udall, with Bayh, Harris, and Shriver running far behind. From nowhere, the Carter campaign seemed to gain momentum and serious campaign contributions as he rolled up one primary victory after another. Many of his volunteers had never worked in a campaign before, let alone a presidential primary. By April 6, the contest had turned into a stop-Carter movement.

In early April in Wisconsin, the home of the Progressive movement and the state where the name La Follette was magic, there seemed to be a perfect opportunity for Udall to halt Carter. On election night, early returns put Udall ahead. By mid-evening, both ABC and NBC projected a victory for Udall. Carter also was ready to concede. But Kenneth R. Lamke, the political writer for the morning *Milwaukee Sentinel*, examined the voting results from 1972 and the voting patterns from early returns and waited until just before the first deadline at 10 P.M. to write a story cautiously suggesting a Udall win. The newspaper published the story under the headline, "Carter Upset By Udall." As it turned out, Carter eked out a slim victory, 37 to 36 percent. The next morning a photographer from the Associated Press urged Carter to hold up the *Sentinel* with the erroneous headline, à la Harry Truman and the *Chicago Tribune* in 1948. Newspapers nationwide carried the photograph and a story about the *Sentinel* gaffe. The stories hardly mentioned that the two networks had projected a Udall win much earlier in the evening and that the *Sentinel* had corrected the headline in later editions. After existing in the shadow of the *Milwaukee Journal* for too many years, the *Sentinel* was finally nationally known, much to the disgust of the staff.

For Udall, Wisconsin was the end of the line, and although Carter lost New York the same night, there seemed to be no one to stop him. He easily defeated Jackson in Pennsylvania three weeks later, ending Jackson's hopes. Brown and Church entered the race in April, but Carter split the remaining primaries and earned a lock on the nomination.

While Carter had come from nowhere to win with relative ease, on the Republican side, Ford warded off Reagan, who needed to overcome the tendency of the party to support the incumbent. Money was a factor. The two candidates split the primaries, but Reagan's hopes of overtaking Ford received a setback when he stopped campaigning in Wisconsin a week before the primary there and flew home to Los Angeles to rethink his campaign spending priorities. As a result, Reagan lost Wisconsin but won North Carolina and Texas. Ford's people left for the convention just a few delegates shy of winning on the first ballot, but controlled the few remaining uncommitted party delegations and managed to defeat Reagan on the initial vote, 1,187 to 1,070. Reagan, however, had lost little. He had established a conservative base of strength in a time when the country was steering to the right.

As the general election campaign opened, Carter led Ford in the polls by as many as seventeen points. But with a volatile, post-Watergate electorate, polls ten weeks before the election meant nothing. Scientific sampling had been around for forty years, but a plethora of polling results seemed to spring from the earth in 1976. Every news organization in every state conducted its own poll, it seemed. Daily chronicling of changes in voting preferences replaced speech and issue stories. Who was ahead seemed more important than what candidates had to say. Yet in August 1976 and into October, the polling tallies reflected only inclinations. A large percentage of the electorate refused to commit. Ford was heartily disliked and Carter was a loose cannon, a nominee who had served a few terms in the Georgia State Legislature and four years as governor. What did he know about foreign policy or the budgeting of hundreds of billions of dollars? If Ford's Washington connections were a drawback, Carter's lack of experience and unknown agenda were disquieting. Early polls, even those in mid-October, could not be trusted. Voters were too confused and too skeptical to be pinned down.

Television images played a major role in the 1976 general election campaign, chronicling the infighting at the GOP convention and then broadcasting three Ford-Carter debates. The first debate on September 28 was interrupted for twenty-seven minutes when the television audio signal was lost. Both candidates stood staring into space, until the sound was recovered.

But it was the second debate that made history and created a trend in campaigns. On October 6, Ford and Carter met in San Francisco. The theme was foreign policy. Max Frankel, *The New York Times* correspondent, asked Ford if the Soviet Union had not succeeded in its quest to dominate Eastern Europe. Ford answered: "There is no Soviet domination of Eastern Europe, and there never will be under a Ford Administration." Frankel, a smirk on his face, asked Ford for clarification. Given a second chance, Ford nonetheless plowed ahead with a long, rambling answer asserting that none of the Eastern bloc nations felt dominated. When his turn came, Carter hammered at Ford mercilessly, pointing out over and over the fallacy of such an argument. In the days immediately following that debate, Ford at first refused to repair the damage with modifications and then belatedly tried to recover with explanations of what he really meant. The man who had demonstrated so little political acumen by pardoning Richard Nixon had badly misspoken during a crucial moment in the campaign, when tens of millions were watching closely in their living rooms. A third debate two weeks later seemed to be anticlimactic. The impact of this gaffe was to solidify the historical judgment that Ford was too slow-witted and had too little grasp of complex issues to serve in the White House. In truth, he had simply misstated his argument and then compounded the problem by refusing to back down. Perhaps in a television age, that is proof of inadequacy for office. The long-range effect of the Ford miscue, however, was its chilling effect on free discussion in future debates. This had been the first series of polemical confrontations in the general election since the Kennedy-Nixon debates in 1960, yet they did not have that same magic. Television was not new anymore, and the two candidates lacked magnetism. The Ford gaffe seemed to take the rest of the luster off the debate concept. Remembering Ford's disastrous misstatement, later candidates would not take chances on extemporaneous comments in debates. Everything said would be carefully choreographed and guarded. Voters would never again hear a free-wheeling, open discussion of issues by major party candidates. For the candidates, it became too risky.

During the time of the three debates, *The New York Times* reported that Secretary of Agriculture Earl Butz, during a plane trip with former Nixon advisor John Dean and singer Pat Boone, had told off-color and racially insensitive jokes. Dean, then a correspondent for *Rolling Stone* magazine, had reported the incident in the magazine days before the *Times* story but without identifying Butz. Ford, who had hoped to keep the incident quiet, was forced to ask for Butz's resignation, an unpopular move with the nation's farmers, whom Butz had championed.

In the end, the turmoil over the pardon, the Ford image, and the worries over the future of the economy proved to be deciding factors. Carter won the election, 50.1 to 48.0 percent and 297 to 241 electoral votes, an electoral college margin less than Kennedy's in 1960 and Nixon's in 1968. The 54 percent voter turnout was even more telling. It was the lowest participation since 1948 and an even more obvious reflection of public disenchantment than the defeat of an incumbent. Only the third sitting president defeated in office in the twentieth century, Ford joined William Howard Taft, who lost in 1912 after a ruinous split in the Republican Party, and Herbert Hoover, who was handily defeated amid the nation's worst depression. Prior to 1976, only six presidents were rejected in their bids for second terms. Between 1976 and 1992, three more presidents were defeated in office. It should be added that many nineteenth-century presidents were denied reelection bids because lack of support within their parties prevented renomination, but the turnover in the White House that began with Ford's defeat is an obvious indication of the public's political unhappiness in the 1970s and again in the 1990s.

Similarly, press coverage lacked fire in 1976. After an unpredictable Democratic primary campaign, the Carter candidacy engendered doubts among editorial writers and commentators. The Carter family contradicted the Southern stereotypes that had dominated mainstream media in the North since the Freedom Rides in the early 1960s. Not only was Jimmy Carter a rural Southerner with a liberal ideology, but he and all the Carters spurned historical convention and reveled in their Southern heritage and parochial backgrounds. This confounded national reporters, who had come to expect a presidential candidate with Kennedyesque credentials. But many correctly raised questions, too, about Carter's qualifications and preparedness for the White House. The candidate had never adequately addressed those concerns. He promised never to lie and never to favor "big-shot crooks" over the little guy. If Carter had won, he had certainly not prevailed convincingly, nor had he persuaded official Washington, especially reporters, of his ability to lead.

During the campaign, voters turned more frequently to CBS with its venerable anchor Walter Cronkite, who had replaced David Huntley and Chet Brinkley of NBC as the TV news personality of choice. Television advertising played a small role. Both candidates opted for "visionary" ads that portrayed one or the other as a savior who would re-discover the greatness of America.

Because it is image oriented, television seemed to favor Carter with his colorful campaign and family. It is questionable that he was given preference because of his more liberal philosophy. There was a certain distaste for the Carter candidacy that was apparent in the coverage, and not just because he was a Southerner or because he was inexperienced. Carter had not needed reporters. They had ignored him early in the primaries, and before he had caught on with the elite media, he was an established political force. At that point, attention to the Carter phenomenon was a great story and the candidate had indeed received much favorable press. Still, there was a natural antagonism and suspicion. The candidate who reached voters without the media hype and the correspondents who found the Carter organization to be unhelpful and snippity were mutually distrustful. Besides, reporters were testy about charges that the national media were a group of elite liberals. They went out of their way to criticize Carter whenever possible, establishing a tone for his Administration.

At the outset of the general election campaign, Carter granted an interview to *Playboy* magazine. Why a presidential candidate with aspirations for attracting large numbers of women voters, many of whom were just realizing their hopes at personal independence, would grant an interview with a men's magazine is still a mystery. Carter said he hoped it would show a human side. It did just that. Carter was quoted as saying he had sometimes "looked on a lot of women with lust." In the interview, Carter also revealed that he was a born-again Christian, a statement that made liberals and non-Christians nervous. Carter was quoted as criticizing Lyndon Johnson and referring to him as a liar, a quote he later said was inaccurate.

After the magazine's publication, an angry Jody Powell, Carter's youthful press secretary, pointed to the interview as an example and lectured reporters aboard the Carter plane, telling them that they had a double standard that favored Ford.[1] After years of accusations that they were liberals who favored Democrats, reporters were now informed that they were unfair to a Democratic liberal and in favor of a conservative Republican.

In truth, print and broadcast coverage in 1976 reflected a public disenchantment with both candidates. Stories often dealt with their foibles or voter reluctance to cast ballots. At the same time, as is customary, neither candidate engaged in forthright discussion of issues. Neither offered blueprints for reducing inflation or for implementing peaceful school desegregation. They dodged specifics about the Middle East and about the Soviet Union.

Ford, the most conservative president in over forty years, was weakened by a challenge from the right and a distrustful public. What is most surprising about the 1976 results, given all Ford's troubles, is the slim margin of victory, pointing to less than a mandate for Carter and suggesting that the electorate was still reluctant to vote against an incumbent. It is likely that the narrowness of the victory, too, was a measure of a nationwide move to the right. Was it the debate lapse, the pardon, Reagan's stubborn candidacy, the image of slow-wittedness, or the economic climate that offset this drift to the right and cost Ford the White House? Probably all these factors, but certainly it was not unfair media coverage. The reporting was poll oriented and susceptible to candidate agenda setting, but Ford had made his errors on his own and the press corps had treated Carter as an outsider with much to prove. Neither the candidates nor the reporting in 1976 was memorable. Ford's time in office was the fifth shortest among U.S. presidents. Those presidents serving shorter terms were Zachary Taylor, William Henry Harrison, James Garfield, and Warren Harding. In their cases, death cut their administrations short. Still, like them, Ford will barely be remembered in generations to come.

NOTE

1. Martin Schram, *Running for President 1976: The Carter Campaign* (New York: Stein and Day, 1977), 307.

CHAPTER SEVEN

JIMMY CARTER'S MASTER PLAN

Jimmy Carter did not benefit from the same good wishes and popular support that greeted Gerald Ford in 1974. In the intervening three years, public and press respect for the presidency had sagged. The modern presidency transcends the historic and constitutionally mandated role of executive branch leadership. Symbolism and moral leadership are as important as the capacity to propose policies and negotiate their passage through an often recalcitrant Congress. Between 1967 and 1976, public attitudes toward the president were transformed as many Americans nurtured serious doubts about the office of the presidency itself. Economic uncertainty and Watergate cynicism had drained support and enthusiasm, but the world was still controlled by the World War II generation, many of whom looked back fondly at the presidencies of Franklin Roosevelt and Harry Truman. Time still remained for someone like Jimmy Carter to revive that adoration. This was the real challenge that Carter faced, and the press held the key to establishing a positive image.

Between the election and the inauguration, Carter generated stories from Plains, mostly about his cabinet nominees, whose proposed appointments were generally greeted with positive press endorsements. Although the Carter inaugural speech was not as memorable as the ones delivered by Franklin D. Roosevelt in 1933 and John F. Kennedy in 1961, the Carters did create beneficial television images by walking to the White House from the inaugural speech, while waving and smiling at gleeful crowds. Both the inaugural and the cabinet appointments created an upbeat atmosphere for the first days in office.

During the campaign and in the weeks preceding the inauguration, the nation had come to know the colorful Carter family. The president's mother,

Miss Lillian—as she preferred to be known—had served in the Peace Corps at age sixty-four. She was outspoken and charming, but she carefully refrained from uttering anything that might embarrass her son politically. Jimmy's brother, Billy, was not so judicious. He was the good ol' boy who owned a gas station, swilled beer, and spoke his mind whenever it pleased him. During the Carter years, one innovative marketer, the Falls City Brewing Company, even put out a line of alcoholic brew called Billy Beer. It tasted awful, but the enthusiastic public seemed not to care. At first, Billy was a delightful change from stodgy Washington. Then, in 1978, he visited the radical Arab state of Libya twice and accepted $220,000 in loans from that government. He was forced to register as an agent of a foreign government, creating a public relations headache for his brother. In the 1980s, Billy revealed that he had become an alcoholic. Embittered over the controversy surrounding his public antics, he moved away from Plains. He was not the happy-go-lucky, blue-collar buffoon he had portrayed himself to be, but a troubled individual who struggled with the role of First Brother. Sister Ruth Carter Stapleton, an evangelist, preferred to stay away from the publicity, but her religious fervor worried liberals and prompted repeated assurances from the president that he could adequately separate his same personal religious fervor from his decisions on public policy, such as prayer in school.

Carter's three sons, Chip, Jack, and Jeffrey, were grown, married, and lived quietly away from media attention. Daughter Amy, the youngest, was a precocious youngster, one whom the Carters were not afraid to use as a public relations vehicle. When they moved to Washington, the President and the First Lady decided, amid much fanfare, to enroll Amy in a public school to show their support for public education. Later, during the 1980 campaign, Carter used a conversation between himself and Amy as a way of explaining his stand on nuclear proliferation. Press Secretary Jody Powell wrote later that he was sickened by some unwarranted press attacks on young Amy, but the Carters occasionally invited such criticism by manipulating their roles as parents for public relations points.

Rosalynn Carter campaigned actively, but to the public she appeared to be a typical Southern, supportive wife. After the votes were counted and as the Carter presidency progressed, it was clear that she did not like reporters and actively advised her husband informally on a myriad of public issues. The First Lady was a charming Southern-style woman—likable in public but tough and outspoken in private. Jimmy Carter obviously respected his wife's opinion, and she sat in on cabinet meetings, but her influence in policy matters was informal and quietly unobtrusive.

Once again it became obvious that the country was in a quandary as to what role the First Lady should play: traditionalist or activist. It seemed that each new woman in the White House re-defined the nation's expectations. Rosalynn Carter wisely did not seek a formal policymaking position, because the nation was not certain in the 1970s that it was ready for the First Lady to assume such a role.

It was clear, too, that any time the president's extended family generated news, it could only mean problems for the chief executive. Reporters were usually interested in controversy where the president's family was concerned, and Billy Carter was certainly no exception.

While the delineation between the White House director of communications and the press secretary was not as apparent as it had been under Nixon, Carter did use an advisor for television other than Powell: Barry Jagoda, former CBS and NBC correspondent, and then media consultant, Gerald Rafshoon, in 1979. Powell, age thirty-three, was too young and too inexperienced. He had been with Carter since the Georgia gubernatorial campaign. Prior to 1970, he worked for an insurance company. His memoirs, a series of angry admonishments of the White House press corps, are revealing testimonies to both his inability to deal with the idiosyncrasies of correspondents and his utter loyalty to Carter.

In September 1977 Powell's response to stories about a questionable bank loan to Bert Lance, director of the Office of Management and Budget, perhaps best illustrates the press secretary's lack of seasoning. Illinois Senator Charles Percy spoke publicly about the need for a thorough investigation of Lance. Why don't you check out Percy's use of a private airplane owned by his former employer, Bell and Howell? Powell told a *Chicago Sun-Times* reporter. The ploy exploded when reporters revealed that Powell was the source of the allegation. The press secretary apologized. Eventually Lance resigned, though later he was found not guilty of malfeasance. This incident was particularly unfortunate because Carter needed congressional support. Politics are politics, but Powell's gaffe created doubt among legislators as to the White House's intentions. Press secretaries should tread lightly where Congress is involved. Powell learned on the job.

Meanwhile, suspicion also continued in the pressroom. At best, press secretaries may hope for a standoff with Washington correspondents. Powell and his staff never came close. The press cantankerousness in the post-Watergate era of 1977 was much aggravated by the standoffish and high-handed attitudes and inexperience of Carter and his advisors, including Powell. The press secretary's resentment toward reporters, which had begun with a few confrontations during the campaign, continued unabated for four years.

CARTER PRESS RELATIONS

Carter himself was an affable, smiling, easy-going leader in public, but a steely-eyed, unbending workaholic in private. He refused to delegate detail chores. Often he toiled eighteen hours a day, resolving minor problems that could have been assigned to assistants. He was unswervingly loyal to those around him but unyieldingly demanding of their time. While the official cabinet was composed mostly of career politicians, many other appointees hailed from Georgia. Among those who would later bring grief to the president were Lance, Chief of Staff Hamilton Jordan (former campaign manager), and U.N. Ambassador Andrew Young.

The president disliked dealing with reporters. He met the correspondents twice monthly in televised press conferences early in his administration but dropped the television coverage after the conferences became too confrontational. He would often attend Washington events unannounced, creating problems for reporters expected to cover the president's movements.

When the public on the whole is pleased with the nation's business and economic climate, press relations and minor public relations mistakes are not so important. At such times, reporters, editorial writers, and commentators find it difficult to write negative stories about the president. When the public is disgruntled, such reporting is better accepted by readers, viewers, and listeners. That is, press relations are always important in the modern presidency, but they are more vital for presidents, such as Carter, who govern during times of skepticism and uncertainty. Positive relations with correspondents offered Carter a low-budget insurance policy. As it turned out, discontent among the press corps aggravated Carter's other shortcomings.

That is not to suggest that Carter was unaware of the power of the press, especially television. During another Arab oil embargo in 1977, the president donned sweater and slacks and sat in front of a fire in the White House, informally speaking to Americans of the need to conserve energy. He admonished viewers to make concessions to help the government through a crisis. The fireside chat and the challenge to the electorate did not work. Both commentators and the public saw it as a manipulative ploy. Carter was mimicking both Franklin D. Roosevelt's successful radio fireside chats and John F. Kennedy's inaugural call for Americans to help their country. Viewers do not like retreads or reruns.

Carter was neither Roosevelt nor Kennedy, and, more important, this was not 1933 or 1961. Americans had become accustomed to affluence. Pax Americana—U.S. economic domination of the world—was ending. Production from aging U.S. factories failed to compete adequately with relatively new plants in Japan, Germany, and elsewhere—structures that the United States had helped to build after World War II. Congress could no longer simply appropriate unlimited funding. Corporate and municipal welfare was ending. The government could not continually boost private industry through tax breaks and loans, and bail out faltering local governments. Gerald Ford's decision not to use federal funds to help New York City in 1975 prompted the infamous *New York Daily News* headline, "Ford to City: Drop Dead." Choices had to be made. Prioritizing was painful. Should Congress be urged to fight the stagflation by offering incentives to business? This might not be possible. For example, if defense funding were kept at high levels, schools and entitlement programs might suffer. If taxes were not raised, then inflationary costs would eat into the effectiveness of social welfare programs. Misery would follow. Raising taxes, though, might worsen the economy. The inevitable had been accelerated by the Great Society and the Vietnam War and now in the nondescript 1970s, government had to come to grips with a lid on spending.

This would require careful planning and experienced negotiations. With four years as a government executive, Carter was unprepared for such a precarious assignment. Ultimately the problem was not press relations or public relations, but inexperience. Carter, the most honest and plain-speaking president since Harry Truman, could not handle the job. His inability to establish positive press relations was just frosting for the cake.

There were other failed public relations ploys. Shortly after taking office, Carter addressed a veterans' group and proposed amnesty for draft evaders from the Vietnam War. The choice of audience was geared to show Carter's courage on a tough issue, but the veterans were shocked. The preponderance of opinion writers ridiculed Carter.

Although manipulation of television was not at the heart of the matter, Carter again stirred controversy the next year when he negotiated an agreement with Panama to return the canal to that nation by the end of the century. The canal had been built by the United States after devious maneuvering by President Theodore Roosevelt two generations earlier, but loss of the canal through a treaty at a time when American pride was already wounded was not popular with voters. In another time, Carter might have been accorded grudging respect for such a moral but uncelebrated move. Not in the late 1970s.

When the Soviet Union suddenly invaded Afghanistan in 1979 to support an ineffective communist regime there, an angry Carter railed at the Soviets for their disregard for international law. Relations between the two countries cooled, but the frustrated Carter knew he could not intervene militarily. He settled for a cutback on trade and a U.S. boycott of the 1980 Olympics in Moscow—not a fashionable decision in the sports-crazed United States. These examples illustrate how the president can be manipulated by events, regardless of media strategy. If Carter was inexperienced, he was also president at a precarious time, and the moral high ground was not always safe ground.

Meanwhile, the pace of inflation hastened, reaching an annual rate of over 18 percent a year in January 1980. The prime rate climbed steadily to a peak of 18.5 percent in April, an unthinkable level that halted much bank lending. Gold prices topped $800 an ounce. Unemployment climbed to record levels. Housing construction was stymied, and as the administration faced a re-election campaign, the economy was in the worst condition since the Great Depression had ended in 1940. Carter faced the unpalatable options of stemming inflation by tightening federal credit and risking high unemployment, or letting inflation run its course. He chose the latter.

Maybe he had no choice. Sweeping economic changes would require congressional approval, but Carter confidants—the Georgia mafia, reporters dubbed them—kept to themselves, detesting the social rounds and parties comprising the underground legislative route to powerful elected Washington officials. This and a reluctance by Carter's people to visit Capitol Hill and negotiate legislative initiatives hurt the new president's agenda. Within a year, the administration had its hands full in trying to fend off hostile reporters and attempting to move a balky Congress.

The latter failure was perhaps the most devastating shortcoming of the Carter years. For the first time since Lyndon Johnson's prolific Great Society, a president—and a Southern Democrat, at that—had the opportunity to work with a House and Senate that were both handily controlled by his own party. Carter should have been the person to re-define the public agenda, but his inability to lobby Congress became one of his most obvious shortcomings.

Another failing, which brought more media attention than the ineffective congressional relations, was the president's choice of friends as appointees, some of whom attracted negative attention—justified or otherwise. Clearly, Carter the Southerner had won the support of black Americans for his unmistakable dedication to civil rights. His appointment of Andrew Young, a black leader in Georgia, as U.N. Ambassador demonstrated not only his commitment to blacks, but his loyalty to friends. Young, however, was stubborn and independent. Although he appreciated the confidence Carter placed in him, he was determined to show by defiant acts of autonomy that he would not be subservient. Frequently he spoke out on controversial international issues, diverging from the administration's official policies, a particularly worrisome attitude for a U.N. representative. This tendency finally came to grief in 1979 when reporters learned that Young had met covertly, in violation of promises to the Israelis, with a representative of the Palestine Liberation Organization, a group that Israel considered a terrorist organization. Carter could not resolve this dilemma gracefully. Young had to go, but certainly the dismissal of the highest black appointee in the Carter administration was an embarrassment, engendering resentment among black supporters. The dismissal was followed by a round of media questioning of Carter's overall judgment.

Perhaps the most controversial appointee was Hamilton Jordan. Frequently presidents unwisely name their key political advisors to such high-ranking positions, regardless of their diplomatic acumen. However, Jordan was not only ill qualified, but reputed to be ill mannered. In December 1977, the *Washington Post* reported that during a dinner party at the home of ABC co-anchor Barbara Walters, Jordan had uttered unseemly remarks about the chest of the wife of the Egyptian ambassador. All those involved denied the allegation, but the story bounced around the wire services for several days, and one reporter, ABC's Sam Donaldson, contended he had personally heard the remark. A few months later, it was reported that Jordan spat a drink on the blouse of a woman at a Washington bar, and a year later it was alleged that he had used cocaine at Studio 54, a chic disco in New York. Jordan denied all the allegations but gained a reputation, fair or unfair, as a crude operator.

In the past, an administration boasting better rapport with reporters probably could have squelched or softened these Jordan stories. Maybe Carter and Jordan were being penalized for their failure to establish good press relations. Possibly any president after Vietnam and Watergate inevitably would have been subjected to published gossip. There is no question that stories that quickly gained credence during the Carter years would never have even been considered for publication or broadcast during the Kennedy years and earlier. Certainly the president's chief of staff's inhaling addictive drugs and treating women with disrespect is shameful behavior, worthy of intense scrutiny. Yet no reporter ever adequately confirmed any of these stories; thereby, collectively the press corps abided by a lower journalistic standard than had been acceptable in most instances in the past. Jordan's alleged misconduct hurt the Carter Administration, but it is also apparent that great care was not taken in the reporting of these stories. Such was the environment that existed in the late 1970s.

The silliest episode in the press-president relationship during the Carter years was the great rabbit story. Carter had half-jokingly told Powell that while he was fishing in a boat on a pond near his home in Georgia in 1979, a particularly aggressive rabbit had tried to bite him. Carter used a paddle to fend off the animal. Months later, Powell mentioned the incident in passing to an Associated Press reporter. Once the story hit the wires, it was picked up and re-told over and over. Editorial cartoons featuring the face of Edward Kennedy in a bunny suit and Carter with a paddle were carried nationwide. Carter and the bunny seemed to be the ultimate stretch in press infatuation, a story illustrating the obsession with personalities rather than issues.

So, too, did reporters leap to report assertions that Carter was weakening the military. Logically, after the conclusion of the expensive Vietnam War, military expenditures needed to be reduced. Yet defense budgets are complicated matters. There are defense industry lobbyists from whom campaign contributions have been accepted, military careers to be considered, and thousands of civilian defense plant jobs at risk. During the Cold War, there was also the responsibility for adequate preparedness for a nuclear or conventional military attack, or at least the necessity of appearing to the Soviets to be in readiness. Carter, whose military cuts had been modest, was the victim of a series of stories emanating from official Washington, suggesting that he was soft on defense, allegations Ronald Reagan eagerly exploited in 1980. In retrospect, it has been shown that the Soviet Union's military capabilities had been greatly exaggerated in the 1970s and 1980s, in part because of faulty information provided to the CIA by double agents and in part because of intense interest in certain quarters in maintaining lavish military spending.

Even without such retrospect, allegations of a weakened defense system are always suspect. Figures are so shrouded in bureaucratic paperwork and secrecy that few persons are qualified to offer assessments of a mammoth half-trillion-dollar military budget, particularly not reporters geared to covering the political arena. The bogus defense stories that made the rounds in the late 1970s are typical examples of how reporting could not meet the challenge of the complexities of modern Washington. That is, issues had become so complicated, overwhelming, and fraught with positive and negative political spin that even the most dedicated and intelligent Washington reporters could easily be engulfed. It is doubtful that the most closely connected auditors, administrators, and legislators are fully cognizant of just how this nation spends its resources on defense, let alone a single reporter with only limited access to millions of documents. Usually these stories originated when well-placed congressional or defense sources found it politically necessary to circulate such accusations.

The topic held little allure. Reporters followed tips that led to quick but usually poorly verified stories. This was especially so in the 1970s, because there had arisen a public interest in the personal side of Washington—the foibles and idiosyncrasies of the persons involved, rather than clear discussion of complex issues. Even if there had been enterprising journalists able to explain all the intricacies of the defense budget, few listeners, viewers, or readers would have been interested. Instead, the rash of defense stories were written loosely, based on accusations from political sources, so as to define Jimmy Carter as a dangerously weak individual, a theme that seemed to fit not only the yearning for personalizing the news but one that accommodated the growing disenchantment with the executive office. If the president is seen as impotent or unsuccessful, negative concepts such as a flimsy national defense system are greeted with acceptance. Carter needed not only positive press but also public confidence to ward off such stories. Neither was in place in 1979, and if the president sometimes was treated unfairly, it is also true that he drowned himself with tactical errors, leaving himself open to a rash of negative consequences.

The one clear, unequivocal success of the Carter administration was the Camp David Accord, reached between Egypt and Israel in 1978 through Carter's personal mediation. Arabs and Israelis had fought four debilitating wars in the twenty-five years between Israeli independence in 1948 and the Yom Kippur War in 1973, which ended in a stalemate. This left impressions on both sides that the intermittent conflicts would never end. Egyptian President Anwar Sadat, whose son had died in the 1973 war, had suggested during interviews with both ABC and CBS in November 1977 that he would be willing to negotiate directly with the Israelis. This was the first time any Arab leader had made such an offer. A few weeks later, Sadat visited Israel, and bargaining began.

Acquiescence to negotiations is one thing, but reaching an accord is quite another. Secretary of State Cyrus Vance struggled in vain to bring the two sides together during the summer of 1978. Carter decided to risk another public relations disaster and invited both Sadat and Israeli Prime Minister Menachem Begin to Camp David, where Carter personally arbitrated.

Reporters groused about the silence that surrounded the negotiations, a problem that greeted Truman at Potsdam and Roosevelt at five such meetings before and during World War II. After Israelis agreed to return part of the Sinai Desert and Sadat promised to recognize Israel, negotiations ended in March 1979. Carter enjoyed a major diplomatic victory. The world was stunned. Only sixteen months had elapsed between Sadat's indication of his willingness to negotiate and the completion of an agreement, lightning fast movement for such a momentous diplomatic breakthrough. Although Sadat was assassinated in 1981 and other Arab nations did not follow the Egyptian initiative for twelve years, the Middle East pact was the most significant accomplishment of Jimmy Carter's term in office. Perhaps it was the most astonishing world event of the post–World War II era, until the collapse of the East European bloc and the dissolution of the Soviet Union in the late 1980s and early 1990s.

But Carter had no time to reflect on the majesty of his accomplishment. A most damaging set of other circumstances had come to dominate U.S. public attention. In January 1979, Shah Muhammad Reza Pahlavi, the ruler of Iran, was overthrown. The Shah had led with uncaring brutality, jailing and torturing any who had dissented against his autocratic regime. A month after his departure, a Shiite Muslim cleric named Ayatollah Ruhollah Khomeini ascended to leadership. Iran's government reverted to a theocracy, every facet of life in the country controlled by clerical interpretations of the holy book, the Koran. Suffering from cancer, the Shah in October 1979 requested permission to be treated in the United States, and Carter consented. Angry Iranians spontaneously stormed the U.S. embassy in Tehran on November 4 and took more than fifty American diplomats and embassy employees hostage, a gross violation of accepted international law.

Months later, the government acquired control of the hostages but still refused to release them. For the remainder of the Carter Administration, evening newscasts often led with the story, announcing that "day 35 of the hostage crisis passed without a resolution. Day 67 . . . day 112 . . . day 400." ABC created a late evening news program, *Nightline*, hosted by Ted Koppel. For months on each weekday night, the show summarized the day's events in Iran (usually nothing of significance), airing taped video of Iranian protesters holding up insulting placards in English, shaking their fists, and screaming their defiance at the U.S. network television cameras. If ABC newspeople were manipulated, they seemed not to mind.

Other networks featured specials on the hostage crisis, and newspapers and news magazines explored the story from every angle. For months, Carter personally directed every aspect of the hostage crisis negotiations, to no avail, exhausting himself and preventing adequate review of heightening domestic economic problems. Carter was caught. Any broad-based military action would almost certainly result in the deaths of the hostages and enmesh Americans in a war in the Middle East. Inaction resulted in scathing condemnation. In April 1980, five months after the assault on the embassy, Carter authorized a helicopter raid from the desert outside Tehran. Equipment problems forced cancellation of the mission, but in the predawn darkness as the invaders sought to return to base, the helicopters collided at takeoff, killing eight Delta Force raiders. Later in the day, television cameras rolled as Iranian soldiers stood over charred American bodies and laughed. In the middle of the 1980 presidential primaries, those images struck hard. Eventually the Iranians released all the hostages on the day of Ronald Reagan's inauguration, January 20, 1981, just a few moments after Reagan took office—a final personal insult to Jimmy Carter.

In 1991, Gary Sick, a former Naval intelligence officer, claimed that Reagan's campaign manager, William Casey, had met with Iranian intermediaries, Cyrus and Jamshid Hashemi, in Madrid in the summer of 1980 and in Paris in October. Sick claims that a deal was struck to send military materials through Israel to Iran in exchange for release of the hostages, only *after* Ronald Reagan was elected and then inaugurated. Sick wrote that this closely paralleled the Iran-Contra deal in 1985, an arrangement that Casey was willing to undertake because of the successful effort in 1980.[1] Although Sick carefully establishes dates, times, and places, he does not have documentation to support his thesis, and so his allegations have become part of a collection of conspiratorial concoctions that may have validity but are not yet part of accepted history. In the absence of concrete evidence, this seems to be a figment of a conspiracy-infatuated society. It seems an unlikely scenario, especially since Reagan really did not need such a gesture to win the election. However, as the Iran-Contra arms-for-hostage deal came to light in 1986, skeptical Americans rightly began to believe that politics might dictate any sort of negotiation.

On the other hand, had the media pressure on Carter to release the hostages created such tension that the president was forced to act unwisely? Was Carter treated unfairly by television, radio, newspapers, and magazines during the fourteen months the hostages were in captivity? Jody Powell says yes. News executives say no. The truth, as usual, probably lies somewhere in between.

Terrorism and the expropriation of hostages had become all too frequent in the 1970s. Palestinian terrorists in Munich, West Germany, had destroyed the majesty of the 1972 Olympic Games by taking Israeli athletes hostage and then murdering them. The hijacking of airplanes and kidnapping of business executives during the 1970s had raised American fears. Not only did such actions represent a chaotic threat to everyday life, but the abductions of personnel from an American embassy also constituted an invasion of U.S. soil and a taunting of the United States itself. A story commanding public interest, it was possessed of drama, intrigue, global security implications, national pride, emotional appeal (for the hostages), and economic repercussions (oil). But did it overshadow the increasingly perilous economic situation at home, the resumption of hard-line Cold War attitudes, gasoline shortages, the deteriorating plight of the U.S. poor, racial discord, civil service reform, and the 1980 political campaign? What occurred in the months after the invasion of the embassy was a case study of television's inclination to rely on formula stories. Cameras were in place for the daily hostage drama fix, protesters in Tehran received free advertising for their hate messages, and the unloved Carter Administration offered the wide target. Overkill.

It is not the obligation of television or print news executives to decide what kind of coverage would bring the hostages home the soonest or what stories would be the most likely to protect Carter from undue criticism. As always, their obligations were and are to report stories when and where they occur and to be balanced and accurate. Lacking any additional concrete facts, the story should have died a natural death after a few weeks, or at least the emphasis should have diminished, but certainly no news organization could be faulted for exploring every angle.

One of the reasons for the formula approach was the need for pictorial drama. As television images took on more importance, often as much importance as the content of the message itself, pictorially oriented stories were often overplayed. A routine high-speed chase of a suspected felon became national news because a helicopter captured the pursuit on video. A shark attack was worthy of prime-time attention because an underwater camera was in place as the victim was killed. Sports programming drew high ratings because the pictures usually evoked drama along with winners and losers. Television led the overkill of the Iran-hostage story because cameras, to some extent, had come to dictate news judgment.

At the same time, the tragic events of the final months of the Carter Administration also pointed to an unresolved dilemma in the press-president relationship. The president could not call in reporters and ask them to tone down coverage, so that the U.S. negotiating position would be strengthened. As representatives of a strong, independent press, they would not accept such a notion. He could not give them advance warning of the impending rescue effort in April 1980 because he feared the story would leak. There was anxiety in the White House that even if the rescue were successful, the Iranians would simply take more prisoners from among the hundreds of reporters still in Tehran covering the story. Still, the president did try to suggest in vague terms that reporters should vacate Tehran, but to no avail.[2] There was not enough trust or goodwill between the press corps and the president to allow Carter to take correspondents into his confidence. Perhaps this was better than the mutual admiration that led to a decision by *The New York Times* to refrain from reporting the Bay of Pigs story in 1961, but the simple lack of mutual respect can never be positive in a chaotic crisis situation. After Carter left office, the press-president antagonism continued, even heightening during the Reagan and Clinton Administrations. This atmosphere leaves the potential for an inadvertent national disaster fostered by an ill-advised press report that could not be squelched because the president did not possess even a small bond of trust with reporters.

The marred hostage crisis seemed to be a microcosm of Jimmy Carter's failed master plan to reintroduce optimism in America. Carter's restraint and the eventual return of the hostages in the end represented a diplomatic success story, but Carter's soiled reputation was the result of the president's failure to build a positive public impression and of the fickleness of historical events. Because

Carter was seen as ineffective and indecisive, Americans expected the worst in the hostage situation and discovered the opposite only after it was all over.

THE 1980 ELECTION

By late 1979, more than ten years had passed since Edward Kennedy's automobile had plunged off a bridge into the Chappaquiddick Bay, apparently ending his presidential aspirations. Kennedy nevertheless had remained popular in his home state, continuing an active role in the Senate as a spokesperson for the left. In September 1979, deciding that Carter could not win re-election, Kennedy announced his candidacy. Polls that summer indicated that potential Democratic voters favored Kennedy by a three-to-one margin.

Despite Carter's apparently weakened position with voters, the primaries did not reflect a switch to Kennedy, who had his own problems. His answers to reporters' questions about Chappaquiddick seemed dishonest. His nasty attacks on Carter and his challenge to a sitting president alienated party regulars.

For his own part, Carter decided to remain in the White House throughout most of the long primary season. As the primaries progressed, it was obvious that Democratic voters preferred him. Kennedy managed victories in Massachusetts, New York, and Connecticut and then won five of eight primaries on the last primary Tuesday in early June but still lagged far behind Carter. He refused to release his delegates even on the eve of the convention. Rancor between Carter and Kennedy lasted long after the campaign was over.

Sensing the public's desire for change, candidates eagerly crowded the Republican primaries. They included Bob Dole, the 1976 vice presidential nominee; Ronald Reagan, the former California governor, who barely missed wresting the 1976 nomination from Gerald Ford; George Bush, the former congressman, ambassador, and CIA director; former Texas governor John Connally, a converted Democrat; Tennessee Senator Howard Baker; and John Anderson, a surprise entry, a U.S. Representative from Illinois. They campaigned vigorously in Iowa and New Hampshire, hoping for early victories that would bring the same kind of hefty contributions and momentum that Carter had enjoyed in 1976.

By virtue of his anti-Washington, conservative rhetoric and the national attention he gained in 1976, Reagan was the clear front-runner as the primary season opened. The other candidates made the mistake of trying to gang up on Reagan during a debate in New Hampshire in February, denying him the microphone as the debate progressed. The strategy backfired. Though he barely lost the Iowa caucuses to Bush, Reagan won most of the early primaries and locked up the nomination by the end of March, derailing a late draft Ford movement.

For the fifth straight campaign, the only suspense left for the conventions were the vice presidential selections. Carter kept Walter Mondale. A stirring speech by Kennedy, in which he defiantly declared that he would continue to fight for the causes he championed, upstaged and angered the president at the convention. In somewhat of a surprise, Reagan chose George Bush as his running mate. He had met with Ford and considered putting the former president on the ticket until Ford told CBS anchor Walter Cronkite publicly that he would accept such a position only if he had a guarantee of a meaningful place in decision making.

Anderson proved to be an interesting election-year phenomenon. He was new and different (a liberal Republican from an unfamiliar district), and he finished a strong second in the Massachusetts primary to Bush. The fresh face was a story, but voter preference in Massachusetts, the most liberal state in the Union, hardly reflects the wishes of Republicans elsewhere. The attention paid to Anderson seemed overblown. Conservatives said a liberal media establishment was at fault. Perhaps, but more likely it was that Anderson provided the only oddity of an otherwise disappointing primary season. Encouraged by the positive media attention, if not any tangible delegate count, Anderson decided in May 1980 to create a third-party candidacy. Throughout the general election campaign until the final week, he enjoyed strong press attention. With polls indicating only minimal support, Anderson finally was ignored in the last week before the election. His candidacy related more to liberals' disappointment in Carter than to a movement away from the two major parties. It was not a reflection of the deep mistrust of the two-party system that had developed in the 1968 campaign and would re-emerge in the 1990s.

During the primaries and the general election, Reagan delighted crowds of supporters by delivering speeches laced with conservative rhetoric. He decried court-ordered school busing for integration, promised to reward taxpayers instead of "tax eaters," and stood in front of the Statue of Liberty promising to rejuvenate America. Carter told Americans he would listen more carefully in the next four years and would be more understanding of the needs of the poor than would Reagan.

Ronald Reagan seemed to capture the mood of the country in 1980. Americans were fed up with tight budgets, oil shortages, and government spending programs. They wanted a crackdown on crime, a return to more prosperous times, and renewed respect for a country so scorned that its diplomatic representatives had been held in captivity by a third rate, Middle Eastern demagogue.

The League of Women Voters invited all three candidates to the first debate in Baltimore on October 21, but Carter declined to attend, so just Anderson and Reagan contended. In the second debate a week later, only Reagan and

Carter were invited. During the second encounter in Cleveland, Reagan drove home his point to voters. "Are you better off now than you were four years ago?" he asked his television audience. Clearly they were not. Carter had no convincing answer. Interestingly, the Cable News Network, which had been created only two months earlier, televised the second Carter-Reagan debate and then inserted Anderson's live responses from Washington, creating television history. Anderson, however, won no electoral votes and earned only 6 percent of the popular vote, less than half George Wallace's 1968 vote share.

Reagan scored a landslide victory with 51 percent of the popular vote to Carter's 41 and 489 to 49 electoral votes. Fundamentalist Christian Coalition leaders actively supported Reagan, two-thirds of their members voting for the Republican candidate. Christian fundamentalists had become a powerful force in presidential politics. Also, there had been a large crossover of Democratic voters for Reagan. An incumbent was defeated for the second time in four years, the first time that had occurred in nearly a hundred years. The Watergate-ravaged Republican Party of 1976 appeared to be the new order of the 1980s. Republicans took control of the Senate for the first time since 1953 and gained thirty-three seats in the House. Reagan supporters variously judged the election to be a mandate for Reagan, fundamentalist Christians, and/or the Republican Party. It was, in fact, a sign of the growing conservatism and restiveness among voters. Any party or leader who took voters for granted in the 1980s and 1990s would regret it.

Television exit polling had been perfected during the 1970s so that on election night, all the networks declared Reagan a winner by 7:30 P.M. in the East. This was only 4:30 P.M. in the West, however, and many West Coast voters were angry that the election was a fait accompli before they were even able to cast their ballots. Some suggested that all polls nationwide should close at the same time, but this presented other logistical headaches. The question was left unresolved, so that future lopsided presidential elections would present the same problem.

The Reagan-Carter debate had underscored Reagan's tactical advantage. He could afford to take the high road and simply appeal to voter eagerness for change. Carter was left to justify a shaky record of achievement. The failures of the Carter Administration doomed his presidency, especially the inability to turn the economy around. When Reagan asked his telling question during the debates, he was asking Americans whether *they* were better off than they were four years ago, not whether the hostages in Iran were better off. Americans may have felt less secure with the invasion of the embassy and angry about the insult, but the entire drama was played out thousands of miles away. The reasons voters were not better off were that new homes were unaffordable and incomes were not keeping pace with daily expenses. Reagan won because his honest, home-spun charm and his conservative ideas were preferred to Carter's failed economic policies. Media influenced the election certainly, but inflation decided it.

Some historians have referred to the Carter Administration as a transitional presidency, one that failed to stem the tide of disenchantment sweeping the country. Certainly the admiration Americans expressed for Carter in the years after his presidency and the many diplomatic missions that succeeding presidents asked him to undertake indicate that the former president was not personally disliked. The 1970s was a difficult time to be president. Two chief executives who served all or most of their terms during that decade were defeated in office. A third resigned. This was unprecedented. It seems likely that in such a turbulent environment most mortals would have struggled to lead the United States. Almost immediately after Gerald Ford and Jimmy Carter had taken office, Americans seemed to begin to search for someone else to assume national leadership. In that sense, perhaps the two men led transitional administrations, but both men had chances to be something more than just interim leaders. Neither took advantage of the opportunities afforded them, because neither had the tools to influence Americans through the media and to lead the world.

Ronald Reagan certainly knew how to project a positive image, and he understood television. Unlike the 1970s, his presidency would define the 1980s and set a new U.S. agenda. No person or event seemed to describe the 1970s. Watergate merely delineated the failings of Richard Nixon. Widespread disappointment with Carter and Ford, inflation, and international tensions seemed to define the two presidents as puppets who were manipulated by a series of unfortunate tragedies. Perhaps if there was a clarifying theme for the 1970s, it was the solidification of television as one of the single most influential forces in the lives of Americans. Economics and Watergate decided the 1976 and 1980 elections, but television greatly influenced everything else in between, including world and national events and the presidential primaries. After 1980, American presidents would seek ways to truncate the influence of television newspeople and to manipulate the medium for their own purposes without allowing it to be used to exploit their weaknesses.

NOTES

1. Gary Sick, *October Surprise: America's Hostages in Iran and the Election of Ronald Reagan* (New York: Random House, 1991).

2. See Jody Powell, *The Other Side of the Story* (New York: Morrow, 1984), 228.

III

THE 1980s

MORTGAGING THE FUTURE

CHAPTER EIGHT

THE GREAT
NON-COMMUNICATOR

Few other modern presidents have provoked more historical debate than Ronald Reagan, and no interactions between the press and the president have been more inaccurately portrayed than those in the 1980s. During his presidency, public and press alike marveled at Reagan's speaking style and his popularity. He was often compared to Franklin D. Roosevelt. Labeled the Great Communicator, Reagan was seen as the president who brought his message to the people. But his was a theme of a different sort and it was delivered largely without an intermediary. The Reagan White House was not really what it appeared to be. When Reagan left office in 1989, he was as admired by a majority of Americans as he was when he took office. Yet he had lost a grip on the presidency, and his press relations had deteriorated so much that he hardly spoke with reporters. A president was not supposed to be able to maintain his popularity in the midst of a scandal and without first cementing relations with reporters, but Reagan did. The rules changed during the 1980s. Image and substance became almost mutually exclusive.

Reagan was really the Great Non-Communicator and the Great Delegator. He maintained his popularity by carefully orchestrating his public image and by largely avoiding probing questions. Communication involves the conveyance of information, not the recitation of practiced but meaningless phrases. This was not the kind of communication that FDR had used to gain public sympathy and support. Reagan's communication was the oration of practiced lines. His engaging smile and homespun speaking style were balm for the wounds of the previous two decades, but his lack of substance unremittingly distances him from Roosevelt. There is no comparison, except in that most superficial of measures: style.

But Reagan was more than merely an actor mouthing scripted lines. The "aw, shucks" persona was not synthetic. Any lengthy conversation with Reagan convinced the listener that he was in the presence of a sincere man, who cast himself as the plebeian enemy of the exploitative patricians. The former California governor preached his conservative, populist gospel with the fervor of a missionary, clinging devoutly to the concept of libertarian mores and the basic values of the working class. Reagan was not interested in details and specifics. He left that to others, while he provided the spirit and enthusiasm. Thus, many of his failures relate to his lack of follow-through, not to his convictions or his sincerity.

Reagan was born in Tampico, Illinois, and lived much of his youth in nearby Dixon before attending and graduating from Eureka (Illinois) College. After a brief career as a radio sportscaster in Davenport and then Des Moines, Iowa, Reagan left for Hollywood and a movie contract with Warner Bros. He appeared in a series of what the industry defines as B (low-grade) movies. Always the clean-cut hero, Reagan's roles mirrored his personal values, but he usually starred in low-budget films, lightly regarded by the critics, and he was never the box office draw that could mean automatic success for any worn script. A typical portrayal was that of Notre Dame football star George Gipp in the movie *Knute Rockne—All American*, in which Rockne, after Gipp's untimely death from pneumonia, urged his team to "win one for the Gipper."

After a stint as host of the *General Electric Theater*, a popular television program in the 1950s, Reagan entered politics at a rather elevated level for a novice, defeating incumbent Governor Pat Brown (the same Pat Brown who trounced Nixon in 1962) of California in 1966. Reagan served as governor for eight years. His brief quest for the Republican nomination in 1968 and then the near-miss in 1976 did not discourage him; rather, they convinced him that he needed better timing, a supposition confirmed by his defeat of Jimmy Carter in 1980.

The theme of the Reagan Administration, and, indeed, the 1980s, was "less government is better." In this spirit, Reagan and Congress partially deregulated the airline, trucking, and telephone industries and built a climate for business growth. The public, too, was turning against organized unions. In 1981, when unionized federal air controllers refused to accept a negotiated contract, Reagan fired them and installed replacement workers.

The 1980s were marked by corporate consolidation and "downsizing." Industrial and commercial jobs disappeared amid rising world competition, and some of the most powerful Northern states—Illinois, Ohio, Pennsylvania,

Indiana, and Michigan, among others—became known as the Rust Belt, where manufacturing plants that had operated for the entire century closed their doors. The Reagan years completed a painful U.S. transition from an industrialized society to a computerized one. Steady, full-time, high-paying manufacturing jobs were replaced by part-time, minimum-wage, service industry positions. New economic policies were described as Reaganomics and the changes in societal and economic structure the Reagan Revolution.

But all the fuss over Reaganomics and the Reagan Revolution almost never came about. On March 30, 1981, a mentally unbalanced young man from Denver, John Hinckley Jr., shot Reagan in the chest outside a Washington hotel as the president was walking to his limousine. Press Secretary James Brady, Secret Service Agent Timothy McCarthy, and Washington policeman Thomas Delehanty were also shot. All survived, but a bullet struck Brady in the head, and he has since been paralyzed. The bullet that hit Reagan lodged an inch from his heart, and air entering the wound collapsed a lung. His was nearly the second shortest presidential term of office in history. After the bloody 1960s, the shootings stunned Americans. There had been two attempts on Ford's life during his term of office, but he had not been injured. The repeated assassination attempts suggested to Americans that violence had become the norm in American politics.

Reporters and the public did not learn until much later the seriousness of Reagan's wound. At one point, doctors were unsure if he would live, but as has been universally the case when the president's life is in jeopardy from a wound or from failing health, the White House issued misleading, positive assessments to the press and public. Meanwhile, a genuine outpouring of compassion for the president and for Brady came from every section of the country.

The incident had other consequences. Years later, after he left office, Reagan, an ardent supporter of the rights of Americans to bear weapons, backed legislation that required local authorities to check the backgrounds of gun owners. Known as the Brady Bill in tribute to the former press secretary, it drew surprising bipartisan support in 1994. Reagan acknowledged that he had changed his traditional stance on gun control, and this seemed to be the deciding factor in the bill's passage. For his own part, Brady, years after his recovery, campaigned against some gun rights candidates, occasionally contributing to their defeats.

More pertinent to the Reagan years, the shootings drastically affected the careers of two leaders in the Administration. Prudently, Vice President George Bush assumed a low profile, assuring the press that he was only a caretaker until Reagan was released from the hospital. Secretary of State Alexander Haig, on the other hand, informed reporters on the day of the shooting that because Bush was out of town, he was in control of the White House. His televised comments came after Deputy Press Secretary Larry Speakes responded with flustered answers to reporters' questions about who was in charge of the government. Haig wanted to assure the world that someone was in charge, but his comments backfired. The words were taken out of context from a long statement—he did not really mean that he was assuming control of the government. (Actually, the Speaker of the House is third in line constitutionally. The Secretary of State is fifth.) Yet from Reagan's point of view, the underlying implication seemed clear, and before a year had passed, Haig was replaced.

The incident brought out the worst and best in television news. Regular programming was replaced by on-air coverage of the assassination attempt. Americans, many praying that the nation would not have to endure the funeral of another popular president, watched replays of the shootings and the immediate capture of Hinckley. Despite more than thirty years of televising everything from wars to walks on the moon, it was apparent that the networks were not adequately prepared for such an instantaneous, momentous event. Coverage was chaotic, disorganized, and often marked by false information. At one point, the Associated Press, CBS, and ABC reported that Brady was dead. Beset by conflicting accounts, ABC anchor Frank Reynolds scolded his colleagues on the air and demanded they find out what was happening. Correspondents rushed on the air with jumbled descriptions of the events instead of waiting for accurate information. Television could not comprehend that the shooting of the president was an act that required accurate information ahead of speedy reporting. In her recollection of the incident a year later, NBC correspondent Judy Woodruff berated herself for not getting on the air first.[1] No one outside a small group of broadcasters cared whether ABC was four minutes ahead of NBC. The pressure of the moment was to get it right, and the networks failed, because it was not clear to them why being first was not the priority in such a grievous situation.

SPIN-DOCTORING THE NETWORKS

When Reagan recovered, he named Larry Speakes deputy press secretary and David Gergen, a former Nixon speechwriter, director of communication. Paralyzed and confined to a wheelchair, Brady never returned to the White House, although he retained the title of press secretary throughout the Reagan years. Speakes had worked for small newspapers in Mississippi and served briefly as an aide in the Nixon and Ford administrations before joining a New York public relations firm in the late 1970s. Peter Hannaford and Michael Deaver, partners in a California public relations concern, helped to direct

Reagan's presidential campaign, so it was natural for Reagan to appoint Deaver as his chief White House media strategist with the title of staff director. Consequently, communications responsibilities from the Reagan White House were carefully divided among strategists, propagandists, and press officers. Campaign Press Secretary Lyn Nofziger, a former newsman and a political pro, was not awarded any major administration post because he was considered too coarse and too frank in his dealings with reporters. About a fourth of the entire White House staff concerned themselves only with influencing the media—more than during any previous administration.

Putting spin on the day's news, particularly the evening network television news, was the administration's top priority. From early morning to early evening, Reagan's media staff released information and verbally encouraged television correspondents to report on the White House's chosen topic of the day. After a while, reporters caught on and resisted, but invulnerability was difficult. To influence local newspapers, the White House held more than a hundred press briefings for out-of-town newspeople in an effort to explain policy decisions, while at the same time avoiding regular White House press conferences and inundating the White House press corps with news releases about minor issues. News flow from the White House degenerated into a tug of war. Instead of gathering information through polite questions and answers, reporters were forced to screen most of what was given to them and ask Speakes pointed questions over and over to glean small grains of unscripted information. Leaks replaced press conferences, and reporters learned to find covert ways of prying loose information. The briefing room was organized so that reporters sat in assigned chairs, with preference often given to friendly news organizations. The White House obsession with influencing daily stories, especially television reports, combined with the already skeptical post-Watergate press attitude to create constant press-administration tension.

For his part, Reagan hardly spoke to reporters in the early months. He had met with them a total of only three times by the end of the summer of 1981. Based on Deaver's advice, he was content to have the public see him only through rehearsed speeches and public functions. Such press avoidance ebbed and flowed through the eight years of the Reagan presidency, but avoidance was the norm. During that same period in 1981, Reagan addressed the nation on television six times, mostly to discuss the economy. Two of the speeches were to joint sessions of Congress, and one was his inaugural speech.[2] The televised addresses were twice as frequent as the press conferences. The interaction between the press and the president had come to a virtual halt. Reagan did not know the names of many of the reporters, according to Kenneth T. Walsh, correspondent for *U.S. News & World Report*.[3] Access to the West Wing of the White House was practically closed to reporters, who found it difficult to get even a hint of what was actually happening in the inner sanctums of the Administration.

The Reagan White House, however, was not the same as the Nixon one. Aides all found reporters to whom they could leak information. This convinced certain reporters that the Administration really wanted to cooperate, and it allowed the White House to launch trial balloons, while preserving the usual ace in the hole—deniability—for Reagan and often for themselves. The net effect was confusion, with signals coming from every direction and reporters being used to test policy statements and to help key appointees jockeying for presidential favor. As with many of the Reagan initiatives, communications policy was a combination of television savvy, conservative ideology, amateurish management, and self-interested jostling for position.

But there was still the business of governing. The first two years of the Reagan regime did not bode well for either the president or the country, but fortunately for the Republicans, the nation's economic problems did not last long. In 1981, the governors of the Federal Reserve System tightened federal credit as a means to slow the rate of inflation. The unemployment rate which had begun to rise at the end of the Carter Administration, worsened. By the middle of 1982, unemployment reached nearly 8.4 percent, the highest level in decades, and the prime rate remained over 16 percent. Businesses reacted badly. The steel industry, suffering from both the recession and outdated facilities, shut down many older mills and warehouses, sending whole communities in Pennsylvania, Indiana, Illinois, Ohio, and elsewhere into chaos. Many jobs in several industries were lost during this period, never to be restored. Workers who had been employed all their lives at the same plant had to re-train or remain unemployed. Yet as revenues dipped, the Reagan Administration and Congress combined to increase defense spending and expand entitlement programs, leaving a fiscal 1982 budget deficit of $128 billion, the first time an annual federal deficit had exceeded $100 billion.

Suddenly Reagan was not popular. Opinion polls reflected a rapid decline in public approval of the new president. Both Congress and the White House wanted a quick fix, and, as usual, they turned to the formula presidents had been employing for decades: a tax cut. They hoped that a stratified reduction in income taxes through 1984 would spur economic growth, bring a quick end to the recession, and propel a prosperous stretch. That is what occurred through the rest of the 1980s. Annual inflation dropped to about 2 percent by 1986, and interest rates returned to the 9 to 10 percent level. After the initial tax cut Congress actually raised taxes several times throughout the decade, including a five-cents-a-gallon gasoline tax to provide money to replace a crumbling interstate road system originally built in the 1950s. A 1984 income tax change also eliminated a number of itemized deductions, in effect raising taxes for many in the middle class. But the emphasis was on the return to normal fiscal times, and when that occurred, Americans hardly noticed the rest.

The prosperity came with a price, however. Many unemployed or marginally employed and poor Americans did not share in the economic growth. As mergers and expansion built up a number of large corporations, the percentage of Americans living below the poverty line increased from 20 to 26 percent.

More important to the future of young Americans, Congress failed to control spending on defense or any other budget category, particularly entitlement programs such as Medicare, Medicaid, social security, Aid to Dependent Children, and welfare. In 1983, the deficit ballooned to $208 billion and remained above $110 billion annually until 1996.[4] By that time, the federal government had accumulated $5 trillion in debt, and too much of the budget was spent on interest. Reagan supporters point out that, by 1989, revenues had actually returned to their 1981 levels, but congressional spending had continued unabated. Congress had not controlled spending, but any experienced politician would have anticipated this. Reagan and his advisors did not understand Capitol Hill. Regardless of who was responsible, the Reagan years were marked by a false prosperity that provided comfort to the wealthy and the upper middle class in the 1980s but mortgaged the future of an unsuspecting young generation of the twenty-first century. Even after a Republican-backed bill to reduce the deficit, the Gramm-Rudman-Hollings Act, was signed in December 1985, the spending did not abate. Congress and the White House kept extending the deadline for mandated reductions, virtually ignoring the measure they had voted into law.

In March 1983, Reagan announced his support of a project to protect the entire country through an impenetrable defense system that could obliterate without fail any missile launched against the United States. The system would rely on a collection of lasers that could be launched through space by a system of satellites, ground radar, missile silos, supersonic jets, and other high-tech military hardware. Military advisors warned Reagan that this Strategic Defense Initiative was both extremely expensive and based on technology that did not yet exist. It was a highly improbable gamble, but Reagan pressed ahead, requesting billions from Congress. He wanted to dispel any residual image of the nation as a militarily declining power. The plan, dubbed Star Wars by headline writers (after the box office smash hit), cost tens of billions of dollars but was never implemented.

In many ways the tax cut and the ill-advised Star Wars plans were typical of Reagan's ideological, scatter-gun approach to problem solving. He developed ideas based on his conservative precepts and then turned them over to others to iron out the details. Often the details could not be resolved, no matter how hot the iron. Sometimes the plan was ill defined or unfeasible. Yet Reagan plowed ahead anyway. Press criticism of such ideas met with public disfavor because times were good in the mid-1980s and Reagan still appeared to Americans to be the earnest, sensible leader they had been seeking for twenty years. Many of Reagan's proposals went unchallenged or barely contested for other reasons too. Details were too technical, reporters were not given adequate facts, the language of the bills was clouded, or the public uninterested. In the later Reagan years, columnists and editorial writers themselves claimed that Reagan was not criticized harshly enough or that disparagement seemed to slide off him. Thus came the phrase the "Teflon presidency."

What of this Teflon presidency? Were reporters too soft on Reagan, too deferential as author Mark Hertsgaard argues,[5] or was he so skilled at communications that he could not be criticized effectively? Actually, Reagan was heavily censured in the first year of his presidency, when unemployment reached uncomfortable proportions. There were times when the entire press corps and the media establishment turned against Reagan too. Much of the journalistic community was greatly angered in October 1983 when U.S. armed forces invaded the tiny Caribbean island of Grenada, to oust a Marxist government that ostensibly was a danger to 1,000 Americans there, most of them medical students. While Americans cheered the successful invasion, reporters angrily denounced a policy that banned them from the island until days after the skirmish. The overt censorship seemed to be a reaffirmation of Reagan's hostility toward the free flow of information. The furor died because the public reacted with disinterest, but the president was still excoriated by journalists and media owners.

In 1986, after it was revealed that arms were being shipped covertly to the rebel forces in Nicaragua through a U.S. deal with the hated Iranian regime, Reagan's public popularity dipped some twenty points, to below 40 percent approval. It rebounded, but in that instance public outrage seemed to be the determining factor in how criticism struck the president. If there was a "liberal slant" or an "anti-Reagan slant" on the news, as it was reported, it seemed often to be mutually exclusive of public perception. During the Reagan years, media was not the message. Most Americans seemed to form an opinion about Reagan early in his Administration and cleave to that opinion, no matter what was broadcast or published later. Reagan had ended the economic chaos for the present, and he was perceived generally as honest and successful, at least in comparison with Carter, Ford, Nixon, and Johnson.

By the end of the 1980s, the World War II generation had begun to reach retirement age. The new generation was accustomed to comfort. More than a clean environment, world peace, a balanced budget, a future for their children, better schools, programs for the poor, an integrated society, fewer nuclear weapons, better international relations, and a renovated defense system, the majority of the baby boomers wanted one thing: a continuation of their comfortable lifestyle. The generation that ironically had been typecast as irreverent, idealistic, worldly, uninterested in wealth, and liberal by definition actually put its greatest emphasis on economic security. Had family responsibility changed the peace generation? More likely the confusion was due to a misinterpretation of just who grew up during the 1960s and what they stood for. The "peace" generation was a myth. In essence, the Reagan "revolution" was a recognition that, above all else, jobs and finances still counted most. Reagan had provided what Americans wanted, and in return he was insulated from some of the public criticism that had plagued his predecessors. There was no Teflon coating around the president, but there was some no-stick spray. The concept of a Teflon Reagan presidency is partly mind-set, partly myth, and partly a misunderstanding of why a president is popular in the post-Watergate, post-Vietnam era.

As the tough years of recession gave way to a mood of optimism that pervaded the country by 1984, Reagan looked forward to re-election. Nearly the entire 600-member White House staff gave priority to the campaign. The staff dedication to the 1984 re-election drive closely resembled the organization of the Nixon 1972 campaign, minus the dirty tricks.

On the other side of the aisle, the Democrats seemed unable to locate a credible candidate after the Carter failure. None of the hopefuls from the 1976 campaign was interested. Former astronaut and Ohio Senator John Glenn stepped forward, as did Jesse Jackson, the civil rights advocate and Chicago antipoverty agency director. Carter's Vice President, Walter Mondale, was a nationally recognized leader, and Colorado Senator Gary Hart was a handsome liberal who had helped direct McGovern's campaign in 1972. Not one appeared to be a person who could lead the Democratic Party or defeat Ronald Reagan, however.

Mondale was touted by reporters as the front-runner, gaining early attention. Then he lost the New Hampshire primary and was forced to fight Hart all the way to the convention. Early primary success propelled his candidacy and provided much-needed financial donations. Yet the 1984 primaries seemed to epitomize everything that had gone wrong with the presidential selection system. Reagan used the power of the incumbency to solidify his relationship with the electorate, Mondale benefited from the wide-open primary system and name recognition to gain the advantage, Glenn's bland television person-ality jettisoned his campaign despite his place in aeronautic history, and Hart's good looks boosted an otherwise unimpressive career and placed him second after an early challenge. Mondale had locked up the nomination before the convention. The open primary system, which had been devised to encourage candidacies, had become a costly gauntlet that actually discouraged competi-tion in favor of name recognition. After Carter's repudiation in 1980, the last candidate the Democrats should have been awarding the 1984 nomination to was Walter Mondale. Jackson's modest showing and the lack of interest by party regulars in a possible vice presidential nomination for the black leader disap-pointed and discouraged the African-American electorate too.

Soon after Mondale had the nomination in hand, he announced that he was considering placing a woman on the ticket. Once having so hinted, he was obliged to follow through or leave himself vulnerable to charges that he was simply manipulating the female electorate. Mondale named Geraldine Ferraro, a U.S. Representative from Upstate New York. Reagan kept Bush.

The campaign was listless. Coverage, as had become the norm, was marked by weekly poll stories indicating over and over that Reagan would score a landslide victory. This trend continued throughout the campaign, interrupted only by Reagan's confused debate remarks. Press coverage of a Bush-Ferraro debate was punctuated by analysis of Bush's post-debate comment that he had "kicked some ass." At every point in the campaign, spin doctors from both sides influenced reporters by explaining their versions of daily events.

A scholarly study of election coverage in seventeen newspapers nationwide showed that both Reagan and Mondale received overwhelmingly positive coverage by a two-to-one margin. Similarly positive coverage was detected in network reports. Two of the three networks carried more Republican stories than Democratic, however. Leading newspapers endorsed Mondale more often than Reagan, 41.2 percent to 29.4 percent, suggesting that the major newspapers were more liberal than voters, but a hefty 29.4 percent offered no endorsement at all. The last statistic suggests that newspapers were frequently shying away from offering partisan editorial opinion.[6] The press did not figure strongly in the 1984 election. Reagan swamped Mondale, winning all but one state.

REAGAN'S SECOND TERM

Reagan's inner circle transfigured as he began his second term. Deaver left Washington (he was later found guilty of perjury in connection with post-ad-ministration lobbying on behalf of his public relations firm), advisor Edwin Meese became attorney general, former Nixon speechwriter Patrick Buchanan took over as White House director of communications, and Chief of Staff James Baker swapped responsibilities with Treasury Secretary Donald Regan. The last change turned out to be the most problematic for Reagan, when his chief of staff squabbled with Nancy Reagan and resigned in 1987.

The changes in the White House in 1985 suggested a new outlook for the Administration but actually signaled trouble. Because Reagan delegated so much authority, he desperately needed aides on whom he could heavily rely and who could continue to burnish his image. The White House deteriorated into a repository for palace gossip and internal bickering. Regan and Buchanan, two relative novices, were left to direct communications policies. This anarchy had some disastrous results.

Press relations deteriorated. Contact with reporters slowed after the campaign, and eventually the press corps had to resort to shouted questions as Reagan left the White House to board a helicopter. Reagan would hurl a shouted response back, barely heard over the noise of the whirring helicopter blades; if he did not like the question, he held his hand to his ear and shrugged, indicating he could not discern the content of the interrogatory. Leaks were substituted for communications policy.

In 1987, Speakes resigned to take a position with the investment firm of Merrill Lynch in New York, and he was replaced by Marlin Fitzwater, Bush's press secretary. Fitzwater turned out to be a much more workmanlike and agreeable press agent, but there were less than two years left in the Reagan Administration, and the change did not affect press perception much. Speakes, for his part, published his memoirs and immediately drew criticism for revealing that he often made up quotes for Reagan while he was press secretary because he thought he knew what Reagan would say anyway.

Reporting about the president sometimes became very personal. In July 1985, doctors operated to remove a malignant polyp from his intestine, and in January 1987, they operated on an enlarged prostate. Reagan's health and his advanced age (seventy-eight when he left office in 1989) became a constant source of press concern. At the same time, his habits, some not so flattering, had developed into more than a matter of inside conversation. Occasional stories carried references to the aging president's falling asleep at some Oval Office meetings or to his lack of attention at other gatherings. His affinity for jelly beans brought good-natured humor, if a bit too much emphasis.

The most serious criticism of Reagan's personal characteristics concerned his inability to speak extemporaneously. This was certainly where Reagan was far different from FDR. Attempts at off-the-cuff answers to questions often brought misstatements or fumbling responses. Perceived by reporters as a cue-card president, Reagan's elocutionary stumbles became a center of speculation. On one occasion, Nancy Reagan whispered in his ear when reporters asked him questions, bringing charges that even she thought he needed prompting and that she was controlling him. Eventually he spoke almost exclusively in public from prepared statements.

Reagan's acuity was of the utmost importance in the mid-1980s for a variety of reasons, not the least of which was that drastic changes were coming about in the Soviet Union. Leonid Brezhnev died in 1982, ending eighteen years of Brezhnev's version of hard-line leadership. His successor, Yuri Andropov, the former head of the KGB, lived only fifteen months after assuming leadership, and Konstantine Chernenko, Andropov's replacement, died in early 1985, just a year after Andropov. This by happenstance brought to an end twenty years of doctrinaire rule in the Soviet Union. A relatively unknown but moderate Politburo bureaucrat, Mikhail Gorbachev, came to power as General Secretary of the Communist Party. Reagan, who early in his administration had labeled the Soviet Union an "evil empire," did not at first relate well to Gorbachev. Nicholas Daniloff, Moscow correspondent for *U.S. News and World Report,* was arrested in the summer of 1986 on apparently trumped-up charges that he had spied for the U.S. government. This brought an angry response from the president, chilling personal relations between him and Gorbachev. Nevertheless, they met in October 1986 to debate the mutual destruction of intermediate-range nuclear missiles. Reagan insisted on continuing with his Star Wars program, and negotiations fell apart, only to be consummated in December 1987. Reagan had developed a distant but respectful relationship with Gorbachev; more important, a partial disarmament had been negotiated, leaving hope for future arms reductions.

This soon became a different kind of consideration. By 1988, the Cold War was ending. The borders between East and West Germany were opened, and the hated Berlin Wall was torn down in 1989. Eastern bloc nations declared themselves free of Soviet domination, and most adopted modestly democratic, noncommunist governments. Arms reductions had been a necessity to Gorbachev, but most Americans, even those in the intelligence community, could not believe that the Soviet Union had been so badly weakened. It was learned in 1994 that a key double agent, Aldridge Ames, had been spying for the Soviet Union and providing the CIA with false information about Soviet strength. Reagan had probably been misled by his own intelligence agency. The diminishing role of the Soviet Union brought assuagement in the 1980s but soon would carry concerns that chaos and nuclear uncertainty could replace Soviet domination in Russia and elsewhere in the coming years.

In retrospect, it is apparent that few within the Reagan Administration and almost no one in the press corps understood the incredible revolution that was sweeping the Soviet republics and Eastern Europe. Arms talks drew a great deal of attention, but the real story was developing within the Baltic area. It was not a story well told until dramatic events in Berlin and the former Iron Curtain countries underscored the changes.

Other foreign affairs problems plagued Reagan. In May 1985, the president traveled to West Germany to develop better relations between the two economic giants and to cement a bond between himself and Chancellor Helmut Kohl. As part of the itinerary, the president agreed to visit a cemetery in Bitburg to honor German soldiers who died during World War II. Then it was learned that SS officers were buried there. They had been members of Adolf Hitler's elite unit who had been in charge of murdering millions of innocent victims, mostly Jews, under Hitler's racial extermination policies. Despite the furor, Reagan went ahead with the visit, reasoning that he had made a promise and that most of those buried at Bitburg were regular army soldiers who had fought honorably for their country. It was a public relations disaster.

This unwise decision was one of many that plagued the second term. The worst apparently was Reagan's confidence in his National Security Advisor, Vice Admiral John Poindexter, and Poindexter's aide, Marine Lieutenant Colonel Oliver North. In November 1986 Attorney General Edwin Meese revealed that the Reagan Administration had violated its own ban on the sale of military parts to Iran and had diverted some of the money from the arms sales to the Contras, a guerrilla band fighting leftist leaders in Nicaragua. Surprisingly, Israel had helped to broker the arms-for-hostages arrangement. The Iran-Contra scandal appeared to be serious enough to generate Watergate-type repercussions. Poindexter, apparently with the blessings of CIA director William Casey, had engineered the arms deal in order to influence Iran into helping to free hostages being held in Beirut and to end the anti-American Sandanista leadership in Nicaragua.

On November 2, 1986, David Jacobsen, one of the hostages held by the Islamic *Jihad* in Beirut, was released. Negotiations had been arranged by National Security Advisor Bud McFarlane, who had traveled secretly to Iran in May 1986. Questions arose about what had been promised or done to gain Jacobsen's release, and Meese, on learning of the negotiations, explained on November 4 that an arms-for-hostages deal had been struck. Casey died soon after, but North and Poindexter, amid much fanfare, testified before a Joint Select Congressional Committee in July 1987. The combative North challenged the committee before a huge American television audience, and his interrogators backed down. In the upside-down televised world of Washington politics, North became a national hero after violating the laws of his own country, illegally intervening in a civil war in Nicaragua, and helping to send arms to Iran—a country under a trade ban for its support of terrorist activities. Eventually the hostages were released, and North escaped punishment on a legal technicality. The furor killed any momentum left in Reagan's second term, and his popularity dropped precipitously. Polls indicated that only 14 percent of Americans thought Reagan was telling the truth about Iran-Contra, and his approval rating had sunk from 60 to less than 40 percent.

Yet public approval of Reagan returned to robust levels by the time he left office. An independent counsel, Lawrence Walsh, was appointed to investigate Iran-Contra, and after seven years of probing, he concluded that both Reagan and Bush knew of the arrangement and had approved of it. Both had always denied knowing of the covert deal while it was being consummated and, after Walsh's report, once again claimed they had not been aware of the secret activities. Reagan escaped the kind of stigma attached to Nixon after Watergate, but Iran-Contra seemed to bring an end to his effectiveness as president.

Why was Iran-Contra so clouded by the question of responsibility? Why didn't Reagan's credibility sustain more damage than it did? What role did the press play in Iran-Contra, and how could public reaction be characterized?

The answers to these questions strike at the core of the Reagan presidency and its relationship with correspondents. The assumption, even by columnists of the time, was that Reagan had somehow outwitted or captivated reporters, the public relations techniques employed by the White House successfully keeping the press at bay. Such was not the case. Iran-Contra was complicated. It involved international arms dealing and covert maneuvering by governments of at least four countries. Too much is easily hidden, and not much becomes public in a timely manner in such cases. After several months, the public became bored with the story. There also existed wide public sentiment excusing the whole mess because it was accomplished in the name of fighting communism in Nicaragua. North's argument that he was only doing what was best for the country engendered a sympathetic response.

That is not to excuse the lack of aggressiveness on the part of the Washington press corps. As the scandal unraveled in 1987, much attention focused on the clean-cut image of Oliver North and his attractive secretary Fawn Hall. Image won over substance, as it had throughout the Reagan administration. Cameras focused on the people involved such as North, Hall, and Poindexter, and in most cases journalists lost track of the overall picture: a government out of control through either the acquiescence of the president or, conversely, his underlings, who were breaking laws with impunity without his knowledge.

Yet even reporters who unflaggingly attempted to uncover the truth about Iran-Contra met with a bored or disinterested public response. It was just too murky and too far away for the public to care. Americans like their government malfeasance clear-cut and plainly spelled out, usually with explanations of who became rich from the scandal. Warren Harding's Teapot Dome scandal was something Americans could understand: greedy oil men and corrupt government officials. Like Watergate, Iran-Contra was not about money; it was about violations of the law for ideological goals. More important, the revelations about the underhanded negotiations came late in 1986, a little more than two years before Reagan was to leave office, with not enough time to affect the waning Administration. And there were no tapes to tattle on the perpetrators. Reagan and Bush could claim whatever they cared to, and for years no one could argue to the contrary. By the time Independent Counsel Lawrence Walsh finished his long-running investigation and named Reagan and Bush as having participated in the planning of the arms deal, his findings were just a footnote to history. The entire matter had lost its impact.

But like Watergate, Iran-Contra was only a symptom of what had gone wrong in the White House. In 1996, the *San Jose Mercury-News* reported that the CIA had been funneling crack cocaine to drug dealers in Los Angeles in the latter part of the Reagan Administration to provide funds to the Contras. The newspaper later recanted much of the story. No charges were issued immediately after the story broke. Many within the Reagan Administration labeled the allegations as preposterous, but the fact that the story was given much credence was testimony to the low esteem in which the federal government was held.

In 1986, Congress passed with little fanfare a measure that guaranteed savings and loan lending. With the assurance that the federal government would repay bad debts, savings and loan companies began to extend credit to all manner of unwise or unprincipled business managers. Not surprisingly, many of the loans turned out to be failures, especially after the Wall Street Crash of October 1987. Many debtors defaulted, causing savings and loan bankruptcies. Taxpayers had to ante up to creditors. But the failures and the ensuing legal entanglements did not come to fruition until after Reagan left office, leaving George Bush to deal with a staggering national debt, increasingly steep annual budget deficits, and the cost of repaying savings and loan obligations, variously estimated at $100 billion to $500 billion over the ensuing decade. Reagan left office still a hero to many Americans, but the underlying issues that plagued Washington during his two terms left a gap between perception and reality.

NANCY REAGAN

By the time the Reagans took office, their children were adults. Both Ronald and Nancy had been married to other spouses and divorced before they were wed to each other. None of their children took part in the Washington scene, except for an occasional public statement or daring pose in a magazine. The Reagan First Family essentially consisted of only Ronald and Nancy. Throughout the two terms of the Reagan presidency, Nancy Reagan was an almost constant source of controversy. It was clear from the time that Reagan entered presidential politics that his wife would be his frequent advisor. Anyone close to the First Couple realized what engendering Nancy Reagan's disfavor could mean.

Her image oscillated. Soon after Ronald Reagan took office, she drew criticism for wearing expensive designer fashion clothing while many Americans were out of work. She insisted on replacing the White House china with a new $400,000 set, an eyebrow-raising extravagance, though private donations had been used, not taxpayer money. Her cool exterior, occasional sharp tongue, expensive tastes, rich friends, and fierce protectiveness of her husband earned her the unwanted moniker "Dragon Lady"—a parallel to Vietnamese President Ngo Dinh Diem's sister-in-law, Madam Nhu, whose untoward remarks after the Kennedy assassination had earned her the eternal enmity of the American public. No one on the White House staff wanted to cross swords with Nancy Reagan; most tried to avoid her entirely. "No one on the staff wanted to hear from the first lady because no one wanted to ever get in her sights. It had long since become a tenet of staff longevity that to offend Mrs. Reagan was suicidal," Fitzwater recalled in 1995.[7]

At Deaver's suggestion, the First Lady tried to polish her image by initiating an anti-drug campaign with the slogan, "Just say no." The well-meaning effort was stifled to some extent by her Hollywood background, wealthy friends, and flashy clothes. How could someone like Nancy Reagan understand the pressures on teens, especially poor youngsters, who sold or used drugs out of economic necessity or intense peer pressure? During the Geneva Disarmament Conference in 1986, reporters leaped on the rumor that Nancy Reagan and Raisa Gorbachev did not like each other and that their estrangement had been affecting the negotiations.

Throughout their years in the White House, the Reagans maintained that the press misunderstood the First Lady. They suggested that reporters directed personal attacks at her to get at the President, whose popularity made him an invincible target. This logic was dealt a crippling blow in 1987 when Chief of Staff Donald Regan resigned under pressure. He quickly put together his memoirs for publication a year later. The book actually was a gushingly complimentary evaluation of Ronald Reagan, but the most often quoted parts were the harshly critical assessments of Nancy Reagan.[8] Regan had been forced to resign because the First Lady had deemed him deleterious to the president.

The most damaging revelations in Regan's book were allegations that the president's entire schedule was arranged by his wife after she consulted with a Los Angeles astrologer. The whole White House schedule was often revamped because the astrologer told Nancy Reagan that the timing was wrong, Regan wrote. Coming soon after the Iran-Contra hearings, the Regan accusations struck at the heart of the Reagan Administration.

The book engendered the usual dichotomous reaction. Reagan's loyal supporters refused to believe such charges, and those who were never Reagan fans seemed to want to accept any such allegation. Four years later, gossip columnist Kitty Kelley published a book alleging that Nancy Reagan had affairs and that she was a conniving, offensive woman.[9] Though Kelley's sourcing and fact gathering were worthy of the trashiest tabloid, the book's revelations were quoted in mainstream media, including the front page of *The New York Times*. It seemed that there was more than objective decision making in the handling of Nancy Reagan stories.

Yet clearly Mrs. Reagan had changed the role assigned to the First Lady. Her frequent advice to and control over her husband raised questions about just where an unelected spouse fit into the environs of power. In an America where women comprise more than 50 percent of the electorate but a tiny portion of seats in elected national government, how are women to obtain a voice among those who make decisions that affect their lives? Surely a First Lady is such a person. But is that how female influence should be most effectively exerted? Through whispered suggestions to the nation's leader and through the rearranging of his travel and meeting schedule, according to the dictates of a reader of tarot cards? Could the leading lady of the land be aggressive and forthright without being seen by both women and men voters as a bitch? Nancy Reagan confused the role of the First Lady more than she defined it, and she, more than anyone else in the White House, contributed to poor press relations during the Reagan years. Reporters, in turn, excoriated her unmercifully.

THE 1988 ELECTION

Because Reagan was constitutionally prevented from seeking a third term, 1988 was to be one of those rare election years that would offer wide-open primaries on both sides of the ballot, the first such campaign in twenty years. Bob Dole, Bush, Haig, former Congressman Jack Kemp, Delaware Governor Peter DuPont, and conservative television Evangelist Pat Robertson lined up on the Republican side. Democratic hopefuls included Jesse Jackson, Gary Hart, Illinois Senator Paul Simon, Tennessee Senator Al Gore, Massachusetts

Governor Michael Dukakis, Arizona Governor Bruce Babbitt, Missouri Congressman Richard Gephardt, and Delaware Senator Joseph Biden.

Hart was decidedly the Democratic front-runner after the 1986 midterm elections. No other Democrat seemed to carry either the national reputation or the allure of Hart. But since Thomas Eagleton's demise as George McGovern's vice presidential choice in 1972, personal problems had been major campaign themes. Though not much had been published, by the spring of 1987 a whispering campaign about Hart's private life had already begun. To dispel these rumors, Hart in May 1987 told reporters that he had nothing to hide and they were welcome to follow him around if they did not believe it. The *Miami Herald* sent reporters to do just that. They staked out his Georgetown town house and reported that twenty-nine-year-old part-time actress and model Donna Rice had come there early in the evening and then stayed until morning. Hart told reporters they had been discussing campaign strategy. Weeks later, a published photo showed Hart aboard a yacht with Rice sitting on his lap. Hart, who was married, withdrew his candidacy. He later returned to the campaign but with no success. Jackson was the nominal front-runner in May 1987.

On January 25, 1988, as Bush was starting his primary campaign, he consented to a live interview with CBS anchor Dan Rather. The give-and-take opened with Rather's telling Bush that CBS had uncovered evidence that Bush had been aware of the Iran-Contra coverup. Angered by the ambush, Bush charged that Rather was being unfair, and he made reference to an embarrassing incident when Rather had walked off the set months before. The interview closed with Rather's cutting off Bush in mid-sentence. The confrontation was ugly. CBS claimed it had a right to question the vice president about his role in a major political decision, while Bush argued that the series of one-sided questions during the opening of a political campaign was unfair and unbalanced. Either way, it was clear that Bush and Rather disliked each other and that personalities had replaced substance in the interview. This, it seemed to conservatives, confirmed that network reporters were liberals out to get Bush.

Bush finished third in the Iowa caucuses behind Dole and Robertson, but as with Bush's victory over Reagan in 1980, the Iowa results proved meaningless. Bush easily won New Hampshire and took all sixteen "Super Tuesday" primaries on March 8 to seal the nomination. Dukakis, with more money raised and better organization, also swept to an insurmountable lead on Super Tuesday. The Super Tuesday phenomenon proved to be a factor during and after 1984 because of the huge number of delegate commitments decided in one day, but the New Hampshire primary still captured the most press because it was the first real test of strength.

The quick end to the primaries with such uncharismatic candidates as Dukakis and Bush was a disappointing result for a wide-open campaign. The 1968 race, marred by assassination and rioting, had also resulted in two conventional candidates, but both had been landmark figures in Washington. Neither Dukakis nor Bush, with low-key personalities and low-profile national careers, seemed to be what voters expected, especially after the upbeat Reagan years.

Although some preliminary polls after the conventions showed Dukakis with a substantial lead, polls in September and October suggested that Bush was comfortably ahead. The 1988 election was particularly disappointing. Bush advisors announced at the beginning of the campaign that they were "creating" a bolder and more assertive Bush. The candidate visited a flag factory to have cameras reflect his image, while he was surrounded by the Stars and Stripes. In his acceptance speech at the Republican National Convention, he used the term "a thousand points of light" to emphasize his broad-based economic and social agenda and "a kinder and gentler" presidency, but he never explained what either phrase meant. Bush also promised, "Read my lips: no new taxes," a promise that would haunt him in 1992. Dukakis's mistake was to assume that the most obvious imagery would influence voters. To combat the notion that he was soft on defense, Dukakis donned army gear and sat at the helm of an Army tank while cameras rolled.

The most overdiscussed and overrated aspect of the election was the Bush advertising campaign. Researcher James P. Pinkerton in the Bush camp (who later became deputy assistant to the president for policy planning) discovered in a transcript of a primary debate in New York that Senator Al Gore had asked Dukakis about a parole granted to convicted murderer Willie Horton. While on parole, Horton had raped a woman and beaten her fiancé. The Republicans charged that a Dukakis-led government in Massachusetts was soft on crime. The much-discussed television ad seemed to hit at the heart of Americans' fears at the time. It is the one aspect of the 1988 presidential general election campaign most remembered. It has been widely suggested that it and a fumbled Dukakis debate response to a tough question on crime made the difference in the election.

These, however, are simply indications of how the media at the time missed the point. Americans were concerned about crime and the economy, but it was Ronald Reagan who seemed to sooth those fears. Bush, the surrogate, was the beneficiary of the Reagan legacy. His campaign tactics served only to underscore the strength of a conservative philosophy at the time. In 1989 he became the first vice president to succeed a president of his own party since Martin Van Buren had followed Andrew Jackson in 1837. Well organized for the primaries, Dukakis emerged as the strongest of a weak field. He was not equal to the task of running for the presidency, however, and despite Bush's mediocre campaign style, being the Vice President during a popular presidency was the inherent advantage he needed. Analysis of the 1988 campaign centers too much around the micro issues of advertising and debate style and too little around the historical time period that controlled the election.

The *Washington Post* declined to endorse either candidate. Major newspapers and news magazines decried the entire campaign as free of any relevant content to the voters. The percentage of voters who turned out was the lowest since 1924. This was a continuation of the voter apathy of the 1980s and, ironically, voter participation was even worse eight years later.

Coverage of the 1988 campaign was equally disappointing. Even the wire services and other national media were becoming aware that candidates were consciously manipulating coverage and that poll results were being used far too often as substitutes for issue-oriented coverage. I mailed a survey to the editors of the seventy daily newspapers in Illinois soon after the 1988 election. About two-thirds of the newspapers replied, and about three-fourths of those said they were disappointed in the presidential election coverage that year. With the exception of the *Chicago Sun-Times* and the *Chicago Tribune*, the newspapers were supplied with their coverage by the Associated Press or the United Press International, the UPI being the preferred choice in the less populous Southern Illinois area and the AP in the north. The editors had little choice as to how the election was covered, and most said they were not pleased with the superficial and issueless coverage they were sent. The wire services were not the only culprits, of course. Network television coverage was the worst offender. At least when Bush visited the flag factory and Dukakis rode on the tank, the news media immediately saw these ploys as manipulation and promptly ridiculed these efforts.

A study of three networks' and seventeen newspapers' coverage of the election showed that, as in 1984, stories were overwhelmingly positive, and half to two-thirds of the stories were about politics and government or about the strength of the candidate. The focus was upon character and politics, not the issues.[10]

Bush, by virtue of his relationship with Reagan and due to the still-strong economy, swept to an overwhelming victory in 1988. He captured 56 percent of the popular vote and outpolled Dukakis in the electoral college, 426 to 112. The Congress remained Democratic, suggesting that Americans once again had not identified success with a party but with a candidate. Coattails seemed to be a concept of the past.

For his part, Reagan left Washington convinced he had brought Americans back to a conservative philosophy with which they could build a future. He was so confident of his hold on the American public that he and Mrs. Reagan traveled to Japan shortly after he left office and accepted a multimillion dollar fee to speak on behalf of Japanese industry, enriching themselves through the office of the presidency. Still, Americans were largely satisfied with the Reagan presidency. The 1980s had brought about a total separation of image from substance.

A careful examination of the Reagan legacy suggests that domestic policies were miserable failures and foreign policy had been largely driven by covert activities or unfolding events over which Reagan had no control. A selfish generation had settled for a false prosperity in the 1980s, leaving a heavy economic burden for which future generations would be responsible.

The image had succeeded, however. Americans felt good about Reagan generally, if not about the presidency itself. If Reagan had alienated reporters, it had not affected his bond with the public, and this was a legacy that would worry reporters. Would presidents of the future imitate Reagan, circumventing the White House press corps and concentrating on building a television image? The presidency changed in the 1980s, with priority being given to creating television impressions. But so had the press. How Americans saw the White House was being determined not only by new presidential priorities but also by changes in the role of the media and the media themselves.

NOTES

1. Judy Woodruff, "*This Is Judy Woodruff at the White House*" (Reading, Mass.: Addison-Wesley, 1982), 24.

2. See "Chronology of Major Speeches" in Kurt Ritter and David Henry, *Ronald Reagan: The Great Communicator* (Westport, Conn.: Greenwood, 1992), 193.

3. Kenneth T. Walsh, *Feeding the Beast: The White House Versus the Press* (New York: Random House, 1996), 54–55.

4. Annual budget deficits from 1977 to 1996 were $53.7 billion in 1977, $59.2 billion in 1978, $40.7 billion in 1979, $73.8 billion in 1980, $79 billion in 1981, $128 billion in 1982, $207.8 billion in 1983, $185.4 billion in 1984, $212.3 billion in 1985, $221.2 billion in 1986, $149.8 billion in 1987, $155.2 billion in 1988, $152.5 billion in 1990, $269.3 billion in 1991, $290.4 billion in 1992, $255.1 billion in 1993, $203.1 billion in 1994, $163.9 billion in 1995, and $107 billion in 1996.

5. Mark Hertsgaard, *On Bended Knee: The Press and the Reagan Presidency* (New York: Farrar, Straus & Giroux, 1988), 102.

6. Guido H. Stempel III and John W. Windhauser, eds., *The Media in the 1984 and 1988 Presidential Campaigns* (Westport, Conn.: Greenwood, 1991), 15–20, 69–70, 179.

7. Marlin Fitzwater, *Call the Briefing! Bush and Reagan; Sam and Helen: A Decade with Presidents and the Press* (New York: Random House, 1995), 168.

8. Donald Regan, *For the Record: From Wall Street to Washington* (New York: Harcourt Brace Jovanovich, 1988).

9. Kitty Kelley, *Nancy Reagan: An Unauthorized Biography* (New York: Simon & Schuster, 1991).

10. Stempel and Windhauser, eds., *The Media in the 1984 and 1988 Presidential Campaigns*, 69–94.

CHAPTER NINE

MEDIA'S CHANGING ROLE AT THE WHITE HOUSE

That speech turned out to be the best thing that ever happened to me.
Imagine where I'd be today if I'd said something really nasty.

—*Shock Jock Don Imus, November 1996*[1]

During his dinner address on March 21, 1996, at the White House, Don Imus insulted President Bill Clinton and wife, Hillary, by referring to the president's alleged extra-marital affairs and to the First Lady's legal problems. During the next seven months, his syndicated radio show expanded its member stations from fifty to ninety. Being rude and insulting to the Clintons had made Imus a popular radio personality. Imus is not a journalist but an entertainer; however, the difference was becoming fuzzier and fuzzier to Americans in the 1980s and 1990s, and shock "journalism" seemed to have replaced traditional issue-oriented reporting. Washington journalists were seen by the public as personalities or opportunists seeking only self-aggrandizement and sensational stories about White House embarrassments. This perception was part of the negative press-public-president relationship that had evolved by the time Ronald Reagan left office. The entire triumvirate had become quite complicated, but historians and journalists who have attempted to delineate this relationship too often over-simplify. The association developed at several levels and was enmeshed in a tangle of social, economic, and political convolutions.

The nature of the media industry itself, and television in particular, changed drastically between 1960 and 1990. Even before John F. Kennedy took office, cables carried TV signals to isolated sections of the country. These communities could not receive the usual airborne video transmissions because towers were too far away or because natural barriers, such as mountains, blocked reception. Ingenious entrepreneurs reasoned that if these areas could be served by cable, so could the rest of the country. Thus, in the 1970s television began its transmutation from a three-network monopoly to a cable industry. For homes and businesses around the country, the average number of channels per outlet increased from seven in 1970 to seventy by 1995. The number of hours that the average person watched television actually decreased by 4 percent between 1985 and 1990, but still Americans, on average, spent 8 times as many hours in front of a television—61/2 hours per day—as they spent reading a newspaper. Washington and the White House were the center of attention for four nightly newscasts (CNN being added in 1980) and numerous cable news and discussion shows. In March 1979, the not-for-profit cable network, C-SPAN, began broadcasting the entire proceedings of the U.S. House of Representatives. C-SPAN 2 was added in June 1986, offering complete Senate committee and floor discussions. A small but hard-core collection of government video junkies, between 1.5 and 3 million, watched Congress in action daily, with about 200,000 tuned in at any given time. The two C-SPAN outlets also broadcast conferences, discussions, speeches, and ceremonies when Congress was not in session. CNN added a headline news network in 1982.

At the same time, the media's influence in Washington and nationwide became a prime topic of discussion. Awkwardly and with mixed results, print and broadcast journalists themselves tried to analyze the intermix among the press, the presidency, the Congress, and elections. Commentators and editorial writers referred to the "media" as if it were some abstract mass with which they had no connection. Journalism was as much a topic of debate as was government. During presidential elections, coverage on television and radio and in newspapers and magazines focused on "media" as often as it did the issues. Political advertisements, usually negative and of little informational value, were carefully scrutinized in numerous articles and broadcasts.

This attention generated public interest in reporting and media relations, a positive development. The electorate benefits anytime media are closely monitored and held accountable, particularly when press coverage replaces the party structure as the primary influence on voters. One of the downsides of such attention, however, was the focus away from candidates and their obligations in the late 1980s. Every president from Nixon to Clinton complained about Washington reporting and its penchant for negative images. Although some of this criticism was justified, it was exaggerated for effect. Censuring the media was a convenient way of deflecting criticism. "That's not what I said or what I meant" or "my words were twisted" have always been battle cries of politicians, but after the Nixon era, attacking the media became nearly a science. Portraying oneself as a victim of shoddy reporting not only generated sympathy but also shifted attention away from the issues at hand and the administration's shortcomings.

The other downside was media baiting. Certain groups used this tactic as a way to secure attention for their causes. These usually were conservative groups, such as Reed Irvine's Accuracy in Media, which claimed that the "liberal" media were not in step with the country, or they were single-issue groups—feminist, religious, or pro-life organizations, for instance—that sometimes blamed the media for a whole host of social and political ills. Each partisan throng monitored the media and spoke up, rightly, when unjust coverage was detected. Often, though, the grievances were more a matter of perspective. Just as journalists were really too involved to be objective, political and advocacy groups were too self-interested and unschooled in the inner workings of media to be impartial or accurate. How can a person or persons who have never been involved in putting together a half-hour news show or a daily or weekly news roundup accurately assess the intent of a news story? Can a conservative or liberal watchdog group be taken seriously when it launches a diatribe against media coverage? The impetus for the criticism is too suspect.

This is not to say that broadcasters and print journalists should not be taken to task or that they do not make errors or possess biases, but who is the person to point out these shortcomings correctly? If not watchdog groups or the press itself, then perhaps media researchers? Possibly. But if those researchers have never been involved in day-to-day journalism or if they accept large grants from interest groups to conduct their research, their positions mirror those of the advocacy watchdog organizations. The age-old problem that philosopher John Milton addressed in the seventeenth century about safeguarding the market-place of ideas and censoring the censors still applied in the late twentieth century. Much was being written about the press and the presidency, but almost all was laced with bias. Journalists' and politicians' memoirs were usually filled with self-serving anecdotes and postulations, advocacy group arguments were saturated with self-promotion and shrill rhetoric, and think-tank analyses were not only often slanted ideologically but often too narrowly focused or too abstract to provide a proper overview.

Yet the press and the presidency became a topic of unending debate—the subject of thousands of books, academic and newspaper articles, television discussions, and magazine reports. So much was being written and said that sometimes the esoteric debate about communications overshadowed the business of running the country.

At the same time, ownership and the nature of the media was transformed in the mid- to late 1980s, the Big Three television networks all came under new ownership. Capital Cities bought ABC, the Tisch family (hotels) CBS, and General Electric NBC. In the 1990s, Westinghouse acquired CBS and the Disney Corporation bought out both Capital Cities and ABC. With these corporate takeovers, the networks lost their identities and their independence.

By the late 1980s, network budgets had been chopped, and bureaus were closed in the nation's smaller metropolitan areas and in cities around the world. In 1987 CBS laid off 215 news department employees, and the "tiffany" network's nightly news ratings dropped to third place. NBC lost a quarter of its news staff. Both CBS and NBC cut their Washington correspondent staff from thirty in the mid-1980s to thirteen by 1994. The Big Three share of all television viewers for all programs tumbled steadily from 90 percent in 1960 to 55 percent by 1995, mostly because of cable. Broadcast news directors, along with network entertainment czars, scrambled to hold viewers, including news audiences. Nightly news audiences dropped 20 percent from the beginning of the Carter years to the end of the first Clinton term—10 percent in the first four years of the Clinton administration.

Anchors Dan Rather of CBS, Peter Jennings of ABC, and Tom Brokaw of NBC had remained in place for nearly two decades by the late 1990s. All had been trained in television news only. Most television newspersons were this new breed of on-air "personalities," who had always been in television and knew that good looks and a winsome style were as important as aggressiveness, insight, and writing quality. With the budget cuts and the new species of network journalist, national television news became more style than substance. The self-centered baby boom generation demanded more news about their own personal interests: health, business, fitness, lifestyle. This coverage replaced traditional government and political news. The stand-up thirty-second summary in front of the White House every day was shortened or eliminated altogether, to be replaced by soft news segments or tragedies with impact and drama, the O. J. Simpson murder case being a prime example. This trend was not limited to national television news—it extended to every type of media— yet national television, with its heavy influence and reliance on visuals, was the most obvious example of the change. Prime-time broadcast magazine formats, modeled after the long-running CBS *60 Minutes* show, replaced documentaries and extended news programs. These often were marked by fluffy stories and interviews with entertainers. The mix diluted the impact of the hard-news stories, confusing viewers as to whether the magazine programs represented investigative journalism or light-hearted entertainment.

Print media, including newspapers, newspaper chains, national news magazines, and the wire services, also metamorphosed. United Press International nearly ceased operations in the late 1980s. A series of ownership changes managed to save the wire service, but it lost most of its subscribers, becoming only a shell of its former self by the late 1990s. AP remained healthy, but as a confederation of member media organizations that not only subscribed to the service but also contributed to it with their own local and national stories, it had an advantage.

At the same time, a news service is interested in reporting most stories briefly and without elaboration, so it is not a leader in impact stories or investigative pieces. Larger news organizations use AP as a starting point for their own stories, and they usually are the most effective counterbalances to presidential spin doctoring. The smaller newspapers and radio and television stations rely on the wire service or network for Washington coverage.

Consequently, the largest newspapers and AP dominated print coverage of the White House, and many of the breaking stories from Washington originated with *The New York Times, Washington Post,* or *Los Angeles Times,* each newspaper also having its own syndicate of subscribers who used the stories one cycle after they appeared in the flagship newspaper. All three major mainstream newspapers with flagship cities contained liberal editorial leanings, and many conservative organizations used this as evidence that the media covering the White House had a left-wing bias (a question addressed in detail in chapter 12). Many of the more influential newspapers that covered the White House during the Kennedy Administration had cut back on Washington coverage or had folded by the late 1990s. Few communities had more than one daily, English-language, mainstream newspaper. Only New York had more than two. Because of the softening of news coverage and the reduction in the number of newspapers actually interested in their own Washington coverage, the press corps had grown in numbers but shrunk in terms of diversity. A blasé public and the sheer magnitude and complexity of covering such a terrifying animal as the federal government and the presidency was overwhelming the journalistic community.

Superficiality became a hallmark of Washington print coverage. This shallowness stemmed from a trend in reporting generally. One of the most drastic changes was initiated by the founding of a national newspaper in 1982, *USA Today.* The leading publication in the Gannett Newspaper chain, much of its financing came from profits earned by Gannett's local dailies. Most were monopolies in small communities. *USA Today* emphasized graphics, brief stories, statistics, and polls. It sampled American public opinion on every topic from favored foods to expectations for the next thirty years. Frustrated staffers were not allowed to write more than eight paragraphs per story. Although the newspaper did not engender much profit, it raised the chain to new levels of respect and recognition and provided it with a most influential national marketing tool. *USA Today* became the second largest daily, general circulation newspaper in the country, behind the business-news-oriented *Wall Street Journal.*

The newspaper also touched off a scramble among many other papers to change their writing and layout styles. Clones of *USA Today* appeared nationwide, especially in the expanding Gannett chain. Newspapers, which had been steadily losing customers to television and profits to newsprint costs, concentrated on entertaining readers and enticing them to subscribe through the use of splashy color layouts. Content suffered, as did interest in national news. With the end of the Cold War, foreign policy news also declined. Similarly, news magazines mutated. Cover stories less frequently dealt with presidents, Washington policy, or foreign affairs.

Only when a new personal scandal was brewing did newspapers, magazines, or television take great notice. By the middle of the Clinton Administration, the president was finding it difficult to gain the attention of any medium, except when a new personal embarrassment surfaced.

The personality trend in both newspaper and magazine journalism began in the early 1970s with the founding of *People* magazine. The public had always been fascinated by the quirks and personal lives of entertainers. *People* magazine took this trend a step further by reporting from a personal perspective on all manner of public figures, including politicians. The public wanted to know everything about everyone famous, including the president. Developing during the era when revelations about John F. Kennedy's private life became public, this penchant gained both widespread acceptance among mainstream publications and the approbation of the public. The taboos of the past gradually gave way during the 1970s and 1980s. With the reporting of Gary Hart's indiscretions, it was clear that the private lives of presidents and presidential candidates were wide open to scrutiny. It was obvious, too, that such invasive journalism was much more popular than issue-oriented traditional coverage. What was of interest to the largest numbers of viewers and readers supplanted, in large part, what they needed to know about government.

Radio made a comeback in the 1980s, but not as the national news medium it had been. On Saturday mornings, Reagan addressed the nation informally by radio. Clinton followed suit. Yet, talk radio was the really raging craze. Listeners loved to call in and sound off about almost any topic. By the late 1990s, more than 25 percent of informational content on the radio had been given over to talk. This meant more access to the average listener, but less accuracy (anyone could argue or allege just about anything that was not libelous) and a reduction in serious journalism.

One favorite talk format, pioneered in the 1960s by raucous broadcaster Joe Pyne, was the combative ideological talk show, where the host paraded his biases and berated any guest with opposing views. Rush Limbaugh, a transplanted Midwesterner, arrived in New York in 1989 and became an instant success with his syndicated, conservative fulminations. His populist appeal and simplified solutions to the most complex problems pleased his audience, many of whom were fed up with government rules, oily politicians, declining job income, and what they perceived as liberal bias in the media. Limbaugh's program was somewhat unique in that he talked the whole program to a carefully selected conservative audience, while inviting no guests and conducting no interviews.

Limbaugh's show expanded greatly during the Bush Administration, and reached its zenith when Bill Clinton took office. Clinton's smarmy personal conduct was just the foil that Limbaugh needed, and, like Imus, he found that skewering the president and the First Lady was not only great fun but quite popular. The program boasted more than 20 million listeners in 1995. If conservatives could not keep the White House, they could win the radio waves. Limbaugh became so celebrated that even Clinton complained occasionally that he was at a disadvantage, constantly being upbraided by Limbaugh with no chance ever to respond.

THE WASHINGTON PRESS CORPS

Washington journalism and journalists also transformed. Not only were reporters more skeptical, but they found their employment less secure. Since the New Deal era, Washington had attracted the brightest and most aggressive correspondents and commentators the nation had to offer—perhaps the most talented collection of journalists in the world. In an industry marked by low wages, long hours, and irregular recognition, capital journalists stood out as the most acclaimed, best-paid, and most powerful members of the Fourth Estate. But with financial cutbacks in the news industry, Washington reporting was not the secure pedestal it once had been. Now print journalists had to contend with being transferred "back home," shifting capital assignments, and even sudden unemployment resulting from downsizing or cessation of publication.

With this uncertainty, many skilled journalists searched for more secure employment or larger nest eggs. A few well-known columnists and print correspondents took much higher-paying positions in television, serving as interview show panelists, broadcast commentators, political broadcast correspondents, and ideological debaters. Some used their inside Washington experience to write books and collect large royalties. Others, including both print and broadcast journalists, traveled the lecture circuit, charging as much as $45,000 per speech—money often paid by wealthy lobbyists. The money grab among journalists caused ABC, whose news personalities were among the worst abusers, to issue a partial ban on paid speech fees for its correspondents.

On the one hand, journalists found the speeches and discussion show stints a partial answer to economic uncertainty. On the other hand, in a time when the entire Washington press corps was being criticized and placed under intense scrutiny, the book royalties, the exorbitant speech fees, and the changeover to television convinced many that journalism equated with hypocrisy and journalists were for sale. How could reporters investigate and piously pontificate against legislators and White House underlings who accepted fees for books and speeches or who took money from lobbyists, if they were guilty of the same practices?

And what was a journalist anyway? By the late 1980s, America had somewhat divided into two camps: viewers who watched several hours of television daily and "personalities" who were frequently seen on the screen. The latter camp was composed of actors, actresses, entertainers, athletes, politicians, and journalists. While most television journalists were local on-air personalities, the elite reached the network level after working their way up from the meanest, poorly paid street reporter positions at tiny stations. They all became part of the parade of faces seen daily. When they debated senators and congresspersons during forum discussions and offered ideologically charged arguments, they became to the viewers another part of the "Beltline Crowd," not journalists protecting the public's interest.

In some cases, the television commentators were just well-known ideologues with no training in journalism. When speechwriters such as Patrick Buchanan hosted their own television discussion shows and then, as in the case with Buchanan, ran for president, the public became confused as to who was a journalist and who a politician. The same thing occurred when a former press secretary co-hosted a discussion show (Clinton's press secretary, Dee Dee Myers, for example) and when a correspondent offered himself or herself as a television analyst, or when a pollster or media advisor hosted a television program.

Journalist, lobbyist, politician, pollster, advisor: they all changed seats and were getting rich at the expense of the taxpayers, in the view of many. Washington, always a strange hybrid of insiders and transferees from the heartland, had become a world unto itself, one that too many Americans saw as an isolated island of self-centered personalities. Television brought Washington into millions of living rooms, and many did not like what they saw or were confused by the interchangeable roles.

The divisions engendered by Vietnam and Watergate had palliated by this time, but the contentiousness between press and president and the ingrained distrust of both by the public had grown like a malignant tumor. By 1990, the public skepticism sprang as much from knee-jerk instinct as from any activity or wrongdoing. To the voter, national government and the scenario in Washington had evolved from a source of protection, to a threat to public good, to a source of self-serving corruption at all levels. Presidential politics and national elections drew less interest and fewer voters each year. The parade of faces on television confused the electorate as to who was watchdog and who was law keeper, engendering nationwide anger and suspicion.

The Washington press corps itself had doubled to nearly 2,500 persons from Kennedy's time. Despite the public's perception of the press corps as a wealthy elite of self-promoting antagonists, most Washington reporters lived on modest incomes and worked long hours without recognition beyond their small circulation areas. About 75 of the 2,500 correspondents covered the White House regularly, the elite who commanded more prestige than the "regional press reporters," the same system that had existed since the Eisenhower era. But during Reagan's time, even the elite media had a stratified pecking order, with wire service and network television correspondents getting the most attention from the White House, the largest circulation newspapers and the national magazines the second most, and the remainder of the regulars the least attention.

The pressroom was more spacious after the Nixon era, but it was still cramped and uncomfortable. The briefing room was a demilitarized zone where much information was passed along, but rarely was anything of substance. Beset by a shower of information and overwhelmed by a bewildering collection of domestic and foreign policy agencies, Washington correspondents increasingly concentrated on personal innuendos and mini-scandals rather than issues and irregular government spending.

There were several reasons for this. First, to unearth fiscal wrongdoing or to explain a complicated foreign policy initiative took hours, days, weeks, and even months of research and interviewing. Reporting on a whispered innuendo about a politician, particularly a president, with a curt response from the press secretary, required only about an hour of work. Such a story would likely top the news, too, where the budget analysis would find itself buried at the end of the newscast or on an inside page.

Second, despite the Watergate lesson, White House reporters tended to wait for news to be served up through daily advisories. Hard-nosed journalism took the form of heated confrontations in the briefing room. Departing from the White House to unearth other sources or stories about the president would leave the journalist at risk of missing the rare blockbuster story generated from traditional sources. No correspondent could risk being away from his or her desk for any length of time. Alhough it was occurring with less frequency in the 1990s, it was possible that a president could announce a major decision any time. Even with backup correspondents available, not always a possibility with tight media budgets, the lead White House correspondent would not want to miss a major story, especially a television journalist to whom airtime was a precious commodity.

Third, White House reporters often had orders to chase down stories emanating from other media sources: "Let's follow on this and get our own angle" or "why didn't we get this first?" This "pack journalism" was just as prevalent in the 1990s as in the 1960s. Many stories over the wire or in major newspapers began, "Published reports indicate . . ." or "During an appearance on *Meet the Press* . . ."

Covering the White House, then, had its own reward and punishment. Although they enjoyed the most prestigious jobs in journalism, correspondents worked long hours, experienced increasing pressures from both sources and bosses, and then dealt with the complications of a skeptical era. They were at the mercy of the communications establishment around the president, but in a post–Vietnam-Watergate era they were almost obligated to clash with that establishment at every turn. They could not leave their cubicles in the basement of the White House for fear of losing a breaking story, and they spent endless hours analyzing nearly useless press releases and following the president on vacations and politically oriented tours of the world and nation.

During elections, these correspondents followed the incumbent around the country, sharing the long days and nights on the road in airplanes and sometimes trains and buses. Yet the loose camaraderie among the candidate and correspondents that had once existed seemed lost. During the Carter and Reagan Administrations, the president did not fraternize with journalists and josh with them lightheartedly on the long and unending flights aboard Air Force One. Reagan and Carter stayed in the forward cabin, sending press people back to pass out terse, written communiqués. Often the good campaign stories came from the home office or from correspondents still in Washington, who were free to roam and ask questions of a myriad of sources for campaign perspective.

Some of this perspective came from unending polls and public opinion samplings, which also supplanted the stump speech and the daily press briefing as the lead story. Yet as the electorate became more skeptical and less interested in political campaigns, the polls became more fragile. The undecided vote was larger, the party vote smaller, and the number of nonvoters greater. A poll might indicate one candidate ahead, but if a reasonable portion of the sampling changed their minds at the least provocation, this poll could be meaningless.

Or if the majority of the sampling never bothered to vote, the poll could also be incorrect. Scientific sampling is supposed to take this into account, but as the number of disaffected voters increased, polling accuracy came to be a difficult proposition.

Still, White House reporters dutifully asked press secretaries and presidents what they thought of the latest poll results. No matter whether the candidate found the results favorable or unfavorable, the answer always took the form of: "We don't pay attention to polls. We wait for the American people to speak at the ballot box." And all of this provided the foundation for a large percentage of election stories, albeit useless stories.

Presidents themselves, from Nixon to Clinton, used polls for a myriad of reasons. They tested public reaction to domestic and foreign initiatives. They sampled reaction from certain segments of the public, such as ethnic groups or women. They checked issues or ideas. Polls often were employed to separate the president's personal popularity from his public stances on issues. The trick for the president was to react to the polls without voters' knowing this was his motivation. No president wanted to be seen as a marionette, whose strings were pulled by the latest public inclination. Yet knowing how the electorate felt at a given time allowed presidents to play on certain desires or fears and to manipulate voters with reassurances and promises that fit the latest public opinion sampling. The key for the president was to appear to be doing this extemporaneously. Reporters were saddled with not only translating their own polls but also with the responsibility of having the clairvoyance to know when the president was leaning on his public opinion surveys.

The greatest press-president problem in the 1980s and 1990s centered around the information flow from the Oval Office. During the Franklin D. Roosevelt administration, Stephen Early, the press secretary, was a tactician who provided written information and made travel arrangements for correspondents. Because Roosevelt met with reporters three times a week in a reasonably informal and mutually rewarding setting, working in the White House was a satisfying and rewarding experience. This press conference setting became more formal under Harry S. Truman, when conferences were moved to the State Department auditorium, and even more formal under Kennedy, when literally thousands of reporters attended. By the 1990s, contact with the president was sporadic, confrontational, and usually unrewarding. It was apparent by the time Reagan left office that avoiding reporters could be more beneficial for the president than meeting with them and answering their questions. Would ensuing presidents emulate Reagan's avoidance theory? Would the task of covering the White House lose its magic entirely?

Under Kennedy, the president had held the upper hand over television, but Lyndon Johnson, Richard Nixon, Gerald Ford, and Jimmy Carter had watched as television grew stronger than the presidency. In essence, Reagan and his staff cut television down to size. While every other elected official in Washington pandered to the networks in every conceivable way in hopes of being seen positively during the nightly news, the president plotted ways to use television without being on the nightly news at all or by being seen more than heard.

The media relationship with the president had always been different. House members developed a relationship with the home district media and were rarely quoted nationally. Frequently the politics of the representative matched that of the leading newspaper or newspapers in the home district. The exceptions might be the suburban representatives in metropolitan areas, where the big city daily was likely to be liberal editorially in keeping with its urban readership but the representative conservative in response to his or her more affluent constituency.

The local television and radio stations often used the U.S. representative for reaction to issues or national policy decisions. Reporters would call or interview on camera the local congressperson for reaction to a foreign affairs policy decision, a budget cut, a miscue by the president, an inter-party spat, or any other Washington-based story. Usually the answers were predictable but provided filler. The representative received free television or radio exposure, and the station was able to obtain comment on a timely topic from the area's most powerful politician. This relationship between local media and representative rarely caused the kind of harsh confrontation that occurred daily in the White House.

Senators of less populous states followed similar patterns. Usually one or two statewide newspapers, typically in the state capital, carried editorial leanings that mirrored the senator's. The few television and radio stations could often reach the senator and obtain comment almost as easily as they could communicate with the U.S. representative.

In the larger states, senators were more responsive to the larger newspapers and broadcast stations, while usually allowing aides to respond to inquiries from the less prestigious media. Only with major issues or events did the senator field questions from the smaller stations and papers. The politics of the senator could differ from the state's largest newspapers, depending on the part of the state from which the senator drew his or her political base. Being interviewed in a positive vein on network television or being quoted on issues in the big three magazines or newspapers were coups that even these large-state senators sought anxiously, however. Governors and senators from populous states usually were the persons who later sought the presidency, and they especially treasured national television exposure. Juggling media interviews and learning how to manipulate television was a game that all elected Washington politicians learned to play, but different levels of office had different rules.

The modern presidency has always been unique in this regard. Reporters flock to the White House. Media, especially television, are a chimera, whose heads constantly have to be lopped off by those aides who advise the president. Except during elections, the president does not seek out reporters but aspires to control the media. Imagery and media management were all important to Reagan. His success at strengthening his personal popularity operated on a different level from his success at managing government, but it was apparent by 1988 that the public could not discern the difference, at least in Reagan's case. Ultimately his triumph or failure was judged by his ability to maintain a strong economy, but his appeal to voters originated with his ability to portray himself as a David aiming his slingshot at the media Goliath. Thus, undercutting the power base of television specifically and media generally was the real triumph of the presidency in the 1980s, just as the expansion of television offered one of the greatest changes in the lives of Americans in the 1970s.

Consequently, reporting on the modern presidency had many unique trappings by the time George Bush came to office. A haze of suspicion between journalist and White House staff seemed to linger everywhere. Correspondents faced the possibility of abandoning their traditional roles in the pressroom and simply wandering to other places for stories. Kenneth T. Walsh, White House correspondent for *U.S. News and World Report*, wrote in 1996 that providing a steady flow of news, or "feeding the beast," was a responsibility of the president, and those who did not found themselves at odds with reporters. Perhaps during the 1990s and in the years to come, reporters would not have the luxury of waiting for news but would have to leave the pressroom to find stories on their own, despite the risk.

Stories that reveal government malfeasance or waste in spending or interpretive articles that provide a complete picture of policy trends in Washington are usually infinitely more valuable than stories about dignitaries visiting the White House or the latest gossip about the president's private life. An investigative piece not only saves taxpayers money but serves as a warning to others in government, who realize that they eventually may come under scrutiny too. The watchdog theory for the press is not just a theory; it works when practiced. By the 1990s, investigative journalism, even in Washington, was drowning in a river of gossip, lifestyle, and business news, however.

Yet because of the declining role of columnists in Washington, that well-versed interpretive piece from the White House reporter had taken on added importance. Writing and reporting that combined earnest legwork with intelligent insight provided a focus that the complicated policies inherent to Washington desperately needed but were only too infrequently written.

Would George Bush continue to manipulate reporters and answer their questions sporadically? Would media recede as the most frequently discussed and most often considered influence in Washington? Would reporters return to hard-nosed reporting, keeping themselves in the background? Would office-holders, including the president, concentrate more on improving the nation's lot economically, politically, militarily, and diplomatically and addressing the problems of individual Americans? This was a challenge that Bush and the White House correspondents would have to consider as inaugural day 1989 approached.

NOTE

1. October 20, 1996, Associated Press story quoting Don Imus from *Satellite Direct Magazine*, October 15, 1996.

IV

THE 1990s

STARTING OVER

CHAPTER TEN

GEORGE BUSH
AND OTHER FABLES

As George Bush greeted well-wishers on inaugural day 1989, he appeared to have much to his advantage. Closely associated with a popular retiring president, he represented a continuation of what Americans apparently sought in the 1990s: the sanctity of personal economic security and insulation from world affairs. Many who were unemployed in the early 1980s had just begun to return to normal working lives. The threat of nuclear devastation was apparently ending with the close of the Cold War. The East European communist bloc was dissipating, and the Soviet Union was nearly bankrupt.

Still, public skepticism toward government and the presidency remained, and beneath the calm surface lay trouble. Federal bailouts for failed savings and loan companies stalled budget deficit reduction. Conservatives regarded Bush's moderate record with suspicion, and his legislative itinerary remained unclear. During the campaign, he emphasized what he would not do—be soft on crime, raise taxes, establish more social welfare programs—but avoided discussing specifically what he would do.

This proved not to be an immediate problem. Early cabinet appointments were readily accepted, with the exception of John Tower for Secretary of Defense. After reports of Tower's reputed womanizing and drinking became public, the Senate rejected his nomination, the first such rebuff of a proposed cabinet officer in thirty years. Although the defeat somewhat overshadowed the other well-regarded nominations, the disappointed Bush accepted the setback with minimal rancor, and the early days of the administration met with public expectations. Bush's selection of former New Hampshire Governor John

Sununu as chief of staff soothed conservatives' insecurities temporarily, though later the choice would also prove to be an embarrassment.

World and national events created dilemmas, but Bush handled them to the satisfaction of both press and public. In December 1989, he revived Yankee gunboat diplomacy. When secret police in Panama killed an American Naval officer, Bush responded by sending 24,000 troops into Panama to "protect" American citizens. President Manuel Noriega was arrested and later tried, convicted, and jailed in the United States on drug-running charges. Questions arose. Arresting a foreign leader and imprisoning him on U.S. felony charges certainly created uncertain international precedents. More important, though, Central and South American peoples wondered about U.S. respect for their national sovereignties. Bush found both praise and stinging criticism with his decision to invade Panama, but as is usually the case with controversial but successful foreign affairs initiatives, he emerged more popular with the public than before. As with the Reagan-directed invasion of Grenada, however, the furor quickly died. The legalities did not concern Americans as much as Panama's perceived assault on U.S. prestige and influence.

On the domestic side, in 1990 Congress approved updated clean air acts. Reagan had adamantly opposed expanding government environmental regulations, including those aimed at alleged polluters, so the Bush initiative was seen as a first step in defining a new administrative agenda. The measures—the first sweeping revision of clean air laws since 1970—were aimed at reducing motor vehicle emissions, smog, toxic air pollutants, and acid rain.

In 1990, a second set of guidelines, the Americans with Disabilities Act, was enacted. The law stipulated that most public buildings and transportation had to be accessible to disabled people. Democrats claimed credit for its passage, arguing that Bush's influence had been minimal, but it was clear that Bush's thousand points of light translated to a more lenient policy toward reformers than had Reagan's programs.

Such legislation is not the basis for building lasting popularity, especially when it created more government bureaucracy amid an anti-government public mind-set. What Americans wanted was the financial reassurance they had been promised. During the first year in office, the Gross National Product increased slightly less than 1 percent, compared to more than 3 percent per year during Reagan's second term. Government spending increased 7.5 percent, seven times the average rate during the Reagan years,[1] and this at a time of record-setting annual deficits.

This was not entirely Bush's fault, of course. With no line-item veto powers, he could not altogether control congressional spending, and the cost of failed savings and loan institutions kept the treasury empty. If world affairs were kind to Bush, domestic developments were not.

When a budget impasse developed in 1990, Bush was forced to renege on his campaign pledge not to raise taxes, a decision that his opponents would flout for the next two years. Taxes and user fees were raised by $137 billion over five years, including a hike in the maximum income tax rate from 28 to 31 percent. With spending and the national deficit climbing, Bush had no choice but to support a compromise. Unlike most other campaign promises, however, the "no new taxes" pledge was one the voters remembered. By September 1990, Bush's popularity had dropped, to where only about a third of Americans thought well of his economic policies.

These reactions should not have been a surprise to the president. He had been around Washington politics since his boyhood. His father was Connecticut Senator Prescott Bush. George was born in Milton, Massachusetts, and lived his youth in Greenwich, Connecticut. A U.S. Navy pilot during World War II, he married Barbara Pierce in January 1945 and graduated from Yale in 1948. He worked his way through the corporate hierarchy in the oil business in Texas and California to become president and CEO of Zapata Petroleum.

His campaign to unseat Democratic Senator Ralph Yarborough in 1964 failed, but two years later Bush won election to the U.S. House, where he served from 1967 to 1971. His Senate bid in 1970 against Lloyd Bentsen failed. (Ironically, it was Bentsen who later joined Michael Dukakis on the 1988 Democratic ticket.) Bush's Washington career continued nonetheless, and he was well traveled in the 1970s, serving as ambassador to the U.N., chair of the Republican National Committee, ambassador to the People's Republic of China, and director of the Central Intelligence Agency before returning to Houston after Jimmy Carter's victory in 1976. Bush too had unsuccessfully sought the Republican presidential nomination in 1980 before accepting Reagan's offer to serve on the ticket.

Dragged from Texas to Washington to New York to Kennebunkport, Maine, the Bush children all grew to adulthood (except for Robin, who died of leukemia at age three) by the time the Bushes reached the White House. Son Neil was an outside director of the Silverado Savings and Loan in Colorado during the presidency, and his name was connected with unsavory business practices there, but he was cleared of any wrongdoing after an investigation. George Walker Bush was a managing partner of the Texas Rangers major league baseball team. Otherwise, the five Bush children remained largely out of the limelight during the presidency, though two years after the senior Bush left Washington, George W. Bush was elected governor of Texas and brother Jeb failed in his bid for the governor's mansion in Florida.

The White House Bush family, then, consisted of only George and Barbara, just as, to most of the world, the Reagans were just Ronald and Nancy. Barbara Bush was a totally different First Lady from her predecessor. For all her adult life before she entered the White House, she had cared for her children and supported her husband in his successful business and political endeavors. Her memoirs are replete with fond references to her children and grandchildren and her admiration for her husband.[2] She seemingly found it difficult to utter unkind criticism of anyone—except perhaps reporters and those who would leak stories to them.

The First Lady did not like journalists or what she felt they stood for. She reasoned that they had badly misconstrued her husband's intentions and unfavorably altered the political process. She claimed later that reporters had heavily favored Bill Clinton during the 1992 presidential campaign. But more in character was her upbeat personality and her motherly instincts. Barbara Bush was a throwback to the political wives of yore, women of determination and strong opinions, who subordinated their goals to their husbands' careers. Her joys in the White House were hosting dinner parties and playing early morning tennis outside the White House. During the 1992 campaign, stories hinted that Bush had had an affair with a younger woman. These stories surfaced as Bill Clinton was forced to explain his private liaisons with women such as Arkansas television journalist Gennifer Flowers. No proof of any amorous relationship outside the marriage was ever presented in Bush's case, however, and the gossipy reports embittered both George and Barbara Bush.

Barbara Bush cut a path that she insisted on following, regardless of outside criticism. Her snow-white hair made the First Lady look much older than her husband, but she quietly ignored snickers about "the president and his mother." When she told a reporter that she favored a ban on the sale and possession of automatic weapons, a minor row developed. Her husband, a member of the National Rifle Association, opposed such a measure, but she did not back down. In June 1990, the First Lady and Raisa Gorbachev, wife of Soviet leader Mikhail Gorbachev, jointly addressed the graduating class at Wellesley College. More than 150 female students signed a petition against the commencement speech, arguing that the president's wife had distinguished herself only through her husband's career and was not qualified to be a commencement speaker to 1990s graduates. She responded without enmity, saying that she understood their feelings but did not agree. She delivered the speech as planned.

That was as much controversy as the First Lady experienced. Barbara Bush was a radical change from Nancy Reagan and an even greater contrast with Hillary Clinton. Many young people, both men and women, were disappointed in her and what she appeared to stand for. Times had changed, they reasoned, and they longed for a woman in the White House who was more assertive in her support for women's causes. But the First Lady steadfastly refused an assigned role. Her feelings apparently generated sympathy among most Americans, because for the next several years, she perennially topped polls as the most admired woman in America.

The press secretary changed not at all. Marlin Fitzwater had clearly been on loan to Ronald Reagan for the final two years of his Administration. After the election, Bush asked for the return of his press secretary, and Fitzwater continued as White House spokesperson, dealing with reporters competently though not necessarily promoting his boss as effectively as some of the most successful press secretaries. His relationship with the press changed, however. Unlike the Reagan years, the press secretary was the primary source for information to reporters and media advice to the president. Imagery was not at the top of Bush's agenda.

"Of the three presidents I have covered, George Bush was the one I liked best," wrote Kenneth T. Walsh, White House correspondent for *U.S. News and World Report*.[3] That is certainly not surprising. Bush was generous in providing quotes and more understanding of the needs of reporters than any other president had been since Kennedy. He held more than 250 press conferences in four years, an average of more than one a week, mostly in the briefing room, where he patiently answered any and all questions. During flights aboard Air Force One, he mingled with correspondents and answered more questions, even allowing the informal give-and-take to be televised. Personal interviews were frequent. Bush also appeared on news shows and sometimes talk shows. No other president had ever been so considerate without actively seeking to control reporters by punishment and reward. Bush simply felt it his duty to respond to inquiries. Fitzwater sometimes thought Bush was too accessible. The question of whether every president after Reagan would seek to guide press coverage and create an image without allowing reporters opportunities for inquiries had apparently been answered—or so reporters hoped.

Yet his accessibility certainly did not tone down press criticism, keep embarrassing questions off the agenda, or make the American public feel all warm and fuzzy about their president. In fact, from Bush's perspective, being understanding and cooperative with the White House press corps had gained him nothing. Why? Probably because journalists wanted to reassert themselves as keepers of the Fourth Estate, but also because the relationship among president, press, and public had started over. Declining interest in world and national affairs and a lack of legislative initiative from the White House placed White House news in a secondary role. Bush was seen on television about one-third as often as Reagan. For the first time since 1933, the country did not turn to Washington for answers to the complexities of their individual and collective lives, and networks looked elsewhere for leads for news shows.

At the same time, Bush learned that positive press relations do not ensure affirmative public relations. As in the case of the Ford Administration, reporters react more to the mood of the country than to how the White House treats them personally. That is not to say that correspondents are not arrogant or do not expect answers to their questions; they are and they do. Accepting this does not provide insulation in times of public disenchantment, however. Historical events and basic issues supersede press relations. And in the summer of 1990, one set of historical events was to control the presidency for nearly a year, while a second would end the Bush presidency.

THE GULF WAR

On July 16, 1990, the Kuwaiti government decided to recognize Iran, the nation Iraq had fought from 1980 to 1988. Angered by the insult, Iraqi President Saddam Hussein ordered his troops to mass along the mutual national border of Kuwait and Iraq. U.S. Secretary of Defense Dick Cheney responded by sending a telegram to Hussein warning him that the United States would take seriously any threats to U.S. allies in the Middle East. On July 25, April Glaspie, U.S. ambassador to Iraq, was called to Hussein's office. He asked her what the telegram meant. Glaspie responded that the United States would take no position on an Arab-Arab disagreement. She explained later that this did not mean the United States would stand by idly during an invasion of Kuwait, but historians have interpreted the meaning of her response differently.[4] Historically, the Iraqis considered Kuwait a province of their country that had unlawfully broken away and established its own government, and they were looking for excuses to reclaim their lost province.

Whatever Glaspie's intent, the Iraqis interpreted it loosely enough to initiate an invasion of Kuwait on August 2, 1990, overrunning the oil-rich country within days. Suddenly, world attention focused on a country that had drawn almost no notice since World War II. U.S. Middle East policy in the 1980s had decidedly favored Iraq over Iran, though Hussein had been a ruthless and cruel dictator. Now some of the richest oil fields in the world were under his control, with the threat of even more economic chaos as the Iraqis marched toward Saudi Arabia.

Over the next five and a half months, Bush carefully brought public and world opinion against Hussein and Iraq, while a U.N. force comprised mostly of U.S. troops deployed to the region. As Hussein rejected peace overtures and withdrawal recommendations from both the United States and the U.N., the world edged closer to a full-scale war. Bush constructed a diplomatic base for the inevitable conflict, even obtaining Arab support of a U.N. embargo and the eventual bombing of Baghdad (though no Arab nations participated in the military action). Bush set a deadline of January 15, 1991, by which time Iraqi forces were to evacuate Kuwait. On January 12, the Senate voted, 52 to 47, and the House, 250 to 183, to support military force, a resolution similar to one that had already been approved by the U.N. Hussein, with the sixth largest army in the world, seemed bent on a confrontation with the United States and the combined forces of most of the rest of the developed world. The industrial nations agreed to reimburse the countries that sent military forces to the Persian Gulf, most of the estimated $50 billion being paid to the United States.

On January 16 (U.S. time), coalition forces began to bombard military targets in Kuwait and Baghdad. The incessant bombing continued for six weeks until more firepower had been unloaded in the Gulf than in any other war in history. The sky over Baghdad at night was lit by tracers, as mission after mission struck the hapless city. In an attempt to divide coalition forces, Hussein ordered the launch of Scud missiles against Israel, a nonbelligerent. At the urging of the United States, the Israelis reluctantly remained neutral. Israeli intervention would likely have caused Arab nations to withdraw their support. U.S. bombing missions continued around the clock. Neither the firebombing of Dresden at the end of World War II nor the air barrage over Hanoi during the Vietnam War could match the intensity of the air assault on the Iraqi capital. Still, Hussein stood firm.

In late February, U.S.-led coalition ground forces entered Kuwait. The Iraqi army crumbled as thousands deserted or laid down their guns. The ground war was over in three days. A total of 244 coalition soldiers were killed during the entire conflict, while more than 100,000 Iraqis died, according to U.S. estimates.

Hussein's forces were driven from Southern Iraq and Kuwait, but Arab allies would not allow any further military encroachment, so Hussein remained free and the Iraqi government humbled but unchanged. At least three times in ensuing years, Hussein threatened military action in the Middle East, and the decision not to press the advantage in 1991 haunted U.S. policy in the Middle East.

Press coverage was nearly as controversial as the war. The Bush Administration warned American reporters in Baghdad to evacuate. All but a small CNN camera crew had already left, and with Hussein's permission they stayed, ignoring admonitions about their safety. They continued to send live television reports even after the bombing began. The CNN pictures offered Americans a spectacular view of the Iraqi capital city as the tracers lit up the sky. It was the first time in history a nation's people could watch from their living rooms, live and in color, hostile warfare against an enemy from the enemy's perspective.

Also, for the first time in its brief ten years of broadcasting, CNN captured the attention of a large portion of the viewing public. The major networks turned over their regular programming to war coverage the first day but settled for sporadic reports after that. CNN, the only all-news network, aired uninterrupted coverage. The majors had geared their programming and advertising to entertainment, and network executives decided they could not afford to yield the advertising dollar to an ongoing war, so many Americans turned to CNN.

Hussein was allowed to manipulate CNN, dictating where cameras could be carried and what could be broadcast, an orchestration that angered many Americans and provided CNN with an ethical dilemma: Were they giving aid to the enemy by broadcasting information back home, while under the exploitative control of the Iraqi censors? At one point, hundreds of Iraqi civilians were killed when a bomb struck a bunker where they were sheltered. U.S. military leaders argued that the aerial attacks had been aimed at a military target and had struck the bunker by mistake. Others suggested that Hussein had placed the civilians there, purposely exposing them to harm and hoping to use their deaths as a public relations gambit. CNN broadcast live shots of the destruction in the bunker, offering pictures that seemed to confirm the Iraqi argument.

Still, military experts later conceded that CNN had not given the Iraqis an advantage by their broadcasts. Nothing shown on American television had compromised the military effort. The camera crew had provided valuable insight during the bombing while literally risking their lives. However, they operated willingly while under the control of the enemy, and this was difficult for many Americans to accept. Perhaps a more enlightened decision would have been to leave Iraq before the bombing, but it was not the U.S. government's place to dictate what a television team should do in such a situation. It was a delicate determination, and news executives probably made the wrong decision. They were legitimately subjected to second guessing and may have had second thoughts themselves, in retrospect, but by acting autonomously, they protected their independence from U.S. government edicts. Perhaps in the long run this was more important than the short-term question of whether they were used as tools of the Hussein censors, especially in view of the tight restrictions placed on the press generally by the U.S. military.

As for the other reporters, Desert Shield and Desert Storm proved to be as infuriating to them as the Grenada incursion in 1983. The U.S. military required pools, where hundreds of news organizations were represented by a few reporters at a time. At televised briefings in Saudi Arabia, only the pool reporters were allowed to attend. They asked detailed questions but were usually rebuffed with "no comments" or evasions. The truncated synopses kept the news media scraping for any factual data and reporters seething. At one point, a CBS news crew wandered away in search of a story and were captured and held captive by Iraqis for a month. Leading news executives complained bitterly about the censorship. After the war, a joint commission was formed to explore ways of handling news flow during future incursions, but the committee disbanded with little agreement.

Americans watched the televised question-and-answer sessions during the war with distaste as some reporters asked ridiculously obvious questions or repeated the same ones over and over. To the many viewers who were unaccustomed to press conferences, the whole process seemed unnecessary. Sympathy fell largely with the military spokespersons who held the briefings. In truth, press conferences never have been good theater. Reporters often are redundant or tend to ask uninformed questions, but that is the nature of an imperfect process. What is important is that a few well-chosen interrogatories do emerge, and if they are ignored, then the public is placed at a disadvantage, no matter what viewers think from watching the procedure on television.

With the intense television coverage, it would seem logical that Americans did not read newspapers and magazines, having satiated their interests through video reports. Such was not the case. For once in the post–Cold War era, Americans were following world news with great interest. Almost everyone had a friend, relative, or acquaintance in a place that few could locate on the map. Television and radio only whetted war news appetites, and newsstand purchases increased dramatically. When news is followed avidly on instantaneous media, television and radio, it serves as a springboard for more complete print coverage. Broadcast media ideally do not supplant print media so much as they complement, and the Gulf War seemed to underscore that point.

Bush initially emerged from the war as an unqualified icon. The few Allied casualties and heavy Iraqi losses pointed to an undisputed military success. Hussein's army was smashed and his plans to plunder the oil fields of Kuwait and perhaps Saudi Arabia were turned aside. Both Colin Powell, the chairman of the Joint Chiefs of Staff, and Desert Storm Commander Norman Schwarzkopf were celebrated heros.

Yet after the initial exhilaration, questions remained. If the U.N. motive was to drive Hussein from Kuwait, why hadn't coalition forces marched into Baghdad and captured him, putting an end to his aggression? And had Bush been forthright with Congress when he urged war? Had Hussein been given assurances by April Glaspie that the United States would not intervene, only to refute those promises? Had the CIA backed Hussein for years? Why were U.N.

troops really in Kuwait? Would they have been there if the richest oil deposits in the world had not been located there? After all, the United States had not opposed some of the most repressive and aggressive regimes in the world in impoverished Central and Southern Africa. What of the soldiers who complained that they suffered from nerve system disorders and other symptoms that were commonly described as Gulf War syndrome? As late as six years after the war, the U.S. government reported that no chemical weapons had been used against these soldiers but that they were suffering from stress. These troubling questions took some edge off the euphoria once the war had become history.

The real saga of Desert Storm, however, was not the ease with which the invasion had achieved its goals or the minimal American casualty count but the potential catastrophe that had been averted. It was known that Iraq possessed chemical weapons and it was believed that Hussein was disdainful enough of human life that he might be willing to unleash such terrible destructiveness. The Gulf War was not the great little Spanish-American War of 1898. Americans could have died by the tens of thousands in the Middle East, regardless of their superior numbers, and the fear that kept Americans watching, listening, and reading about the war was the real possibility that their friends and relatives could suffer painful deaths inflicted by chemical weapons or by some other banned weaponry.

When Bob Woodward published his book, *The Commanders*, months after the war's end, he claimed that military advisors had warned against an invasion. His book raised other questions about the efficiency of the Bush government and its policies in the Middle East. Once again, Woodward had personally redirected the perception of the American presidency, requiring that conventional wisdom be re-examined.

In retrospect, Americans should have had second thoughts about the glory of the war. The policies that favored Iraq in the 1980s and had led to a misunderstanding between Glaspie and Hussein in July of 1990 were badly flawed. But once the invasion had begun, Bush pursued a diplomatic resolution and then a military one with great patience and resolve. Not standing up to Hussein could have been a disaster of global proportions.

Media coverage of the war was, by and large, outstanding. Despite the bitter complaints from news organizations and the reservations about CNN's role, coverage was thorough and responsible, though certainly jingoistic at times, as one might expect during wartime. Watching, listening, and reading about the war during its most critical stages not only allayed many Americans' fears but provided a united front for the U.S. soldiers in the Middle East. It was a time of tragedy marked by great U.S. and U.N. courage, diplomacy, and will and by reasonably proficient U.S. reporting, despite severe limitations.

THE 1991 RECESSION

As is typical of the presidency, Bush had no time to savor the victory in the Gulf. Although his personal popularity was at its highest just after the war—a nearly 90 percent approval rating—within months after the conclusion of the fighting, Americans turned against the president. After a decade of apparent prosperity, the nation slipped into recession. The Gross National Product in 1991 decreased by 1 percent. Added to this was a quirk in the economic process. What had occurred in the 1980s did not parallel the 1920s and 1950s. The beneficiaries of good times in the 1980s were mostly the wealthy and upper middle class. Mergers and acquisitions had forced downsizing in American industry and many middle-aged Americans found themselves scrambling for jobs in a hostile workplace environment. Still others, mostly poor and lower middle class, found work only in minimum wage positions, mostly part time. The American underclass had grown, as had the number of millionaires. Stock manipulation and fraud appeared to be rampant on Wall Street, and the earning power of the average American had decreased significantly.

The 1991 recession confirmed the submerged fears of many Americans who had experienced the tumultuous days of the early 1980s and had been plagued by downsizing ever since. No job was safe in the new corporate world. Not only had the public, the press, and the president been forced to re-define their relationships, so had Americans been required to re-examine their associations with their employers. No amount of celebrating over the Persian Gulf victory could mask the skepticism and disenchantment that had ensnared America. The basic tenet of politics—guns and butter—had been re-interpreted as just butter.

In 1991 Bush nominated a conservative African-American jurist to the Supreme Court. Before the celebrating in the black community could get underway, however, a former aide, Anita Hill, stepped forward to say that the nominee, Clarence Thomas, had sexually harassed her when she had worked for him. Both Hill and Thomas testified before televised hearings of the Senate Judiciary Committee. The accusations divided the country. Although Thomas was narrowly confirmed, the divisive process had not only devastated Thomas but wounded Bush and intensified public skepticism about Washington politics.

Shortly after, a minor White House scandal broke. Chief of Staff John Sununu, whose abrasive manner had alienated legislators and reporters alike, was reported to have used government aircraft for private excursions. Sununu refused to acknowledge wrongdoing, claiming to have been unjustly pilloried by reporters. Bush asked for his resignation in late November 1991, however, creating embarrassment just as the economic malaise was at its worst.

By the beginning of the 1992 political campaign, the Gulf War was forgotten. Once again, Washington politics and economic uncertainty occupied the attention of mainstream America. Reporters sniped at Bush for what they perceived as his lack of initiative and his indecisiveness, a theme that bounced back and forth for months: Bush could not handle the job; Bush could not settle on a course of action; Bush had no ideas or agendas; Bush's appointees were a disgrace.

Actually, Bush had been paralyzed early in his term of office by the excesses of the Reagan Administration and again later by the Gulf War. As with Gerald Ford, he had been weakened by world and national events and his own inability to create a lasting, positive image. The criticism from reporters was, as usual, a natural outcropping of the public disenchantment that preceded it. Put simply, the scent of blood was in the water, and Bush was suddenly shark bait.

To the president, whose approval ratings had soared just months earlier, this seemed quite puzzling, but it should not have been. What was apparent in the skeptical 1990s was that polls and approval ratings were nearly useless. With only loosely formed ideologies and minimal party allegiances, voters change their minds about presidents quickly. The timing of the recession was probably the most disastrous turn of events Bush could have imagined. Pundits who had been predicting a smashing Bush victory in 1992 were backpedaling. Bush, they now reported, was in trouble. How much trouble, everyone agreed, would depend on whom the Democrats nominated.

The downturn in the economy had caught not only Bush but also prominent Democrats unprepared. A run for the White House costs a great deal of money. By 1992, advertising, staff, travel, printing, and a myriad of other expenses in a full-blown primary and general election campaign topped $150 million total—$55 million in the primaries alone. Raising that kind of money took planning and preparation. Many Democrats did not want to squander their careers and incur huge debt in a futile race against a popular incumbent. By the time it was clear that Bush was vulnerable, it was too late. Most of the leading candidates had no organizations for such an expensive undertaking and declined to run. New York Governor Mario Cuomo, Representative Richard Gephardt, Senator Albert Gore, and Reverend Jesse Jackson all announced their noncandidacies. The only person left was the seven-term governor of Arkansas, Bill Clinton, and a few no-names or has-beens, who would not have even considered a campaign in other than a nearly bankrupt 1992 primary field. It was ironic that the opposition party could not muster a field of credible candidates to challenge a wounded incumbent. Yet the field of Democrats willing to enter the primaries had been unimpressive for twenty-four years and

a dark horse candidate emerging from the convention—as had occurred in 1924 and 1952—was no longer feasible.

Despite his lack of national stature and an embarrassingly awkward and poorly received nomination speech during the 1988 Democratic National Convention, Clinton had demonstrated an amazing political acumen and popularity during his years as governor. He seemed to provide the fresh face and legitimate executive skills that had evaded Democratic candidates for a generation. Before the first votes were cast in the first primaries, reporters were already conceding the nomination to Clinton.

Yet from the moment that Clinton had acknowledged his aspirations for the White House, he was surrounded by controversy. During an appearance on the Arsenio Hall television show, he played a saxophone and later appeared on MTV, establishing a new level in undignified campaigning. Despite his obvious political and public relations talents, Clinton was a lightning rod for negative stories about unsavory or immoral conduct. Because he was relatively unknown, he eagerly sought out reporters early in the campaign, granting interviews liberally and appearing on television as often as television would allow. In February 1992 allegations surfaced about his relationship with Arkansas TV journalist Gennifer Flowers. The Clintons appeared on CBS's *60 Minutes* and conceded that there had been marital problems in the past, but the two told viewers the infidelity had ended. This seemed to defuse the issue for the moment, but Clinton grew more distant from the press.

Later he danced around charges that he had evaded the Vietnam draft during his younger years and then he admitted that he had smoked marijuana. He tried to mitigate the culpability by adding that he had puffed but not inhaled. Because of Clinton's thin skin and the invasive nature of the stories, the Arkansas governor remained at odds with reporters throughout the rest of the campaign and never again felt comfortable in their presence.

Clinton's challengers included Senator Bob Kerrey of Nebraska, former Senator Paul Tsongas of Massachusetts who had retired from politics six years earlier to fight cancer, Virginia Governor L. Douglas Wilder, Iowa Senator Tom Harkin, and former California Governor Jerry Brown. Wilder, the only African-American candidate, withdrew four weeks before the New Hampshire primary.

Patrick Buchanan, the former Reagan media advisor and Nixon speechwriter, declared himself a Republican alternative to Bush, as did David Duke, an ultra-right-wing legislator from Louisiana. All the candidates except Clinton and Bush conducted poorly organized and underfunded campaigns. Every state and territory had a primary or caucus in 1992; North Dakota had both. And although there were thirty-six primaries and twenty caucuses, the results

of the interminable voting seemed only to confirm that Clinton and Bush had no peers within their parties. Harkin won the Iowa caucuses, but the other contenders hardly bothered to campaign there since Harkin was a favorite son. When Tsongas won the New Hampshire primary with a pro-business and balanced-budget appeal, reporters speculated that Clinton was finished.

As it turned out, however, the tradition of the early primaries and caucuses had changed. New Hampshire and Iowa no longer spelled victory. The important balloting came in March, with eighteen primaries and eleven caucuses. Buchanan won a surprising share of the New Hampshire, Georgia, and Maryland votes, but his mild success in the face of his defiantly conservative rhetoric and low-budget campaign served only to underscore Bush's weakened position. Duke, a former American Nazi Party leader, was thoroughly repudiated at the polls. Brown won 608 convention delegates but proved no match for Clinton. The rest of the Democrats, including Tsongas, withdrew by early April. Ironically, Tsongas died five years later, in 1997, two days before Clinton's second inauguration, from complications of pneumonia after having survived his long bout with cancer.

Clinton and Bush spent $56 million each on the primaries (excluding political action committees). The rest of the field combined spent $40 million. Money was influential in the 1992 primary campaign; more to the point, the front-runners had, as usual, attracted the free spenders at the expense of the rest of the field. The 1990s seemed to renew the value of being the early leader fifteen years after George Romney had initiated the ignominious string of failed front-runnerships.

In late February, billionaire Ross Perot announced on CNN's "Larry King Live" talk show that if his supporters could place his name on the ballot in all fifty states, he would be an independent candidate. Perot eventually spent $60 million of his own money on the campaign, and a disgruntled electorate turned to the feisty Texan in surprising numbers. It was speculated that he might attract even more votes than John Anderson's 6 percent in 1980, but in May few took his candidacy seriously, especially campaign correspondents.

As the Democratic and Republican conventions approached, that attitude changed. Some of the early summer polls, always unreliable but still fodder for stories, showed that Perot actually was leading. His pointed criticism of both parties and the political system seemed to be in sync with the mind-sets of many voters in the summer of 1992. Yet just when it appeared that the campaign could not get any more bizarre, Perot appeared on the "Larry King Live" show again, announcing to the astonishment of his loyal followers that he was withdrawing. He explained in vague terms that he did not think he could win. Later he claimed that he was being followed by government

operatives, who planned to disrupt his daughter's wedding. Perot re-entered the campaign in October, reversing his surprise withdrawal, but he found it difficult to shake the notion that he was too eccentric to be president.

The conventions proved to be uneventful. Clinton chose Tennessee Senator Albert Gore as his running mate. The only controversy surrounded Bush's decision to keep Dan Quayle on the ticket. Quayle had been vilified by reporters since the onset of the 1988 campaign. Conservatives accused the liberal media of crucifying another right-wing national leader. Quayle had problems other than ideology, however. Bush selected him in 1988 because he wanted a youthful counterpart—someone the baby boomers could relate to. Quayle seemed more inexperienced than youthful, however, and especially tentative when speaking in public. He, like Clinton, had backpedaled while explaining how his family had pulled strings to allow him to avoid the Vietnam draft. In May 1992, just after rioting in the Watts section of Los Angeles had once again evoked agonized debate over racism in the country, Quayle told reporters that much of the problem could be attributed to a "poverty of values." Americans had lost their traditional sense of right and wrong, Quayle said, citing a popular television situation comedy, "Murphy Brown." The fictitious character, a supposedly highly regarded television reporter and working woman, had chosen to have a baby out of wedlock. Quayle cited this as an example of how television was corrupting values. This led to a debate between a real vice president and a fictitious television character, played by Candice Bergen. Weeks later during a spelling bee at a junior high in Trenton, New Jersey, Quayle told a twelve-year-old to spell the word "potato" as "potatoe." More silliness and inane television and wire stories.

Was Quayle unfairly singled out on frivolous topics? Perhaps, but other national leaders seemed to weather media fascination with such trivial matters (witness Jimmy Carter and the rabbit and George Bush's announced dislike for broccoli). Quayle, like Gerald Ford, seemed to invite the snickering. An intelligent and articulate spokesperson for the Bush administration, he seemed unable to project this image in public. Despite performing well in the vice presidential debates, Quayle was a liability—a person who found only unhappiness from the vice presidency.

The 1992 general election campaign was a 1990s-type television production. When the three candidates debated, the outspoken Perot gained the advantage. Obviously the underdog, Perot was a free-wheeling sniper who used fiery rhetoric similar to George Wallace's in 1968, promising to get rid of party politics and cut Washington down to size. More Americans watched the three 1992 debates on television than any other debates in history. Vulnerable on the economic issues, Bush seemed defensive. His television advertising attacked

Clinton's record in Arkansas. The ads warned that the rampant poverty there would become the heritage of the entire country if Clinton were elected.

Clinton and Perot hammered at the economic theme. A sign above a desk in Clinton's home headquarters in Little Rock read, "It's the economy, stupid," and he followed that precept. Clinton refused to allow his personal idiosyncrasies to be the focus of the campaign. Before Perot re-entered the race on October 1, both Clinton and Bush studiously avoided discussing specifics about budget deficit reduction. Perot made that his theme and used an unusual technique, half-hour infomercials, to explain to Americans how the huge deficits were harming them and what he would do to correct them. The lengthy discussions drew 12 million viewers, a large number for a thirty-minute political message. Perot seemed to be defying the logic of the image makers. Conventional wisdom dictated that the television advertising message had to be short, simple, and visual. Perot trotted out charts and lectured as if he were an economics professor addressing a freshman class. If nothing else, he refused to let the budget deficit issue die, and as a result, many Americans became keenly aware of its future implications. No president or presidential candidate would be able to finesse that issue after 1992.

In the strange and unusual mix of Perot, Bush, and Clinton, all on seemingly equal footing, Bush seemed to disappear in the shuffle. His "read my lips" commitment echoed. The economy had also faltered, though it actually had begun to rebound by the fourth quarter of 1992, a point that Bush argued frequently, to no avail. Some have speculated that without Perot's candidacy, Bush would have won. This is a myth. The facts dictate otherwise. Polls indicated that Clinton's share of the potential vote increased after Perot dropped out. The mood of the country in the fall of 1992 militantly dictated against Bush. Even in 1980 when Carter lost badly to Reagan, there was a strong feeling until the last few weeks that the contest would be close. From the beginning of the 1992 campaign, an air of inevitability pervaded. Perot simply made the debate discussions and the campaign more interesting.

Indeed, the 1992 campaign was the liveliest since 1976, when Carter defeated Ford. Both Clinton and Perot seemed to represent a break with the politics of the past, suggesting that the 1990s would bring a new start. Clinton shunned the liberal image that Dukakis, Mondale, Carter, Johnson, and Kennedy accepted. Describing himself as a "New Democrat," Clinton hugged the center, turning his back on the poor and the minority community and appealing instead to the middle class. He promised a tax cut for the middle class, but also committed himself to reducing the budget deficit and spending more to combat crime.

Reporting seemed to be more spirited than in 1988. All three candidates drew large media contingencies. Yet for all its drama and color, the give-and-take between press and candidates was severely limited. Both Perot and Clinton loathed reporters. Not only did they not attempt to hide their disdain, but they bragged about it to voters. Bush was less hostile, but many of his campaign staffers became edgy as the campaign progressed and they read stories emphasizing Bush's unelectability. Unlike 1988, press coverage suffered from a lack of input from candidates rather than a lack of aggressiveness. In fact, at the beginning of the campaign, NBC news executives announced that no broadcast sound bite from a candidate on a news show would be less than 30 seconds—this to avoid the meaningless video snippets that had come to dominate campaigns. Others did not follow, but the search for meaningful themes after the 1988 campaign did affect all media.

After the campaign, Bush supporters argued that the media had been biased. Critics employed statistics that illustrated a much higher degree of negative reporting about Bush than Clinton. Yet that negativism was characteristic of the electorate at the time, and it would have been dishonest of reporters to indicate otherwise. There certainly was a feeling of dissatisfaction with Bush—an impression independent of media coverage—and if stories about Bush were negative, they did not intentionally distort mainstream public attitudes.

For those who relished political campaigns, more than 1,200 hours of campaign coverage was shown on C-SPAN. Clinton's personal foibles and Perot's wacky, outspoken public utterances added color. The drama of a president who only recently was revered as the leader of the Gulf War assault but now teetering on the brink of rejection also generated interest. Both Clinton and Perot employed an unusual "town hall" approach to campaigning, answering questions from callers on talk shows and accepting questions from live audiences of citizens rather than reporters.

Yet, as is usual for presidential politics, the general election turned out to be a referendum on the incumbent. And for the third time in four elections, the incumbent was shown the door. Clinton won with 43 percent of the vote to Bush's 38 percent and Perot's 19—the fourth lowest percentage for a winning candidate in history. (Woodrow Wilson earned 42 percent in 1912, Abraham Lincoln 39.8 percent in 1860, and John Quincy Adams, 31 percent in 1824.) Despite his large popular vote share, Perot did not win a single electoral vote.

What had happened to George Bush? It was the economy, stupid. But how badly had Americans suffered during this brief malaise? The recession lasted less than a year. True, the downturn came at the most unfortunate time for the incumbent, but other presidents had survived minor recessions. Other presidents had not been in office in the 1990s, however. It was as if Americans had expected failure, as if they had been conditioned to expect Bush to let them down. They stood at the voting booth lever, ready to substitute someone else in the White House at the first sign of trouble. Bush was not without culpability, of course. He was tentative in the middle of the economic down-turn and unable to tout his political successes with a winning personal style and organized media campaign.

Yet mediocrity has been common in the White House in the 200 years of the presidency, especially in the modern presidency. Historically, it is rare for Americans to reject an incumbent at the polls. Why was Bush so unyieldingly singled out? Because in the 1970s, 1980s, and 1990s, the economy had come to be the defining issue for the preponderance of the electorate. Winning re-election was about pocketbook issues, and Bush had not recognized this soon enough or was unable to control the economy long enough to win re-election. Consequently, little more than a third of the electorate voted for him. His percentage of the vote total was the lowest of any other incumbent since William Howard Taft in 1912.

For correspondents, Clinton's victory spelled trouble. Not only had an accommodating president lost handily, but this candidate who reviled the press and avoided reporters with town hall interviews would now occupy the Oval Office. Whatever good relations had developed between the press and the president would be lost in the middle-1990s. Like voters, the White House press corps had to start over again.

NOTES

1. David Mervin, *George Bush and the Guardianship Presidency* (New York: St. Martin's, 1996), 109.

2. Barbara Bush, *Barbara Bush: A Memoir* (New York: Charles Scribner's Sons, 1994).

3. Kenneth T. Walsh, *Feeding the Beast: The White House Versus the Press* (New York: Random House, 1996).

4. Bob Woodward contends that Glaspie was noncommittal. Historians such as Alex Hybel argue that Glaspie was firmly negative in her response. Glaspie herself told Congress she had been clear about a hostile U.S. reaction. See Bob Woodward, *The Commanders* (New York: Simon & Schuster, 1991), 211–12. Also see Alex Roberto Hybel, *Power Over Rationality: The Bush Administration and the Gulf Crisis* (Albany: State University of New York Press, 1993), 37–38.

CHAPTER ELEVEN

BILL CLINTON'S BAD IMAGE

If a public relations expert in 1993 had set out to rebuild nationwide confidence in the personal values of the presidency, Bill and Hillary Clinton would have been one of the last couples he or she would have hired. Bill Clinton did for presidential moral leadership what Al Capone accomplished for good government. Even before he took office, questions about Clinton's sex life and his and Hillary's business dealings dominated the news. Reporters accorded Clinton no presidential honeymoon, and he offered them no olive branch. Unlike Bush, Clinton had a clear agenda and a dogged determination to pursue it, but each serious policy initiative and each national and international issue was bestowed secondary coverage in favor of fresh stories, and sometimes not so fresh ones, about the Clintons' personal conduct.

Contentiousness dominated between press and president, between president and Congress, between public and press. Presidential-press contact was almost nonexistent, mirroring the atmosphere that existed during the most antagonistic days of Watergate. Allegations about the Clintons' personal shortcomings and the president's aborted policy initiatives only escalated the verbal warfare. Voters reacted with a growing restlessness, and eventually both political parties suffered. Given the post-Watergate mood of the press corps and the public, the 1990s was the wrong decade for such a controversial president.

Through it all, Clinton fought back cleverly and with resolute determination. By the end of his first term, it was clear that both journalists and political Washington had underestimated his acumen and his political gamesmanship. Yet though he survived, Clinton's trials had implications far beyond the 1990s. Like Lyndon Johnson and Richard Nixon before him, Bill Clinton may have been clever enough to win presidential elections, but his behavior carried ramifications beyond the 1990s.

Immediately after the inauguration, Clinton's staff informed reporters that White House access would be restricted. Senior presidential advisor George Stephanopoulos moved into the press secretary's office. Dee Dee Myers, the press secretary, was assigned to a smaller office usually reserved for the deputy press secretary. Reporters were kept away from both rooms and confined to the press and briefing areas in the basement. This restriction, certainly unwelcome to the correspondents, signaled the beginning of a long siege. Although the Clinton staff relented in a few weeks and returned to the usual access rules, the tension remained. After a few months, Stephanopoulos was replaced by former Republican media advisor David Gergen, editor-at-large of *U.S. News and World Report* at the time. Gergen lasted only a few years, and press relations never eased during the first term.

A series of public embarrassments followed the election. Within a few weeks of taking office, Clinton was forced to rescind Zoe Baird's nomination for attorney general. News stories revealed that she had employed domestics in her home illegally. A second nominee, Kimba Wood, was forced to withdraw on similar grounds. Janet Reno was eventually named to the post after a long, drawn-out public relations disaster.

When Clinton nominated Ruth Bader Ginsburg to the U.S. Supreme Court six months later, ABC White House correspondent Brit Hume asked a politely worded but tough question about whether Clinton had hesitated in appointing her. The president exploded, denouncing the question and aborting the press conference. His tantrum was revealing: "I have long since given up the thought that I could disabuse some of you from turning any substantive decision into anything but political process," he told the press gathering and stalked away.[1]

Clinton decided to circumvent the White House press corps by continuing his town hall, talk show, local-press-access strategy begun during the campaign. The goal no longer was to influence Washington correspondents but to make them irrelevant. The youthful Myers had worked with Clinton for seven years in Arkansas and during the campaign, and she reflected the president's contempt for Washington reporting. She was also disorganized and poorly qualified, and her lack of organization caused a myriad of logistical headaches, especially when the president traveled. By September 1994 senior advisors were leaking suggestions that Myers was on her way out. Clinton met with Myers and, in an abrupt turnaround announced that not only was she staying but that her duties would be expanded. The unexpected reversal only delayed the inevitable. By January 1995 Myers was replaced by State Department spokesperson Michael McCurry, who was more reliable and less grating to reporters.

The press and the presidency seemed to be mutually exclusive in the first two years of the Clinton Administration. As Clinton had observed during his 1993 outburst, reporters were looking for specific stories, and they were certainly not the ones the White House wanted on the air or in print. On the other hand, Clinton was providing them with all the ammunition they needed.

Old innuendos perpetually stayed in the news, and new ones seemed to materialize daily. In July 1993, presidential deputy counsel and long-time friend of the Clinton's Vincent Foster was found dead in a park just outside Washington, the apparent victim of a self-inflicted gunshot wound. Foster left what appeared to be a suicide note that blamed his death on reporters and political opponents and their unrelenting invasiveness and insinuations. A former law partner of Hillary Clinton at the Rose legal firm in Little Rock, he had grown up in Hope with his friend Bill Clinton. Reportedly files disappeared from his office, and certain inconsistencies and missing evidence from the investigation of his death fueled conspiracy theories. Controversy surrounded Foster's death for years and, despite independent counsel Kenneth Starr's declaration in 1997 that Foster's death was no more than a suicide, conspiracy conjecture continued.

Other investigations plagued the early Clinton Administration. A few months after the inaugural, the entire White House travel staff was fired and replaced with Clinton associates and friends. The reasons cited for the dismissals were obtuse. It was reported that the First Lady was responsible. Long-term congressional and grand jury investigations followed.

In December 1993 two Arkansas state troopers told reporters that they had procured women for Clinton while he was governor and had then stood guard outside the rooms where Clinton had his trysts. It was also reported in 1994 that Clinton had tried to keep the troopers from speaking out. Then in May 1994 a former Arkansas state employee, Paula Jones, filed a sexual harassment suit against Clinton, claiming that in 1991 troopers had escorted her to a Little Rock hotel where Clinton, then governor, had asked her to commit sexual acts with him. Presidents are generally immune from personal litigation while in office, so the lawsuit languished. In 1997, however, the U.S. Supreme Court ruled that the lawsuit could proceed while Clinton is in office. A May 1998 trial date was set.

It was alleged in 1996 that the White House had requested FBI files on more than 900 ranking Republicans in the Bush and Reagan Administrations. The Army civilian employee, Anthony Marceca, who was alleged to have gathered the background files told the Senate Judiciary Committee in June 1996 that he would not answer any questions, invoking his constitutional right not to incriminate himself. This raised one more investigation and hardened

Capitol Hill attitudes toward the White House. In a separate matter, some of Hillary Clinton's law files from Arkansas were subpoenaed in 1994 and then reported lost. In 1996 they were suddenly found in a seldom-used room of the White House and turned over to a grand jury.

The most serious threat to Clinton came from a land development company, the Whitewater Land Development Corp. Clinton had grown up in Hope and Hot Springs, and many of his business dealings as governor involved friends from his two home towns or acquaintances he made in Little Rock, including James and Susan McDougal. James McDougal had dabbled in politics. He had helped to manage political campaigns for some of Arkansas's most powerful politicians and had run for Congress himself. In 1978, the McDougals and Clintons jointly purchased 3,600 acres of land along the White River just north of Little Rock, thanks to a loan provided by a friendly bank. The investment failed, and most of the 3,600 acres remained undeveloped, but questions about the financing and its commingling with other financial deals drew the attention of prosecutors.

About the same time, Hillary Clinton invested in cattle futures. Unlike most other commodities investors, she transformed her modest original investment of $1,000 into a $100,000 bonanza, guessing right every time in the risky market. Analysts later said that Hillary had to be a genius to have earned such an astonishing return on her investment, or she had information that should not have been available to her.

In 1983, McDougal acquired a modest savings and loan company, renaming it Madison Guaranty Savings and Loan and moving its headquarters to Little Rock. In the heady days of free speculation in the 1980s, he made all manner of questionable loans to high-flying investors. The savings and loan failed, as did the Whitewater Development. The Clintons lost thousands of dollars—anywhere from $42,000 to $76,000, depending on who asked and when the answers were provided. Questions remained about the Clintons' relationships with the McDougals, federal loan regulation violations by Madison Guaranty, loans to both the McDougals and the Clintons, Clinton's influence in protecting McDougal, commissions on loans that McDougal took for himself, and money funneled through the Whitewater Development Corporation.

In 1994 Kenneth Starr, a Republican, was named Whitewater independent counsel with the responsibility for investigating charges of wrongdoing in the White House, especially Whitewater. The House Banking Committee initiated its own investigation. On January 26, 1996, Hillary Clinton was summoned to testify before a Whitewater grand jury. Her long-lost billing records indicated that she had completed a great deal of legal work for the Madison Guaranty—much more than she had ever conceded prior to that time. James

McDougal began cooperating with Starr after being convicted of fraud and conspiracy in 1995. Susan McDougal also was convicted on Whitewater charges, but while she awaited sentencing she was sent to jail on contempt-of-court charges for refusing to testify before a special Whitewater grand jury. Susan McDougal refused to say exactly why she would not testify, except that she would not turn on friends. Even Clinton's successor as governor, Jim Guy Tucker, was found guilty of financial irregularities and faced a prison sentence in 1997. James McDougal was also sent to prison in 1997.

It is no wonder that within a few months of his taking office, curio shops began selling T-shirts, golf balls, jogging shorts, and other memorabilia mono-grammed with Clinton's likeness and the two-word moniker "Slick Willie."

If the media were crucifying Clinton, he and the First Lady were providing the wood, the hammer, the nails, and the ladder. Perhaps no other president had ever been pursued by personal scandal so vigorously. Other presidents, such as Andrew Jackson, Ulysses S. Grant, Grover Cleveland, Warren Harding, John F. Kennedy, and Richard Nixon, had been bedeviled by personal and public scandal, but all but Nixon had shrugged off the claims (Harding died before the public learned of the oil leasing and bribery exposé that was brewing). Times had changed. Eagerly, reporters now sought out personal presidential ignominy, and obligingly the Clintons provided a new disgrace almost every week.

Why did the Clintons seem to attract controversy? Part of the reason was their drives to succeed. During both their early lives, they were taught to strive to be better, by lesson and by example. Bill Clinton's father, William Jefferson Blythe II, was killed in an auto accident before his son was born. Blythe's widow, Virginia, married Roger Clinton before her son was four years old. His mother had Billy take his stepfather's last name in hopes of bringing the family closer, but it was not a happy household. Roger Clinton, a car dealership owner, was a heavy drinker and a gambler, and he physically abused his wife. When the family moved to Hot Springs in 1953, the son was so troubled by his stepfather's behavior that he divided his time between his parents' home and his grandparents' house in Hope. A stepbrother, Roger, was born in 1956. Roger Sr. died in 1967, and years later Virginia married Richard W. Kelley, a retired food broker, with whom she lived until her death in 1994. Bill Clinton's half-brother was as wild and undisciplined as his father. In and out of trouble for years, he was convicted on drug charges and sent to prison during Clinton's first term.

It is amazing that Bill Clinton was able to prosper in such an environment, but his disadvantaged home life was the force that drove him to be the best, not a failure like his stepfather. He was graduated from Georgetown University, attended Oxford in England on a Rhodes scholarship, and eventually received his law degree from Yale University, where he met Hillary Rodham, a graduate of Wellesley College. Rodham had grown up in the affluent Chicago suburb of Park Ridge. Her father, a demanding man, drilled into his daughter the virtues of being independent and having respect for money.

These two overachievers, Bill and Hillary, were married in 1975 in Arkansas. Bill taught briefly at the University of Arkansas law school. Only after a few years in the governor's mansion, and as her husband's political career was sprouting, did Hillary add Clinton to her name. Chelsea was born in 1979. From the time of her birth, she was shielded from the press. The Clintons successfully avoided stories about her for most of the first term.

The first couple were a paradox. Taking advantage of some of the best educational institutions in the nation, they set the foundation for two brilliant careers. In Bill Clinton's case, with all that he had to endure, this seemed particularly admirable. Baby boomers who had taken advantage of the prosperity of the 1950s and 1960s, the Clintons' lives seemed to epitomize the advantages afforded to the young people of the post–World War II generation. Yet they seemed also to embody the "anything goes as long as I'm the one who benefits" philosophy of the 1970s and 1980s. Both were obsessed with money, whether for campaigns or their personal use. They squeezed cash from every opportunity. Their speculative investment ventures and fund-raising schemes seemed to taint whatever good they accomplished otherwise. And they always had cover stories or ways of diverting attention. Like many other baby boomers, they were standing on their tiptoes all the time to see over the rest.

If the Clintons epitomized the worst of the grasping, middle-class high rollers of the postwar generation, they were atypical in many ways too. Few others attended Wellesley College or Yale Law School or earned Rhodes scholarships. Rarely did even the most successful become active in politics at age twenty-six or enter the governor's mansion at age thirty-two. Only a few persons in history have ascended to the White House before reaching age fifty. The two Clintons were typically self-centered baby boomers, but atypically the best, the most determined, the most ingenious, the brightest, and the most canny.

For instance, others had finagled to escape the military draft during the Vietnam era, but Bill Clinton was more adroit and persistent. The family pressed the head of the draft board to delay Bill Clinton's induction. Then an ROTC commander arranged for Clinton to enter the University of Arkansas ROTC program where Clinton was to attend law school. After the draft lottery in 1969, Clinton's high number freed him from the threat of military service, and he turned his back on the ROTC program to attend Yale Law School.

If the first baby boom couple in the White House represented a generation, they represented the best and the worst of that generation. They were the reincarnation of the Chevy Chase lead-in for a news show skit on "Saturday Night Live": "Good evening, we're Bill and Hillary Clinton . . . and you're not." The Clinton smugness angered Americans. That helps to explain the furor over Clinton's $200 haircut aboard Air Force One in 1993 while the jet sat on a runway at Los Angeles International Airport. For security reasons, no air traffic was allowed in or out of the airport during the long delay. The Clintons claimed the incident was exaggerated, yet Americans believed Clinton could be arrogant enough to shut down air traffic at a busy airport while his hair was trimmed.

The perceived haughtiness explains as well the national reaction to Hillary Clinton, the woman who apparently embodied the independence, self-confidence, idealism, career success, and devoted motherhood sought by many young females. Those were traits many had wanted in the First Lady, but arrogance was not one of them.

Soon after the 1992 election, the Clintons publicly discussed a "shared presidency," something never mentioned during the campaign. The First Lady would be a partner in decision making. Clinton named her chair of a national committee on health care reform. To the disappointment of reporters, the committee met privately and developed its proposals in secret. Angered by what was perceived as high-handedness in the management of a crucial national domestic issue, public, press, and Congress attacked the committee and Hillary Clinton. Congress rejected Clinton's health care initiatives, and the president and First Lady backpedaled on Hillary's role in government. By 1994, on advice from White House aides, she had assumed a low profile.

Did this mean that a brilliant and forceful First Lady could not win public acceptance in the 1990s? Perhaps. More likely, it was Hillary Clinton who could not earn public endorsement. If the First Lady was a powerful and forceful woman in a man's world, she was still Hillary Clinton first. She was the person who seemed to look down on contemporaries and who connived to enrich and empower herself. If the experiment with a liberated First Lady had failed, it was as much the fault of the president's wife as that of an America divided over her role.

THE FALL OF THE SOVIET UNION

Clinton's foreign and domestic records in his first term of office drew mixed reviews. After a coup attempt by hard-line communists in the Politburo failed in the summer of 1991, the Soviet Union dissolved in December of that year.

Most of the nation became Russia, while outlying states spun off as independent republics. The Cold War ended. Boris Yeltsin assumed the presidency of Russia, ending seventy-three years of communist rule. No longer did the United States have to contend with the imminent threat of a nuclear war—or at least it seemed that way in the heady days after the breakup of the Soviet state. Unfortunately, the new republic foundered. Gangsters literally ruled many cities, and the nation adjusted poorly during the transition from a managed to a free-market economy. Joblessness and inflation impoverished Russians from one end of the country to the other. U.S. policymakers feared that the financially strapped government might sell its nuclear weapons to other countries or market its nuclear resources. There were similar concerns about the smaller nations in the former Soviet Union, such as the Ukraine, which had inherited nuclear arsenals.

U.S. foreign policy emphasis changed drastically in the post–Cold War effort. Many Third World countries that had been playing the United States off against the Soviet Union had to rely on U.S. financial and military support. Prodded by the U.S. military dominance in the Middle East after the Persian Gulf War, Arabs and Israelis negotiated for settlement of their differences. Terrorist attacks and mutual mistrust disrupted the negotiations time and again, however. After five years, the only tangible results were better communications between the two historical enemies and limited autonomy for Palestinians in selected cities in Israel.

The new world order presented a dilemma for Clinton: How would the United States, as the pre-eminent military power, deal with internal strife and open warfare around the world? Should the United States intervene and risk American lives in attempts to settle obscure Third World disputes? Could a supposedly humanitarian country stand by idly while thousands of innocent civilians were slaughtered? Just before leaving office, Bush had committed U.S. troops as part of a U.N. force to settle civil strife in the African nation of Somalia. Amid the glare of television lights and much fanfare, U.S. Marines waded ashore. Although normal life returned in Somalia, not much was settled, and Clinton waffled while U.S. military forces dallied for months with loosely defined responsibilities. Clinton hesitated again in 1993 when a military junta ousted democratically elected President Jean Bertrand Aristide in Haiti, but eventually the U.S. president committed troops there for a short time too.

In 1994, civil war in the former Yugoslavia brought pleas for a multination peacekeeping force. Once again Clinton hesitated before acting. Charges of wanton killing and genocide by both Serbs and Croatians had intensified the pressure on Clinton. Despite uneasy truces in Bosnia, Croatia, and Serbia, protests and scattered violence continued for several years, and the prospect of a long-term troop commitment in the former Yugoslavia remained a distinct possibility. In 1996, Clinton also sent troops to Central Africa to protect more than 1 million refugees fleeing to escape tribal warfare that affected Burundi, Rwanda, and Zaire.

The four peacekeeping missions underscored the fragile nature of post–Cold War peace. Clinton and future presidents would have to decide whether to ignore fratricidal wars in obscure parts of the world and risk charges of an inhumane foreign policy, or commit U.S. soldiers to wars that might result in American deaths and draw the United States into interminable unwanted conflicts.

At the same time, the four military incursions underscored a Clinton weakness: indecisiveness fanned by an apparent reliance on public opinion polls. More than any president before him, Clinton paid close attention to private surveys that sampled American opinion. In many instances he hesitated, while waiting for a public consensus.

Troop commitment and withdrawal decisions in Somalia, Haiti, the former Yugoslavia, and Central Africa seemed to be heavily influenced by public preference. Secretary of State Warren Christopher admitted soon after the military action in Central Africa in 1996 that television pictures of the suffering refugees on CNN had greatly influenced the decision to send U.S. troops.

A policy on gays in the military also underlines this point. During the 1992 campaign, Clinton promised to eliminate prejudice against gays in the military but backed off noticeably in 1993 when conservatives, military officers, and veterans complained about what they perceived as potential morale problems. Outwardly gay soldiers would harm the image of the military and would pose a threat to straight soldiers, opponents argued. Clinton settled on a policy of "don't ask, don't tell." If soldiers were gay but kept their sexual preferences secret, they could remain in the military under the new Clinton Administration policy. The government could not actively search out gays, but military leaders had a right to weed out enlistees who were openly gay. The compromise satisfied no one and raised questions about Clinton's commitment to his stated policy objectives.

Yet Clinton won on certain key domestic initiatives. He eked out a victory in Congress over the fiscal budget approved in 1994 and held out through one government shutdown after another in early 1996, after neither the Republican Congress nor the White House would give in on budget deliberations. Eventually the Republicans accepted a revised Clinton plan that handed the president both a public relations and legislative victory. Clinton also won the battle in 1993 over an inoculation program for schoolchildren, which in retrospect seemed to be a costly and unnecessary federal mandate.

Perhaps the most controversial legislative measure to be considered during Clinton's first term was the North American Free Trade Agreement (NAFTA). Proposed in 1993, the pact allows unencumbered trade among Mexico, the United States, and Canada. Conservatives worried that the agreement would flood the United States with inexpensive products from Mexico. Labor leaders felt that U.S. companies would be encouraged to relocate in Mexico, where workers earned lower hourly wages, or that U.S. laborers would have to compete constantly with inexpensive Mexican labor. This would result in loss of jobs for U.S. workers. The Clinton administration argued that the measure would be good for all three countries because Canada and Mexico would be just as interested in finished products and agricultural commodities as the United States would be in obtaining the less expensive consumer goods produced in Mexico. Still, NAFTA seemed to be a lost cause with such a powerful and unusual coalition lined up against it. Surprisingly, the president was able to squeak out a victory in Congress, and trade barriers were removed in North America. Three years later, the impact of NAFTA was still being measured, and Chile was seeking a similar agreement in South America.

The overriding success of the Clinton Administration was the reduction of the annual budget deficit, which dropped to $107 billion in 1996, the steady decline in joblessness, and the ever-strengthening U.S. economy in the mid-1990s. Unemployment figures tumbled monthly, and in late 1994 the stock market began a surge that lasted more than three years, more than doubling in that time. Three weeks after Clinton's second inauguration, the Dow-Jones Industrial Average soared past the 7,000 mark, less than two decades after the average had first broken through the 1,000 barrier. The U.S. workforce continued to separate into haves and have-nots, with the number of millionaires and billionaires increasing and the real income of most Americans declining. Full employment seemed to be an obtainable goal in the first term.

Yet Clinton was not able to follow through on his pledge during the 1992 campaign for a middle-class tax cut. Indeed, although he had abandoned poorer segments of the population with his middle-of-the-road rhetoric, Clinton could not satisfy middle-class voters either until such a package was passed in 1997. Dissatisfaction with the president's indecisiveness, his personal indiscretions, and his failed campaign pledges created problems.

Despite a firm rebuke at the polls in the 1994 midterm elections, Clinton had a power base from which to work. He needed only to convince Americans that the relative prosperity stemmed from his policies and initiatives and that the charges about his private life were nothing more than journalistic meddling with the facts or just so much Washington blather. Despite his personal shortcomings and the profusion of scandals and political imbroglios, Americans in 1996 were ready once again to vote their pocketbooks.

If political observers were disappointed in Clinton's apparent indecisiveness, his combative attitude toward the press, and his personal indiscretions, the public generally seemed more than willing to overlook them under the right circumstances. The shortcomings that seemed so important to reporters and commentators and on Capitol Hill merely disgusted Americans with the political process itself. There seemed to be a resigned acceptance of moral turpitude and government underhandedness. One was as bad as another, voters reasoned. To correct the ills of government, they voted against candidates instead of for them, and the topsy-turvy events of the 1994 and 1996 campaigns would punctuate clearly this growing negativity among voters.

NOTE

1. Stanley A. Renshon, *High Hopes: The Clinton Presidency and the Politics of Ambition* (New York: New York University Press, 1996), 109.

CHAPTER TWELVE

THE 1994 AND 1996 ELECTIONS

During the last quarter of the twentieth century, the nation drifted to the right politically. The liberal editorial policies of the nation's most influential newspapers—*The New York Times*, the *Washington Post*, and the *Los Angeles Times*—fell out of step with the attitudes of most Americans and this led to complaints about the "liberal press." Resentment against political coverage generally heightened. Americans in the 1990s wanted fewer government rules and restrictions and a legislative agenda friendly to middle-class wage earners and to middle-of-the road values. They also wanted media whose editorial arguments fit with that perspective. Many smaller and medium-sized newspapers stopped issuing political endorsements. Bill Clinton adroitly gauged this drift and separated himself from both the perceived liberal media and liberal issues.

The conservative atmosphere can be attributed to a complex combination of historical and socioeconomic trends that led to a restructuring of the political balance of power in Washington. The social safety net assembled in the affluent 1960s seemed burdensome in the parsimonious years of heavy budget deficits and declining U.S. world economic hegemony. Under the Clinton administration's proposed 1998 federal budget, 56 percent was pigeonholed for entitlement programs. The most expensive—social security, Medicaid, and Medicare—would cost forty cents of every federal tax dollar. Only 15 percent would be spent on defense and 15 percent, a quarter of a trillion dollars, on just the cost of paying interest on the national debt. Seventy-one percent of the proposed budget was earmarked for spending on social services or interest on debt.

Younger Americans were being asked to finance the retirement needs of the elderly, the health care and welfare costs of the indigent, and the interest on the accumulated debt obligation left over from the free-spending excesses of the 1980s. That trend was expected to accelerate when the baby boomers began to retire ten years later and the national debt reached $7 trillion and then $8 trillion. It was one thing to guarantee in the idealistic 1960s (when the 1969 budget showed a surplus) that all Americans would receive proper health care and a minimal standard of living. It was another to build up budget deficits in the 1980s and then to try to pay the national mortgage and social welfare expenses in the 1990s—this especially when the average income, adjusted for inflation, had decreased 20 percent from the previous generation.

Middle America had other grievances. Affirmative Action laws, in effect for thirty years, had not substantially changed the plight of African Americans. Some had risen to comfortable middle-class status, but the preponderance remained either unemployed or in subsistence-level jobs. Upper-echelon management positions and business ownership remained solidly in the hands of white males.

Similarly, women made strides in the job market between the late 1960s and the late 1990s, but the average female wage earner still took home seventy-six cents for every dollar earned by her male counterpart. The woman manager or professional was still a rare sight by and large. Equity was a matter of perspective. The gap had narrowed, but prejudice remained just below the surface, and women and minorities largely endured in the lower echelons of the workforce.

Still, a majority of Americans had grown weary of the unending rules and regulations aimed at changing this imbalance—guidelines that sometimes defied common sense. Job hiring quotas seemed to violate basic tenets of fairness. The constant worry over a labyrinth of bureaucratic rules drove business owners and managers to distraction. Pundits placed a sardonic name tag on the entire process of mandated fairness in both action and speech: political correctness.

When the rules of political correctness were applied too rigorously, outrage spilled over—ironically the same kind of anger that had met racism in the heyday of the civil rights movement in the South in the early 1960s. Perceptions had shifted 180 degrees. Californians in 1996 approved a referendum to eliminate state equal employment opportunity guidelines. The measure was immediately challenged in court, but the depth of the backlash against government-mandated affirmative action was unmistakable. In 1993, when a college student at Brown University yelled at three female students to be quiet while he was studying, he called them "water buffalos." He was suspended, because the university ruled that the name could be construed as racist. A six-year-old boy was placed in detention in 1996 for kissing a female fellow student on the cheek. School officials deemed such a gesture "sexual harassment." Guidelines with serious intents had been misconstrued by overzealous educators and government regulators. A few extreme examples of government intemperance were given excessive attention, because these extremes seemed to strike at the heart of middle-class dissatisfaction. Reading and hearing about such imprudent interpretations re-confirmed the already firmly held misgivings of many Americans. Although the Reagan era of business deregulation had passed, government was still big and bureaucracy was detested.

There were other basic concerns that seemed to rile voters in the 1990s. First, crime seemed never to be under control, though FBI figures indicated that violent crime had actually begun to decrease slightly in the mid-1990s. Many held the notion that violence was a by-product of a permissive society, dominated by liberal ideology.

Second, beset by government restrictions, some established corporations failed or moved their manufacturing facilities to other countries, leaving older, middle-income workers jobless. Third, family values seemed to be disappearing. Decreasing wages forced both parents into the workplace, splintering the family unit. The average American moved every three years, destroying the traditional bond between family and community. Fourth, religious values seemed at odds with the secular community, particularly in schools, where prayer had been banned, as had religious pageants and displays. Many had had enough of what they considered an environment hostile to basic values. Differences over legalized abortions also seemed to reinforce the division between religious and secular communities. Politicians ran from the label "liberal."

Bill Clinton's "new Democrat" spin had cleverly maneuvered him away from the liberal tarbrush on nearly every issue. The last thing Clinton wanted was to be linked with the failed Democratic leaders of the past: George McGovern, Ted Kennedy, Jimmy Carter, Walter Mondale, and Michael Dukakis. He carefully cultivated an anti-liberal image. He attacked the "knee-jerk, liberal media" to enhance his own claim to be a moderate, if not conservative, ideologue in an obvious ploy to win public sympathy.

Despite his rhetoric, Clinton's record showed that he was the most liberal president to serve in office since Lyndon Johnson. If the nation's leading newspapers were liberal editorially, their conflict with the most liberal president in three decades proved that their news coverage was more antagonistic to the White House generally than to conservative philosophy in particular.

To reinforce his moderate credentials, Clinton waffled at the appropriate times. He backed off his 1992 stand on retaining gays in the military, dodged the issue of equal employment opportunity, took tough public stances on crime but waited until his second term to propose additional spending, and developed an aid to education plan in 1997 based on income tax exemptions instead of direct aid—an obvious boon for the middle class but a virtually worthless gesture for the poor. At various times during his first term, he had proposed to balance the budget in six, seven, eight, or nine years. By the beginning of his second term in 1997, Clinton put forth a five-year spending plan that would provide a surplus by 2002, many of the budget reductions coming after he left office. Most voters do not follow such obfuscation carefully, however, and Clinton's ambivalence actually won him support. He was perceived as a champion of the middle class, though he had not followed through on his campaign promises, by and large, to address the problems of middle-income wage earners.

In 1994, however, Clinton's personal embarrassments and his suspected liberal leanings were still much on the minds of voters. Because of the conservative mood of the nation, the midterm elections of 1994 heralded what appeared to be a new era in Washington politics and a warning of a possible denouement to the Clinton presidency. The engineer behind the "revolution" of 1994 was conservative Congressman Newt Gingrich.

For more than sixty-five years, through war, depression, prosperity, and world dominance, the Democrats had controlled Congress as no other party ever had in American history. In the forty years between 1952 and 1992, voters elected Republican presidential candidates seven times and Democrats only four. But between 1933 and 1995, Democrats controlled both houses of Congress for all but three terms. Americans turned to their senators and representatives to provide entitlements and social services but generally elected Republican presidents to build strong defense systems and ride herd on the free-spending Congress. Yet the role of Congress in the late twentieth century was changing. In the 1980s and 1990s, the task was no longer how to divide the financial pie, but how to live with a smaller pie.

This atmosphere favored the more fiscally conservative Republicans on Capitol Hill, but until 1994 the altered national mood had yet to affect the balance of power in Congress. In the 103d Congress, the Democrats held a comfortable 256-to-176 advantage in the House (there was one independent and two vacancies) and a 56-to-44 majority in the Senate. The Republicans had grown accustomed to playing the role of the loyal opposition.

Gingrich wanted none of that. In the fall of 1994, he drew up an agenda for the 104th Congress and asked fellow Republican congressional candidates to sign their assent to this list of promises. Those who agreed were taking the extraordinary step of pledging in writing to pursue certain legislation, leaving no room to maneuver when they took office. In September 1994, 367 incumbents and challengers signed Gingrich's "Contract with America." The pact consisted of two sections, one addressing reforms in Congress and the other dealing with fiscal and social legislation.

The reforms included promises that Congress would not be exempted from laws applying to others (a mea culpa for abuse of congressional mailing privileges, among other things), a call for an independent audit of Congress for "waste, fraud, or abuse," reduction of congressional committees and limits on chair terms, a ban on proxy votes, a promise to hold no secret meetings, a pledge to invoke a three-fifths majority requirement for passage of a tax increase, and institution of an honest accounting in federal budgeting (Congress usually cooked the books to make the annual budget deficit appear to be less than it was). The contract also promised a balanced budget, a line-item veto so the president could remove the pork from otherwise desirable legislation, an anticrime package, welfare reform, tax deductions for working parents, removal of any American troops serving under U.N. auspices (a swipe at Clinton's uneven troop commitment policies), increased social security benefits, small business incentives, reform of product liability laws, and limits on congressional terms.

Included but not listed in the publicly promoted version of the contract were increased spending on the Reagan administration's Strategic Defense Initiative, capital gains tax cuts, tax cuts for business, and restrictions on abortion clinics. The last four items were rarely discussed openly.

Polls indicated in October 1994 that only 24 percent of Americans had even heard of the Contract with America and only 4 percent said they would be more likely to vote Republican because of it. Press reports on the Gingrich initiative were sketchy. The entire program was underreported and poorly explained in the media, but Gingrich was able to generate enthusiasm because the Clinton White House attacked the contract before public announcement of the details. Clinton claimed the contract would harm the poor and the middle class and favor business. The president's strategy backfired. He lent legitimacy to the Republican gambit. With that publicity, the Republicans were able to create a platform for the 1994 election campaign that established a distinction between the Republicans and the Democrats.

The GOP recorded a surprising landslide victory in November 1994, gaining control of both Houses. The Republicans picked up nine seats in the Senate for a 53-to-47 majority and fifty-four seats in the House for a 230 to 204 advantage (one seat went to an independent). The swing to the Republicans extended to the governors' mansions and to state legislatures nationwide. Democrats were repudiated at every level.

Had Americans bought the contract, so to speak? Because so few had even heard of it and even fewer knew of its provisions, it seems more likely that Americans were disgusted with the Clinton-led Democrats and wanted change. The existence of the contract may have had some impact, because it represented something out of the ordinary and tangible evidence to voters of a new direction, but it is unlikely that the public rushed to the GOP banner because of a list of poorly understood promises.

Once the 104th Congressional session opened, reforms proved to be the most difficult provisions for Capitol Hill to pass. Term limits were dealt one setback after another. As late as February 1997, the House defeated a version of the proposal to cap the number of years senators and representatives could serve. Welfare reform, a crime-fighting package, and increased social security payments did win limited approval, however.

Surprisingly, the one historic measure that gained acceptance was the line-item veto, something that strengthened the presidency and weakened Congress. Republicans apparently expected to win the White House in 1996. The veto affords the president greatly enhanced powers to eliminate wasteful spending, but also the authority to punish and reward members of Congress. The danger of the law is that provisions in future bills designed to boost federal spending in certain districts may be eliminated by the president's pen if those districts are represented by presidential adversaries. The president can use the veto for penance or political payment, as well as for elimination of wasteful spending. The long-term legacy of the 104th Congress may be the unheralded line-item veto, depending on how presidents of the twenty-first century use it and whether the courts consider it to be constitutional.

The contract met with reasonable success, but the whole process was poorly interpreted and understood, a significant failure of the Washington media. Instead, reporters focused on Gingrich and his personality. Many lauded him as a genius—a man behind one of the most astounding political success stories in history. For several months, the new Speaker of the House was quoted more often than the president, elevating the usually behind-the-scenes role of the House leader to that of a nationally recognized political figure. Voters wanted to know everything about this individual, from his politics to his personal life. They soon learned that his sister was gay and diametrically opposed to her brother's politics but that his mother was more like him.

The fascination with the family led to an embarrassing moment for the Gingriches, the White House, and CBS. Connie Chung had joined Dan Rather as co-anchor on the *CBS Evening News*, in 1993, but the experiment was not working well in 1995, and ratings had slipped. Chung, who had hosted morning shows and had been best known for her personality interviews, seemed out of place anchoring and introducing stories about Washington politics.

Newt Gingrich's nominal success with his Contract with America agenda and his swaggering demeanor had created friction between the Republican congressional leadership and the White House. It was a touchy relationship that was kept alive by polite daily phone calls back and forth from the Oval Office to the Speaker's office. In March 1995, just weeks into the 104th congressional session, Kathleen Gingrich, the speaker's mother, agreed to an interview with Chung. Shortly into the interview, Chung asked what Newt thought of Hillary Clinton. Mrs. Gingrich demurred, but Chung persisted. "Why don't you just whisper it to me. It's just between you and me," Chung assured Mrs. Gingrich.

"She's a bitch," Newt's mother whispered. In a normal voice, she added, "That's about the only thing he ever said about her." The comments were aired nationally. The Gingriches apologized to Mrs. Clinton, and, in the long run, it was Chung who lost. Her tactics drew public ire. CBS's sinking ratings were enough for network executives to re-consider the co-anchor experiment, but the public outcry over the interview was the final prod. Eight weeks later, Chung and CBS parted ways.

The nation too sustained damage. The incident had to affect the daily interaction between Gingrich and Clinton, and the entire exchange was unnecessary. It underscored the press fascination with personalities, but it also raised troubling questions about where network news was headed. Why was someone like Connie Chung placed in an anchor position with a major network in the first place? Her Hollywood persona and soft-news orientation only reiterated suspicions that ratings concerns had come to dominate national television news executives' judgments. Why not find a hard-nosed woman reporter for the anchor job, one who had earned the position?

Logically, if one interviews the mother of a powerful legislator, one asks about his personality and his values, so Americans can understand the philosophy of the influential person helping to create laws and allocate billions of dollars. Generating a division between the executive and legislative branches by coaxing an unwary elderly woman into revealing some privately held attitudes about the First Lady damaged CBS in particular, television news generally, and Washington reporting overall more than it harmed Gingrich or Mrs. Clinton. Yet it kindled even more trouble for Congress and the nation. Encouraging ill will between the Clintons and Gingrich served no national purpose. Even the most casual Washington observer seemed to grasp that. The Chung-Rather combination had not been working, and Chung, feeling the pressure to do something dramatic to boost ratings, had stepped across an ethical boundary.

These slips usually went unnoticed, but with the nation's two most powerful political personalities involved, the Chung miscue was laid bare for all to see. The gaffe, too, tarred Washington journalism generally, convincing many that the search for sensational stories had no bounds. It provided fodder for others who wrongly opposed opportunities for women journalists. Washington correspondents quickly disavowed Chung's behavior, but what remained was a public suspicion that too many in the press had probably used similar tactics in the past. That is not true, but in such sensational cases, the truth or falsity of the generalization is almost immaterial.

The Chung incident aside, Gingrich and the new Republican Congress set about establishing their own agenda, working with mixed results at realizing the promises of the Contract with America. Some mentioned Gingrich as a potential presidential nominee in 1996, talk that Gingrich alternately encouraged and discouraged. Many in the print and broadcast media began to write Clinton's political epitaph. The trend was unmistakable: the administration and the Democrats were on their way out.

Or were they? What Gingrich, the Republicans, and Washington reporters and pundits did not fully understand was that the 1994 vote was one of anger and resentment toward politics as usual, not necessarily a GOP mandate. After all, this backlash vote had awarded independent presidential candidate Ross Perot 19 percent of the ballots in 1992. The electorate was in a surly mood after the Bush administration. In a two-party system, voters can express their disgust in only two ways: vote for the other party or candidate, or stay home. In 1992, Clinton capitalized on Bush's unpopularity. In 1994, the conservative mood won out, and so did the Republicans. In 1996, voters simply stayed home or rotated back to Clinton.

The fluctuation between 1994 and 1996 had some other twists and turns. Clearly Clinton and his advisors were shocked by the midterm disaster. A sober Clinton told reporters that the voters had sent him a message, and he understood. Quickly, the president usurped credit for many Republican proposals, including an enacted bill that turned responsibility for welfare programs back to the states and set limits on how long recipients could collect benefits. Clinton revised and re-emphasized his vision of a balanced budget. He took the lead on crime, middle-class financial packages, and tax reform. What the Republicans had done was force Clinton into reviving the emphasis on the middle class, a focus that had appealed to voters in 1992. Clinton survived by carefully detaching himself from anything perceived as liberal. In the long run, the Republicans had done Clinton a favor.

Gingrich, meanwhile, crowed too much. He attached too much significance to his role in the 1994 balloting. His heavy-handed tactics during the new congressional session and his braggadocio cost him much popular support. The Clinton White House painted the Republicans as draconian penny-pinchers who would balance the budget at the expense of poor and middle-income taxpayers.

Meanwhile, reporters closely examined Gingrich's political fund-raising activity. In late 1996 they discovered that he had used charitable donations to fund political activities, including a politically oriented university class he taught. The infractions seemed minor, but Gingrich stalled a congressional inquiry with false denials and evasions, which he claimed later were due to misunderstandings. In a surprise move, he made an about-face in early 1997, admitting wrongdoing but still claiming the misspent money resulted from misunderstandings of the rules, not intentional fraud. He was reprimanded in January 1997 by Congress and fined $300,000, one of the most severe actions taken by the House against a Speaker. (Jim Wright, a Democrat from Texas, resigned in 1989 as Speaker after being accused of financial irregularities. Because of the resignation, the House never took any formal action against Wright, however.) Gingrich's problems reinforced the notion among the electorate that one party was as bad as another and one supposed reformer as duplicitous as the other.

The Republicans squandered their momentum in other ways. In late 1995, Clinton and the Congress deadlocked over the proposed 1996 budget. Clinton said he could not sign off on the Republican-sponsored version because it cut too deeply into needed programs. Republicans argued that their budget proposals reflected fiscal responsibility. Polls suggested that despite the conservative trend, voters thought the Republicans had gone too far. They generally sided with Clinton. The electorate wanted fiscal responsibility, but they wanted the price to be paid by someone else. It was an old and familiar story to lawmakers.

Traditionally, budget deadlocks are broken after closed meetings at the White House, where both sides give some ground to find a common solution. Neither party would budge in late 1995, and the stalemate dragged into the spring. Nonessential federal offices closed down periodically, including a two-week stretch at the end of 1995, until temporary spending measures could be passed. The impasse, finally resolved in April, roiled voters, especially when Congress agreed to pay the federal employees for their involuntary vacation time, in essence handing the taxpayers a huge bill for the standoff.

Yet in less than two years, the wily Clinton had turned the tables by usurping Republican proposals popular with the middle class and suggesting that the Republicans were out only to protect the wealthy. The budget impasse of 1996 seemed a microcosm of what had gone wrong with Washington politics and how the Republicans had misjudged the voters. In previous years, congressional leaders and the president railed publicly at each other and then quietly but good-naturedly negotiated agreements in private. This system broke down in 1996. The new, young Republican legislators brought to Washington by the 1994 landslide wanted no part of quiet compromises. They wanted change, the step forward that they had promised voters, but the stalemate damaged them and Washington generally. The short-lived hopes of the electorate had been dashed, and Washington politics sunk further into the public opinion mire.

THE 1996 ELECTION

As the 1996 primaries approached, the Republicans were hopeful that despite the budget fiasco, their conservative revolution would sweep them into the White House. Clinton yearned for no new scandals that might abort his comeback. He needed to convince voters that his brand of neopopulism was preferable to the Contract with America. News executives and correspondents were pining for an opportunity to report fully and incisively on a spirited campaign instead of being knocked back and forth by spin doctors.

Ever the fund-raising genius, Clinton had money to fight a vigorous general election campaign. Two of the Republicans had also stockpiled cash. Yet with all the turmoil of the 104th Congress and the instability in the White House, this was not to be a spirited campaign at all. In a time of flagging public interest, the 1996 presidential election represented a new low in public enthusiasm. Clinton faced no opposition, and Republicans seemed to concede the campaign to Bob Dole almost before it began.

Names came and went even before the primaries. Senators Arlen Specter of Pennsylvania and California Governor Pete Wilson announced their candidacies in March 1995 and then withdrew before the end of the year, months prior to the primaries. Former Vice President Dan Quayle, suffering from health problems and a tarnished public image, declined to run. So did Gingrich, former Secretary of Defense Dick Cheney, and former New York congressman Jack Kemp. Expectations built toward a campaign by Colin Powell, former chairman of the Joint Chiefs of Staff and the respected hero of the Persian Gulf War. Powell was a new face in politics, an African American with Republican leanings, and an intelligent person whose autobiography was a best-seller. Yet he too announced in November 1995 that he would not be a candidate.

That left Senate Majority Leader Bob Dole; newspaper magazine heir Steve Forbes; former speechwriter and discussion show host Patrick Buchanan; Texas Senator Phil Gramm; former Tennessee Governor Lamar Alexander; Senator

Richard Lugar of Indiana; Congressman Robert Dornan of California; Morry Taylor, a tire firm executive; and Alan Keyes, a former State Department official. It was a crowded field perhaps, but the names of the seven who decided not to run by and large provided a more impressive list. With the exceptions of Gramm and Dole, the field was crammed with long-shot dreamers, a repetition of the quality of competition in the 1992 Democratic primaries.

Dole found himself in a no-win situation. A heavy favorite he had to worry about: (1) voter apathy; (2) a Jimmy Carteresque dark horse who might come from nowhere to capture public favor; (3) a mediocre showing in early primaries that would undermine his name recognition; (4) hard-edged attacks from desperate opponents who had nothing to lose; (5) a long history in the Senate with an established record that could be easily attacked; (6) a reputation as a hatchet man that he earned during the 1976 vice presidential debates; and (7) the loser tag attached to his career after three unsuccessful runs for the presidency or vice presidency.

The Senate Majority Leader had been around a long time—much longer than Clinton—and his fourth time was not a charm. Gramm had been collecting campaign contributions for nearly a year, and he had plenty of money to sink into his campaign. Because of his war chest and because he co-sponsored the proposed budget balancing amendment in 1986, it was anticipated that Gramm would provide the stiffest competition. Not so.

In the long gauntlet of fifty-six primaries and caucuses, voters react early to catch phrases and simple arguments. Over the length of the primary season, they return to name recognition, unless the leading candidate commits some horrendous mistake. Dole did not do so.

Yet the expected Dole victory in Iowa, a neighboring state of his native Kansas, was narrow: 26 percent to Buchanan's 23 percent. Dole had beaten George Bush badly in Iowa four years earlier. Gramm's money had not helped him at all, but Buchanan's run in 1992, his television show, and his ultraconservative pitch had been more valuable than most observers had thought. Gramm's staid personality and complex fiscal policy ideas did not play well on television. He dropped out after the miserable showing in Iowa. There was trouble for Dole in New Hampshire, however.

Forbes, whose main claim to fame was his family's magazine fortune and the column of opinion he wrote for *Forbes* magazine, struck a sensitive nerve with his tax proposal: the 17 percent flat tax. Everyone should benefit from a flat rate of income tax, Forbes argued. The idea, simple and direct, appealed to voters who had grown weary of the complex income tax system that seemed to favor large corporations. Most middle Americans did not pay 17 percent of their income to the federal treasury in 1996, however. They paid the 15 percent rate, which came to 10 percent or less after deductions. Corporations and wealthy individuals paid at a rate of as much as 31 percent before deductions. They would receive the greatest benefit from the flat tax. Apparently reporters did not understand the tax code because they seemed intrigued by the Forbes concept.

Perhaps in an effort not to concede the election to Dole (which is what had been occurring in the earliest days of the campaign), both *Time* and *Newsweek* carried Forbes' picture on their covers on January 22, 1996. There was a mighty effort by television, magazines, and newspapers to make something of the Forbes campaign.

New Hampshire voters did not buy it. They did not buy Dole either. Buchanan won with 28 percent to Dole's 27, Alexander's 23, and Forbes's 12. But as with the Democrats in 1992, the Iowa caucuses and the New Hampshire primary had lost their significance.

Reporters did not catch on. They emphasized that Dole was heading toward defeat and that he could survive only one or two more primary losses (there were fifty-four left!). Most of what was written about the campaign in late February was myth. Alexander dropped out two weeks later, and Dole buried Buchanan in New York and then in seven Super Tuesday states on March 12. Once again Super Tuesday had replaced New Hampshire primary day as the pivotal primary election day. Within a month of the Iowa caucuses, Dole was thinking about the general election and his choice for running mate. Public attention to the primary campaign lasted only from New Year's Day until mid-March, one of the shortest attention spans since 1956.

Media coverage reflected not only truncated public interest but an incredible lack of historical overview. Lessons from previous campaigns seemed lost on reporters. Actually, the public really did not care much either way, and news judgment reflected that. Evening news programs rarely led with primary campaign stories. Newspapers often buried coverage on inside pages. By the time voters in some larger states cast their ballots after Super Tuesday, interest had waned so drastically that the results hardly drew any notice. Media and voters were quickly bored with the entire process. Both the primary and general election seasons of 1996 brought yawns of indifference.

The intent of expanding the number of primaries and caucuses was to allow voters to influence the party's choice directly, but the system was not working. The cost of campaigning in so many states, in terms of both money and human energy, was limiting the field of candidates. Many did not want to face the task of raising $56 million for a primary campaign and another $100 million for the general election and then have to campaign eighteen hours a day for nearly an entire year.

Too many decisions were dictated by the new primary system. Candidates needed good showings in early primaries to qualify for federal matching funds. They also craved media attention because the party hierarchy had little to say about nominees anymore. The message had to be delivered through advertising and news coverage, mostly by television. Candidates concentrated on putting their spin on the news and on developing slick advertising campaigns instead of devising strategies on issues. The need for millions of dollars in cash for campaigning was keeping qualified candidates away and forcing those in the race to do well or drop out quickly, so many voters in the later primaries had no voice in their party's choice for the presidency. At least with state party conventions, someone from the state influenced the choice for a nominee. With the open primary and caucuses, the issue was settled before anyone in many states had a vote. As a result, in 1996 many states moved their primaries to earlier dates to avoid being left to vote on meaningless contests, but the tactic did not work, because the campaign was over by Super Tuesday anyway.

One side advantage of the brief primary campaign was its lack of repetition in coverage. The quick end to the Republican competition set an early confrontation between Dole and Clinton. In August, Ross Perot won the nomination of the Reform Party, the organization he had helped to found, once again creating a three-way campaign. Coverage between late March and August all but disappeared, creating a less tedious campaign than the long, drawn-out affairs in 1992 and 1988.

It was clear from midspring that the Republican choice was a mistake and that Perot did not appeal to as many voters in 1996 as in 1992. It was also apparent that in the midst of the greatest surge in the history of the U.S. stock market and with unemployment at historic lows, Clinton's personal shortcomings and his erratic approach to issues would be overshadowed by gut issues.

Still, enough voters were disappointed with Clinton's personal behavior and his waffling on issues that the electorate might have replaced him had they been offered just the right person—a new face with anti-Washington credentials. Colin Powell was probably the logical choice, but he stayed home. Usually a strong economy is a ticket to re-election, but the benefits of the stock market boom had not extended to the working classes by and large, and there was still much worry about job security and the future of the economy. If there was full employment, it was 1990s style, with many workers stuck in low-paying jobs.

But Dole failed miserably to capitalize on these shortcomings. His was one of the most familiar faces Washington had to offer: "Beltway Bob." Three times voters had rejected Dole's ambitions for the presidency or vice presidency. As Majority Leader in the Senate, he had been a key player in the deadlock over the budget and the periodic, embarrassing government shutdowns.

Clinton may have been the quintessential political manipulator, whose questionable behavior gave Washington a bad name, but Dole appeared to voters not to be much better. Tweedledee or Tweedledum. From the moment the primaries ended, Dole faced both a strong economy and an indifferent voting public that failed to discriminate between the two major party candidates.

Dole strategists struggled. They needed something dramatic to draw positive media attention and convince voters that their candidate indeed represented a bold, new direction. In mid-May, Dole announced that he would resign from the Senate to concentrate on the campaign. A story or two. Weeks later, he announced that if elected, he would cut taxes by 15 percent and still balance the budget. A serious mistake. Polls showed that nearly two-thirds of the electorate did not believe him, particularly because he offered only vague generalities as to how this would be accomplished. Voters had been educated, more or less, about budget deficits and knew of the danger of accepting tax cuts without detailed plans for reducing spending. The $5 trillion accumulated deficit piled up mostly under Republican presidents in the 1980s and 1990s and was a contributing factor to the general public skepticism. Promises of tax cuts had lost their appeal.

The improbable Clinton juggernaut, badly wounded in 1994, nevertheless had recovered and moved toward an unlikely conclusion. With all his problems, the president still seemed untouchable in the summer of 1996. Even when White House political adviser Dick Morris resigned in August just before the convention, voters avidly read the titillating details but seemed unaffected. A tabloid reported that Morris, who was married, had had a year-long affair with a former prostitute, Sherry Rowlands. It was revealed that she had listened occasionally to telephone conversations between Morris and Clinton, raising questions about whether national security had been compromised. By August 1996, however, stories about sexual escapades in the Clinton Administration hardly constituted startling news, and Morris seemed not to damage Clinton.

Dole hoped the convention might provide him with a forum to reverse voters' leanings. Yet for nearly thirty years, the drama had escaped major party conventions. The turgid displays of support for the candidates and meaningless roll calls left television viewers grabbing for their channel changers. The 1996 versions of the conventions were so dull that media and political observers wondered incredulously about the impact on the democratic process and the future of the conventions themselves. Would there be conventions in the next century after the low ratings in 1996? Reporters interviewed each other to find out if there ever had been such indifference. No, there never had been. The only drama came from the Republican gathering, as the faithful waited to hear Dole's choice for running mate: Jack Kemp. The moderate Kemp, a former professional football quarterback, former congressman, and former Secretary of Housing and Urban Development, had eschewed a run at the nomination himself. It was surprising that he would accept a spot on the ticket, but nevertheless the well-regarded New Yorker seemed to be a good choice.

Yet if Dole expected a boost from the coverage of the convention, or from his proposed tax cut, or from the negative publicity surrounding Dick Morris's resignation, or from Kemp's addition to the ticket, he was to be disappointed. Clinton held a fifteen-point lead in the polls throughout the summer and kept an iron grip on that lead in the fall.

Three debates provided no dramatic shift either. Amazingly, after the first one, commentators and supporters criticized Dole for not being sleazier and not harping at Clinton for his and his aides' personal indiscretions. Dole had been roundly criticized for his hammering of Carter in 1976, and now he was being lambasted for *not* pursuing such a tack. The second debate format was a town hall meeting, where voters asked the questions. This added a democratic ambiance to the entire process, but the questions were of poor quality and the debate unrevealing.

In all, general election campaign coverage picked up where the primaries left off. Often, daily television news coverage relegated the campaign to the third or fourth story. Stump speeches drew little or no interest. It was as if someone had thrown a party but no one had deigned to come.

Some positive trends in news coverage did develop, however. Poll reporting was muted because the results hardly seemed to change. Since the 1988 campaign, print and broadcast media executives had been searching for a way to downplay the horse-race coverage and emphasize discussion of issues. Many finally did something about this in 1996. Some newspapers grouped together and submitted written, issue-oriented questions to both candidates with mixed results. The *Chicago Sun-Times* offered both candidates two full pages of its newspaper to offer whatever statements they wished to make on the issues and the campaign. Both candidates largely reiterated meaningless campaign statements, and disappointed *Sun-Times* editorial writers lambasted both Dole and Clinton for not being more forthcoming. Networks offered free airtime for both candidates during broadcasts a week before the election. They were allowed to speak to the voters with no restrictions. Again, they largely reiterated their campaign themes.

At various points in the campaign, writers attempted to make the generational difference between Clinton and Dole an issue. Voters seemed uninterested. Dole drew World War II–era voters not because of his age but because of his politics, and Clinton's appeal to baby boomers seemed to relate more to his guidance of the economy than his age.

What had been low-key but reasonably responsible reporting on the election ended with a disappointing performance by ABC's David Brinkley. Brinkley, a fixture in national television news for forty years, was retiring from most of his news reporting duties. At the end of a long election night, he said on camera that Clinton was "a bore" with "not a creative bone in his body." He indicated that he was disappointed with the Clinton victory and that the president's victory speech in Little Rock was "one of the worst things I've ever heard."[1] He apologized to Clinton days later, but the damage was done. Brinkley's gaffe was disappointing not only to viewers but to journalists, who had been criticized by Clinton as biased and unfair to his campaign. Although Brinkley was only one person speaking after a long night on camera, his remarks came at an unfortunate time when press-president antagonism was at its height, and his words seemed to confirm suspicions among Clinton supporters about the entrenched animosity in journalistic circles.

Television advertising was plentiful, but the negative attack ads and the positive, biographical sketches were old hat. With many states comfortably in the Clinton camp, Dole did not even advertise in several areas, and much money was spent to no avail on both sides.

In the end, Perot was hardly a factor, and Clinton maintained a comfortable lead from start to finish. In the final days of the contest, Dole announced that he would campaign nonstop, visiting state after state with virtually no sleep (much to horror of the reporters following the campaign), but the innovations and energy Dole tried to bring to the race were lost on the voters.

Clinton won easily with 49 percent to Dole's 41 percent and Perot's 8 percent, the rest of the votes scattered among minor-party candidates. Clinton carried thirty-one states and the District of Columbia for 379 electoral votes, Dole nineteen states and 159 electoral votes, and Perot no states or electoral votes. The Republicans picked up two seats in the Senate and lost nine in the House but kept majorities in both chambers for the second consecutive term for the first time since 1928. The slim majority in the House was the smallest for either party since 1953.

The low voter turnout set records. It was less than 49 percent, down 6 percent from 1992 and the lowest since 1824. Not since the moribund campaigns of 1920 and 1924, where voters elected Warren Harding and Calvin Coolidge, respectively, had the turnout dipped near the 49 percent mark. If Clinton were to finish his term to inaugural day 2001, he would be only the sixth president in 164 years to serve two full consecutive terms in office. Ironically, three of those presidents would have served in the last half of the twentieth century, when the presidency underwent turmoil and transition.

As in 1992 and 1988, the election revolved on the state of the economy. Always a major factor in presidential elections, pocketbook issues had come to dominate voter preferences in the last elections of the twentieth century. Yet the 1996 election was more complicated than that simple assessment. Primaries had come to lose their contentiousness, and media influence was left in limbo. The concept that "television decides who gets elected" was losing its credibility. Media, especially television, would always be important, if for no other reason than that is how voters most frequently get to see and hear candidates and read about them.

Yet the primping of the Forbes candidacy, the unending focus on reports of infidelity and financial irregularities, and the attention paid to the differences between Dole's and Clinton's ages in stories about the campaign suggest that reporters looked at the 1996 campaign differently from other voters. Main Street seemed more interested in tomorrow's job prospects than the personal foibles of the candidates. In March 1997 a poll indicated that 60 percent of those sampled thought Clinton was doing a good job, while a majority found disfavor with his personal conduct.

Coverage of Clinton in 1997 continued to focus heavily on his sexual adventures and his personal financial woes. Indeed, soon after the Clinton inauguration, stories revealed that many heavy campaign contributors had stayed at the White House and slept in the Lincoln Bedroom as a reward for their support. To avoid federal fund-raising violations, Clinton aides waited until after the guests had left the White House to contact them for donations. Using the White House for fund raising is illegal. The actions may have been technically legal because the requests for contributions came later, but certainly they were unethical.

It was also reported that a Clinton friend who owned a restaurant in Little Rock, Charles Yah Lin Trie, had delivered $640,000 in contributions to a private legal defense fund for both Bill and Hillary Clinton. The money was returned. The Democratic National Party also remitted more than $1 million in contributions raised by Trie and John Huang, an Asian-American Democratic fund raiser. Later reports revealed that Chinese arms dealers from the People's Republic of China, one of whom was accused of gun smuggling, had stayed at the White House during the campaign. It is illegal for candidates and parties to accept funding from foreign nationals, and there were fears that the Chinese nationals who stayed at the White House might have compromised diplomatic security. In his usual style, Clinton downplayed the revelations and partly came clean by admitting that mistakes had been made, but claiming that they would be corrected.

Clinton tried to start with a clean slate with Congress, speaking in concili-atory terms and appointing seven new cabinet members, including a Repub-lican, former Maine Senator William Cohen. U.N. Representative Madeleine Albright was named as the first woman secretary of state.

Americans in the 1990s traveled quickly from the rejection of an incumbent Republican president, to the acceptance of a Republican Congress, to rejection of a Republican presidential candidate and acceptance of a tarnished Demo-cratic incumbent. Clinton had made certain between 1994 and 1996 that the voters perceived his administration as being responsible for the rosy financial picture. Both journalists and political opponents badly underestimated Clin-ton's political skills and his ability to mask his weaknesses. Both Clinton and the Republicans misunderstood the depth of the disenchantment of the electorate, as evidenced by the low voter turnout. Clinton's bad image had dogged him throughout his first four years in office, but taxpayers were concerned about more basic issues. They clearly chose substance, ignoring image in 1996, a direct turnaround from the Reagan years. The two continuous threads from the two presidencies were the deteriorating information flow between press and president and voter preference for the incumbent when economic conditions were positive. The results of the 1994 and 1996 elections suggest that both press and president will be expected to pay attention to basic middle-class concerns in the near future.

The press in the 1994 and 1996 campaigns illustrated a desire to return to more informative, issue-oriented coverage but stumbled badly in under-standing the meanings of the two elections. The usual emphasis on short-term events and the knee-jerk conclusions about the meaning of the 1994 landslide suggest that reporters did not perceive either the depth of the disenchantment with the electoral process or voter concerns with gut issues.

NOTE

1. Associated Press wire story, November 6, 1996.

EPILOGUE

From Kennedy to Clinton, the presidency changed in the last forty years of the twentieth century, especially the presidential relationship with the nation's news media. So did the mind-sets of Americans and their ideas about the presidency. The future promises to be a continuation of the short-term trend in the 1980s and 1990s.

Costly election campaigns and aggressive reporting about the president's personal affairs will continue to limit the field of candidates interested in seeking the White House, ensuring the likelihood that weak presidents will continue to occupy the Oval Office for the foreseeable future. Certainly Clinton and his wife, Hillary, will be dogged by allegations and investigations for the remaining years of his term in office. Independent Whitewater counsel Kenneth Starr announced his resignation in 1997 and then changed his mind when a furor followed, so the widespread investigation will continue to its conclusion. Either way, Clinton's bad image makes him an unlikely candidate for restoration of the prestige of the presidency.

White House reporters will likely have to turn to sources other than daily press briefings for their stories, increasing the chances that the press corps and the chief executive will drift further apart. During the latter part of Clinton's first term, Vice President Al Gore used online computer networks to communicate with voters directly. The 1997 inaugural was transmitted online instantaneously for the first time in history. Computer technology will change delivery systems in the first decade of the twenty-first century, perhaps making Washington reporters' jobs even more insecure, while placing another wedge between them and the White House.

Yet Kennedy had entered the White House amid uncertain support, a new era of communication, and a measure of press cynicism. On the surface, it seems that it will take only one president with exceptional communication skills and above-average political acumen and diplomatic erudition to restore a positive intermingling among press, president, and public. This will be more complicated than it was in Kennedy's time, however, because mind-sets have changed.

Kennedy's personal indiscretions, after all, were worse than Clinton's, and yet he owed his popularity in part to the fact that he served in a different era, when personal excesses were rarely the subject of press stories and the public was willing to forgive the president almost anything. Any successful twenty-first century president will need to know how to communicate with the public and press, raise campaign money quickly and effectively, and negotiate complex legislative and international compromises in an atmosphere of contentiousness. In addition, he or she will have to have conducted an exemplary personal life before and during the term of office and be relatively free of financial irregularities in a world where money buys influence everywhere. That Clinton was able to win re-election despite his personal shortcomings is not necessarily a positive sign for the future. The low voter turnout in 1996 and the decreasing interest in news from Washington means that Americans have concluded that presidential candidates, by and large, are all not to be trusted.

The national news media and the White House press corps also face problems. The generalizations about the press corps suggest that the public needs to be better educated about what journalists generally and Washington reporters in particular do for a living. A Louis Harris poll of 3,004 adults, commissioned by the Center for Media and Public Affairs in November 1996, found that 42 percent felt that newspersons were more arrogant than most other Americans, 31 percent thought journalists were more cynical, 33 percent found them less compassionate, 34 percent said they were more biased, and 20 percent said they were less honest. Only 51 percent said that the media "usually get the facts straight." Fifty-two percent said the media abuse the First Amendment.[1]

Clearly the press had just as many detractors and public relations problems as the presidency as Clinton began his second term. Part of this relates to the general disenchantment with institutions in the post-Vietnam and post-Watergate days. Part of it has to do with the close scrutiny that has been given to both the press and the presidency in recent years. During Kennedy's time, few looked closely at the process and persons who reported on Washington. The number of networks and print organizations constantly reporting on each other and the presidency has brought heightened examination of both. If one looks too closely at anything, one finds warts.

Still, one of the most important aspects of the modern presidency, perhaps only second to the relationship between president and Congress, is the relationship between the White House and the nation's news media. Mutual anger and resentment will only further undermine the confidence of the preponderance of voters. Certainly the excesses of the Nixon, Johnson, and Clinton Administrations have overturned the pedestal on which such revered leaders as Kennedy once sat. Partly responsible for these failures was the barely masked resentment each president exhibited toward his antagonists, the White House press corps.

In the event of an economic downturn or a world crisis, presidents of the future will need the confidence of the electorate and the trust of the press corps to protect the nation from disaster. In the long run, this is the essence of the importance of the press and the presidency. At such moments, there is a very real need for proper lines of communication between the White House and the nation with the assistance of a responsible, critical, and conscientious news media. It is for those moments that the press and the president need to re-evaluate their relationship. This relationship, after all, is no longer marked by a few reporters coming by the White House to ask questions once or twice a month, as was the case in William McKinley's time at the end of the nineteenth century. How this process succeeds or fails in the twenty-first century can determine how the world will fare for the next generation.

NOTE

1. Associated Press wire story, December 4, 1996.

SELECTED BIBLIOGRAPHY

Aaron, Jan. *Gerald Ford: President of Destiny*. New York: Fleet, 1975.

Abernathy, M. Glenn, Dilys Hill, and Phil Williams, eds. *The Carter Years: The President and Policy Making*. New York: St. Martin's Press, 1984.

Abrahms, Herbert L. *"The President Has Been Shot": Disability and the 25th Amendment in the Aftermath of the Attempted Assassination of Ronald Reagan*. New York: W. W. Norton, 1992.

Ambrose, Stephen. *Nixon: The Education of a Politician*. New York: Simon & Schuster, 1987.

Anderson, Jack, and James Boyd. *Confessions of a Muckraker*. New York: Random House, 1979.

Barret, Laurence I. *Gambling with History: Ronald Reagan in the White House*. New York: Penguin, 1984.

Bartley, Robert L., ed. *Whitewater*. New York: Dow Jones, 1994.

Baughman, James L. *The Republic of Mass Culture: Journalism, Filmmaking, and Broadcasting in America Since 1941*. Baltimore: Johns Hopkins University Press, 1992.

Belin, David. *Final Disclosure: The Truth About the Assassination of President Kennedy*. New York: Charles Scribner's Sons, 1988.

Bell, Coral. *The Reagan Paradox: American Foreign Policy in the 1980s*. New Brunswick, N.J.: Rutgers University Press, 1989.

Ben-Veniste, Richard. *Stonewall: The Real Story of the Watergate Prosecution*. New York: Simon & Schuster, 1977.

Berger, Meyer. *The Story of the* New York Times, *1851–1951*. New York: Simon & Schuster, 1970.

Berman, Larry, ed. *Looking Back on the Reagan Presidency*. Baltimore: Johns Hopkins University Press, 1990.

Bernstein, Carl, and Bob Woodward. *All the President's Men*. New York: Simon & Schuster, 1974.

Bernstein, Irving. *Guns or Butter: The Presidency of Lyndon Johnson*. New York: Oxford University Press, 1996.

Berry, Joseph P. *John F. Kennedy and the Media: The First Television President*. Lanham, Md.: University Press of America, 1987.

Bishop, Jim. *A Day in the Life of President Kennedy*. New York: Random House, 1964.

Bjork, Rebecca S. *The Strategic Defense Initiative: Symbolic Containment of the Nuclear Threat*. Albany: State University of New York Press, 1992.

Blumenthal, Sidney. *Our Long National Dream: A Political Pageant of the Reagan Era*. New York: Harper & Row, 1988.

Blumenthal, Sidney, and Thomas Byrne Edsall, eds. *The Reagan Legacy*. New York: Pantheon, 1988.

Boyarsky, Bill. *Ronald Reagan: His Life and Rise to the Presidency*. New York: Random House, 1981.

Bradlee, Benjamin C. *Conversations with Kennedy*. New York: Norton, 1975.

Brands, H. W. *The Wages of Globalism: Lyndon Johnson and the Limits of American Power*. New York: Oxford University Press, 1995.

Broder, David S., and Bob Woodward. *The Man Who Would Be President: Dan Quayle*. New York: Simon & Schuster, 1992.

Brody, Fawn. *Richard Nixon: The Shaping of His Character*. New York: W. W. Norton, 1981.

Bush, Barbara. *Barbara Bush: A Memoir*. New York: Charles Scribner's Sons, 1994.

Calvocoressi, Peter. *World Politics Since 1945*. London: Longman, 1982.

Campbell, Colin, and Bert A. Rockman, eds. *The Clinton Presidency: First Appraisals*. Chatham, N.J.: Chatham House Publishers, 1996.

Cannon, James. *Time and Chance: Gerald Ford's Appointment with Destiny*. New York: Collins, 1994.

Cannon, Lou. *President Reagan: The Role of a Lifetime*. New York: Simon & Schuster, 1991.

Cantril, Albert H., ed. *Polling on the Issues: Twenty-One Perspectives on the Role of Opinion Polls in the Making of Public Policy*. Washington, D.C.: Seven Locks Press, 1980.

Caro, Robert A. *The Years of Lyndon Johnson: The Path to Power*. New York: Knopf, 1982.

Carter, Jimmy. *Keeping the Faith: Memoirs of a President*. New York: Bantam Books, 1982.

Casserly, John J. *The Ford White House: The Diary of a Speechwriter*. Boulder, Colo.: Associated University Press, 1977.

Chase, Harold W., and Allen H. Lerman, eds. *Kennedy and the Press: The News Conferences*. New York: Crowell, 1965.

Christopher, Warren. *American Hostages in Iran: The Conduct of a Crisis*. New Haven, Conn.: Yale University Press, 1985.

Cohen, Bernard C. *The Press and Foreign Policy*. Princeton, N.J.: Princeton University Press, 1963.

Colson, Charles. *Born Again*. Old Tappan, N.J.: Chosen Books, 1976.

Conkin, Paul. *Big Daddy from the Pedernales: Lyndon Baines Johnson*. Boston: Twayne, 1986.

Cornwell, Elmer E. *Presidential Leadership of Public Opinion*. Bloomington: Indiana University Press, 1956.

Cronin, Thomas E. *The State of the Presidency*. Boston: Little, Brown, 1975.

Crouse, Timothy. *The Boys on the Bus: Riding with the Campaign Press Corps*. New York: Random House, 1973.

Dallek, Robert. *Lone Star Rising: Lyndon Johnson and His Times 1908–1960*. New York: Oxford University Press, 1991.

Deakin, James. *Johnson's Credibility Gap*. Washington, D.C.: Public Affairs Press, 1968.

————. *Straight Stuff: The Reporters, the White House and the Truth*. New York: William Morrow, 1984.

Dean, John. *Blind Ambition*. New York: Simon & Schuster, 1976.

Deaver, Michael K. *Behind the Scenes*. New York: Morrow, 1987.

Denton, Robert E., Jr. *The Primetime Presidency of Ronald Reagan: The Era of the Television Presidency*. New York: Praeger, 1988.

————, ed. *The 1992 Presidential Campaign: A Communication Perspective*. Westport, Conn.: Praeger, 1994.

Denton, Robert E., Jr., and Dan F. Hahn. *Presidential Communication, Description, and Analysis*. New York: Praeger, 1986.

Desmond, Robert W. *The Press and World Affairs*. New York: Arno, 1972.

Dickerson, Nancy. *Among Those Present: A Reporter's Viewpoint of Twenty-Five Years in Washington*. New York: Random House, 1976.

Dinsmore, Herman H. *All the News that Fits: A Critical Analysis of the News and Editorial Content of the* New York Times. New Rochelle, N.Y.: Arlington House, 1969.

Donaldson, Sam. *Hold On, Mr. President*. New York: Random House, 1987.

Donovan, Hedley. *Roosevelt to Reagan: A Reporter's Encounters with Nine Presidents*. New York: Harper & Row, 1985.

Dover, E. D. *Presidential Elections in the Television Age*. Westport, Conn.: Praeger, 1994.

Drew, Elizabeth. *Portrait of an Election: The 1980 Presidential Campaign*. New York: Simon & Schuster, 1981.

————. *On the Edge: The Clinton Presidency*. New York: Simon & Schuster, 1994.

————. *Showdown: The Struggle Between the Gingrich Congress and the Clinton White House*. New York: Simon & Schuster, 1996.

Edwards, George. *The Public Presidency*. New York: St. Martin's, 1983.

Ehrlichman, John. *Witness to Power*. New York: Simon & Schuster, 1982.

Emery, Edwin, and Michael Emery. *The Press and America: An Interpretive History of the Mass Media*. 5th ed. Englewood Cliffs, N.J.: Prentice-Hall, 1984.

Erickson, Paul D. *Reagan Speaks: The Making of an American Myth*. New York: New York University Press, 1985.

Evans, Rowland, and Robert Novak. *Lyndon B. Johnson: The Exercise of Power*. New York: New American Library, 1966.

Fairlie, Henry. *The Kennedy Promise: The Politics of Expectation*. Garden City, N.Y.: Doubleday, 1973.

Firestone, Bernard J., and Alexej Ugrinsky, eds. *Gerald R. Ford and the Politics of Post-Watergate Washington*. Westport, Conn.: Greenwood, 1993.

Fitzwater, Marlin. *Call the Briefing! Bush and Reagan, Sam and Helen: A Decade with Presidents and the Press*. New York: Random House, 1995.

Ford, Betty. *The Times of My Life*. New York: Harper & Row, 1978.

Ford, Gerald. *A Time to Heal: The Autobiography of Gerald R. Ford*. New York: Harper & Row, 1979.

Frost, David. *"I Gave Them a Sword": Behind the Scenes of the Nixon Interviews*. New York: Morrow, 1978.

Gallup, George H. *The Gallup Poll: Public Opinion 1935–1971*. Vol. 1. New York: Random House, 1972.

Gardner, Lloyd C. *Pay Any Price: Lyndon Johnson and the Wars for Vietnam*. Chicago: I. R. Dee, 1995.

Gelman, Harry. *The Brezhnev Politburo and the Decline of Detente*. Ithaca, N.Y.: Cornell University Press, 1984.

Germond, Jack W., and Jules Witcover. *Blue Smoke and Mirrors: How Reagan Won and Why Carter Lost the Election of 1980*. New York: Viking, 1981.

————. *Wake Us When It's Over: Presidential Politics of 1984*. New York: Macmillan, 1985.

Glad, Betty. *Jimmy Carter: In Search of the Great White House*. New York: W. W. Norton, 1980.

Goldman, Eric F. *The Tragedy of Lyndon Johnson*. New York: Alfred A. Knopf, 1969.

Gordon, Gregory, and Ronald E. Cohn. *Down to the Wire: UPI's Fight for Survival*. New York: McGraw-Hill, 1990.

Graber, Doris. *Mass Media and American Politics*. 2d ed. Washington, D.C.: CQ Press, 1984.

Greenburg, Bradley S., and Edwin B. Parker, eds. *The Kennedy Assassination and the American Public: Social Communication in Crisis*. Stanford, Calif.: Stanford University Press, 1965.

Greene, John Robert. *The Presidency of Gerald R. Ford*. Lawrence: University of Kansas Press, 1995.

Gross, Martin L. *The Great Whitewater Fiasco: An American Tale of Money, Power, and Politics*. New York: Ballantine, 1994.

Grossman, Michael Baruch, and Martha Joynt Kumar. *Portraying the President.* Baltimore: Johns Hopkins University Press, 1981.

Gutline, Myra. *The President's Partner: The First Lady in the Twentieth Century.* Westport, Conn.: Greenwood, 1989.

Hagstrom, Jerry. *Beyond Reagan: The New Landscape of American Politics.* New York: W. W. Norton, 1988.

Haig, Alexander M., Jr. *Inner Circles: How America Changed the World.* New York: Warner, 1992.

Halberstam, David. *The Best and the Brightest.* Greenwich, Conn.: Fawcett, 1973.

————. *The Powers That Be.* New York: Alfred A. Knopf, 1979.

Haldeman, H. R. *The Ends of Power.* New York: New York Times Books, 1978.

Hannaford, Peter D. *The Reagans: A Political Portrait.* New York: Coward-McCann, 1983.

Hartmann, Robert. *Palace Politics: An Insider's Account of the Ford Years.* New York: McGraw-Hill, 1980.

Harwood, Richard. *The Pursuit of the Presidency 1980.* New York: Berkley, 1980.

Harwood, Richard, and Haynes Johnson. *Lyndon.* New York: Praeger, 1973.

Herring, George C. *America's Longest War: The United States and Vietnam, 1950– 1975.* 2d Ed. New York: Alfred A. Knopf, 1986.

Hertsgaard, Mark. *On Bended Knee: The Press and the Reagan Presidency.* New York: Farrar, Straus & Giroux, 1988.

Hill, Dilys M., Raymond A. Moore, and Phil Williams, eds. *The Reagan Presidency: An Incomplete Revolution?* New York: St. Martin's, 1990.

Hilty, James. *John F. Kennedy: An Idealist Without Illusions.* St. Louis: Forum Press, 1976.

Hoffman, Paul. *The New Nixon.* New York: Tower, 1970.

Hogan, Joseph, ed. *The Reagan Years: The Record in Presidential Leadership.* New York: Manchester, 1990.

Hohenberg, John. *The Bill Clinton Story: Winning the Presidency.* Syracuse: Syracuse University Press, 1994.

Hybel, Alex Roberto. *Power Over Rationality: The Bush Administration and the Gulf Crisis.* Albany: State University of New York Press, 1993.

Isaacs, Arthur R. *Without Honor: Defeat in Vietnam and Cambodia.* New York: Vintage, 1982.

Isaacson, Walter. *Henry Kissinger: A Biography.* New York: Simon & Schuster, 1992.

Jamieson, Kathleen Hall. *Packaging the Presidency: A History of Criticism of Presidential Campaign Advertising.* New York: Oxford University Press, 1984.

Johnson, George W., ed. *The Johnson Presidential Press Conferences.* Vols. 1 and 2. New York: Earl Coleman, 1978.

————. *The Kennedy Presidential Press Conferences.* New York: Earl Coleman, 1978.

————. *The Nixon Presidential Press Conferences.* New York: Earl Coleman, 1978.

Johnson, Haynes. *In the Absence of Power.* New York: Viking, 1980.

———. *Sleepwalking Through History: America in the Reagan Years.* New York: W. W. Norton, 1991.

Johnson, Richard Tanner. *Managing the White House: An Intimate Study of the Presidency.* New York: Harper & Row, 1974.

Jones, Charles O. *The Trusteeship Presidency: Jimmy Carter and the United States Congress.* Baton Rouge: Louisiana State University Press, 1988.

———, ed. *The Reagan Legacy: Promise and Performance.* Chatham, N.J.: Chatham House, 1988.

Kearns, Doris. *Lyndon Johnson and the American Dream.* New York: Harper & Row, 1976.

Kelley, Kitty. *Nancy Reagan: An Unauthorized Biography.* New York: Simon & Schuster, 1991.

Keogh, James. *President Nixon and the Press.* New York: Funk & Wagnalls, 1972.

Kern, Montague, Patricia W. Levering, and Ralph B. Levering. *The Kennedy Crises: The Presidency and Foreign Policy.* Chapel Hill: University of North Carolina Press, 1984.

Kessler, Frank. *The Dilemmas of Presidential Leadership.* Englewood Cliffs, N.J.: Prentice-Hall, 1982.

Kissinger, Henry. *White House Years.* Boston: Little, Brown, 1978.

Kluger, Richard. *The Paper: The Life and Death of the* New York Herald Tribune. New York: Knopf, 1986.

Kolb, Charles. *White House Daze: The Unmaking of Domestic Policy in the Bush Years.* New York: Free Press, 1994.

Kraus, Sidney. *Televised Presidential Debates and Public Policy.* Hillsdale, N.J.: Lawrence Erlbaum, 1988.

———, ed. *The Great Debates: Carter vs. Ford, 1976.* Bloomington: Indiana University Press, 1979.

Kutler, Stanley. *The Wars of Watergate: The Last Crisis of Richard Nixon.* New York: Alfred A. Knopf, 1990.

Kyvig, David E., ed. *Reagan and the World.* Westport, Conn.: Greenwood, 1990.

Lance, Bert. *The Truth of the Matter: My Life In and Out of Politics.* New York: Summit, 1991.

Lang, Gladys Engel, and Kurt Lang. *The Battle for Public Opinion: The President, the Press, and the Polls during Watergate.* New York: Columbia University Press, 1983.

Lasky, Victor. *Jimmy Carter: The Man and the Myth.* New York: Richard Marek, 1979.

Lawson, Steven F. *In Pursuit of Power: Southern Blacks and Electoral Politics, 1965–1982.* New York: Columbia University Press, 1985.

Leuchtenburg, William. *In the Shadow of FDR: From Harry Truman to Ronald Reagan.* Ithaca, N.Y.: Cornell University Press, 1983.

Light, Paul C. *The President's Agenda: Domestic Policy Choice from Kennedy to Carter.* Baltimore: Johns Hopkins University Press, 1982.

Lurie, Leonard. *The Running of Richard Nixon.* New York: Coward, McCann & Geoghegan, 1972.

Lyons, Gene. *Fools for Scandal: How the Media Invented Whitewater.* New York: Franklin Square, 1996.

McCubbins, Mathew D., ed. *Under the Watchful Eye: Managing Presidential Campaigns in the Television Era.* New York: Washington, D.C.: CQ Press, 1992.

MacDougall, Malcolm. *We Almost Made It.* New York: Crown, 1977.

McGinniss, Joe. *The Selling of the President 1968.* New York: Trident, 1969.

MacNeil, Robert. *The Right Place at the Right Time.* Boston: Little, Brown, 1982.

Maglish, Bruce, and Edwin Diamond. *Jimmy Carter: A Character Portrait.* New York: Simon & Schuster, 1979.

Mahood, H. R. *Pressure Groups in American Politics.* New York: Charles Scribner's Sons, 1967.

Mandelbaum, Michael, and Strobe Talbott. *Reagan and Gorbachev.* New York: Random House, 1987.

Mankiewicz, Frank. *Perfectly Clear: Nixon from Whittier to Watergate.* New York: Quadrangle, 1973.

Matalin, Mary, and James Carville. *All's Fair: Love, War, and Running for President.* New York: Simon & Schuster, 1994.

Mervin, David. *Ronald Reagan and the American Presidency.* London: Longman, 1990.

———. *George Bush and the Guardian Presidency.* New York: St. Martin's, 1996.

Meyer, Peter. *James Earl Carter: The Man and the Myth.* Kansas City: Sheed, Andrews and McMeel, 1978.

Milton, Joyce. *The Story of Hillary Rodham Clinton: First Lady of the United States.* Milwaukee: Gareth Stevens Publishers, 1995.

Moore, David W. *The Super Pollsters: How They Measure and Manipulate Public Opinion in America.* New York: Four Walls Eight Windows, 1992.

Morris, Roger. *Partners in Power: The Clintons and Their America.* New York: Henry Holt, 1996.

Muir, William Ker, Jr. *The Bully Pulpit: The Presidential Leadership of Ronald Reagan.* San Francisco: Institute for Contemporary Studies, 1992.

Murray, Robert K., and Tim H. Blessing. *Greatness in the White House: Rating the Presidents.* 2d ed. University Park: Pennsylvania State University Press, 1994.

Nessen, Ronald. *It Sure Looks Different from the Inside.* Chicago: Playboy Press, 1978.

Newfield, Jack. *Robert Kennedy: A Memoir.* New York: Dutton, 1969.

Nixon, Richard M. *RN: The Memoirs of Richard Nixon.* New York: Grosset & Dunlap, 1978.

North, Mark. *Act of Treason: The Role of J. Edgar Hoover in the Assassination of President Kennedy.* New York: Carroll & Graf, 1991.

Osborne, John. *White House Watch: The Ford Years.* New York: Grosset & Dunlap, 1978.

Paterson, Thomas G., ed. *Kennedy's Quest for Victory: American Foreign Policy, 1961–1963.* New York: Oxford, 1989.

Peterson, Mark A. *Legislating Together: The White House and Capitol Hill from Eisenhower to Reagan.* Cambridge, Mass.: Harvard University Press, 1990.

Pierard, Richard V., and Robert D. Linder. *Civil Religion and the Presidency.* Grand Rapids, Mich.: Academic Books, 1988.

Polsby, Nelson. *Consequences of Party Reform.* New York: Oxford University Press, 1983.

Porter, William E. *Assault on the Media: The Nixon Years.* Ann Arbor: University of Michigan, 1976.

Powell, Jody. *The Other Side of the Story.* New York: William Morrow, 1984.

Price, Raymond. *With Nixon.* New York: Viking, 1977.

Quandt, William B. *Decade of Decisions: American Policy toward the Arab-Israeli Conflict, 1967–1976.* Berkeley: University of California Press, 1977.

Rather, Dan, and Gary Paul Gates. *The Palace Guard.* New York: Harper & Row, 1974.

Reagan, Ronald. *Where's the Rest of Me.* New York: Karz, 1981.

———. *An American Life: The Autobiography.* New York: Simon & Schuster, 1990.

Reasoner, Harry. *Before the Colors Fade.* New York: Alfred A. Knopf, 1981.

Reedy, George E. *Lyndon B. Johnson, A Memoir.* New York: Andrews and McMeel, 1982.

Reeves, Richard. *A Ford, Not a Lincoln.* New York: Harcourt Brace Jovanovich, 1975.

———. *President Kennedy: Profile of Power.* New York: Simon & Schuster, 1993.

———. *Running in Place: How Bill Clinton Disappointed America.* Kansas City: Andrews and McMeel, 1996.

Regan, Donald T. *For the Record: From Wall Street to Washington.* New York: Harcourt Brace Jovanovich, 1988.

Renshon, Stanley A. *High Hopes: The Clinton Presidency and the Politics of Ambition.* New York: New York University Press, 1996.

Reston, James B. *Deadline: A Memoir.* New York: Random House, 1991.

Ritter, Kurt, and David Henry. *Ronald Reagan: The Great Communicator.* Westport, Conn.: Greenwood, 1992.

Rivers, William L. *The Other Government: Power and the Washington Media.* New York: Universe Books, 1982.

Rosenstiel, Tom. *The Beat Goes On: President Clinton's First Year with the Media.* Washington, D.C.: 20th Century Fund, 1994.

Rozell, Mark J. *The Press and the Carter Presidency.* Boulder, Colo.: Westview, 1989.

———. *The Press and the Ford Presidency.* Ann Arbor: University of Michigan Press, 1992.

———. *The Press and the Bush Presidency.* Westport, Conn.: Praeger, 1996.

Rubin, Barry. *Paved with Good Intentions: The American Experience In Iran.* New York: Oxford University Press, 1980.

Ryan, Paul B. *The Panama Canal Controversy: U.S. Diplomacy and Defense Interests.* Stanford, Calif.: Hoover Institute, 1977.

Sabato, Larry J., and S. Robert Lichter. *When Should Watchdogs Bark? Media Coverage of the Clinton Scandals.* Lanham, Md.: University Press of America, 1994.

Safire, William. *Before the Fall.* Garden City, N.Y.: Doubleday, 1975.

Salinger, Pierre. *With Kennedy.* Garden City, N.Y.: Doubleday, 1966.

————. *P.S. A Memoir.* New York: St. Martin's, 1995.

Schieffer, Bob, and Gary Paul Gates. *The Acting President.* New York: E. P. Dutton, 1989.

Schlesinger, Arthur. *A Thousand Days: John F. Kennedy in the White House.* Boston: Houghton Mifflin, 1965.

Schorr, Daniel. *Clearing the Air.* New York: Berkley, 1978.

Schram, Martin. *Running for President 1976: The Carter Campaign.* New York: Stein and Day, 1977.

Schwab, Larry M. *The Illusion of a Conservative Reagan Revolution.* New Brunswick, N.J.: Transaction, 1991.

Shannon, William V. *The Heir Apparent: Robert Kennedy and the Struggle for Power.* New York: Macmillan, 1967.

Shogan, Robert. *Promises to Keep: Carter's First 100 Days.* New York: Thomas Y. Crowell, 1977.

Shoup, Laurence H. *The Carter Presidency and Beyond.* Palo Alto, Calif.: Ramparts, 1980.

Sick, Gary. *All Fall Down: America's Tragic Encounter with Iran.* New York: Random House, 1985.

————. *October Surprise: America's Hostages in Iran and the Election of Ronald Reagan.* New York: Random House, 1991.

Sidey, Hugh. *John F. Kennedy, President: A Reporter's Inside Story.* New York: Atheneum, 1963.

————. *A Very Personal Presidency: Lyndon Johnson in the White House.* New York: Atheneum, 1968.

Sidey, Hugh, and Fred Ward. *Portrait of a President.* New York: Harper & Row, 1975.

Simon, William E. *A Time for Truth.* New York: Berkley, 1978.

Smith, Gaddis. *Morality, Reason, and Power: American Diplomacy in the Carter Years.* New York: Hill and Wang, 1986.

Smith, Hedrick. *The Power Game: How Washington Works.* New York: Random House, 1988.

Sorensen, Theodore C. *Kennedy.* New York: Harper & Row, 1965.

Spalding, Henry D. *The Nixon Nobody Knows.* New York: Jonathan David, 1972.

Speakes, Larry. *Speaking Out: The Reagan Presidency from Inside the White House.* New York: Charles Scribner's Sons, 1988.

Spear, Joseph C. *Presidents and the Press: The Nixon Legacy*. Cambridge, Mass.: MIT Press, 1984.

Spragens, William C. *The Presidency and the Mass Media in the Age of Television*. Lanham, Md.: University Press of America, 1979.

Spragens, William C., and Carole Ann Terwoord. *From Spokesperson to Press Secretary: White House Media Operations*. Washington, D.C.: University Press of America, 1980.

Stempel, Guido H., III, and John W. Windhauser, eds. *The Media in the 1984 and 1988 Presidential Campaigns*. Westport, Conn.: Greenwood, 1991.

Stewart, James B. *Blood Sport: The President and his Adversaries*. New York: Simon & Schuster, 1996.

Stroud, Kandy. *How Jimmy Won: The Victory Campaign from Plains to the White House*. New York: Morrow, 1977.

Sullivan, William. *Mission to Iran*. New York: W. W. Norton, 1981.

Sussman, Barry. *The Great Cover-Up: Nixon and the Scandal of Watergate*. New York: Signet, 1974.

Szulc, Tad. *Then and Now: How the World Has Changed Since World War II*. New York: William Morrow, 1990.

Tebell, John, and Sarah Miles Watts. *The Press and the Presidency: From George Washington to Ronald Reagan*. New York: Oxford, 1985.

TerHorst, Gerald F. *Gerald Ford and the Future of the Presidency*. New York: Third Press, 1974.

Thomas, Helen. *Dateline: White House*. New York: Macmillan, 1975.

Thompson, Kenneth, ed. *Ten Presidents and the Press*. Washington, D.C.: University Press of America, 1980.

———. *The Ford Presidency: Twenty-two Intimate Perspectives of Gerald R. Ford*. Lanham, Md.: University Press of America, 1988.

Turner, Michael. *The Vice President as Policy Maker: Rockefeller in the Ford White House*. Westport, Conn.: Greenwood, 1982.

VanDeMark, Brian. *Into the Quagmire: Lyndon Johnson and the Escalation of the Vietnam War*. New York: Oxford University Press, 1991.

Vaughn, Stephen. *Ronald Reagan in Hollywood*. New York: Cambridge University Press, 1994.

Walden, Gregory S. *On Best Behavior: The Clinton Administration and Ethics in Government*. Indianapolis: Hudson Institute, 1996.

Walsh, Kenneth T. *Feeding the Beast: The White House Versus the Press*. New York: Random House, 1996.

Watson, Mary Ann. *The Expanding Vista: American Television in the Kennedy Years*. New York: Oxford University Press, 1990.

Weaver, David, Doris Graber, Maxwell McCombs, and Chaim Eyal. *Media Agenda Setting in Presidential Elections*. New York: Praeger, 1981.

Wendt, Lloyd. *Chicago Tribune: The Rise of a Great American Newspaper*. Chicago: Rand McNally, 1979.

White, Theodore. *The Making of the President 1960*. New York: Atheneum, 1961.

_____ . *The Making of the President 1964*. New York: Atheneum, 1965.

_____ . *The Making of the President 1968*. New York: Atheneum, 1969.

_____ . *The Making of the President 1972*. New York: Atheneum, 1973.

_____ . *Breach of Faith: The Fall of Richard Nixon*. New York: Atheneum, 1975.

_____ . *America in Search of Itself: The Making of the President, 1956–1980*. New York: Harper & Row, 1982.

Wicker, Tom. *On Press*. New York: Viking, 1978.

Wildavsky, Aaron. *The Beleaguered Presidency*. New Brunswick, N.J.: Transaction, 1991.

Wills, Gary. *Nixon Agonistes: The Crisis of the Self-Made Man*. New York: New American Library, 1979.

_____ . *Innocents at Home: Reagan's America*. Garden City, N.Y.: Doubleday, 1987.

Witcover, Jules. *The Resurrection of Richard Nixon*. New York: G. P. Putnam's Sons, 1970.

_____ . *Marathon: The Pursuit of the Presidency, 1972– 1976*. New York: Viking, 1977.

Wofford, Harris. *Of Kennedys and Kings: Making Sense of the Sixties*. New York: Farrar, Straus & Giroux, 1980.

Woodruff, Judy. *"This is Judy Woodruff at the White House."* Reading, Mass.: Addison-Wesley, 1982.

Woodstone, Arthur. *Nixon's Head*. New York: St. Martin's Press, 1972.

Woodward, Bob. *The Commanders*. New York: Simon & Schuster, 1991.

_____ . *The Agenda*. New York: Simon & Schuster, 1994.

_____ . *The Choice*. New York: Simon & Schuster, 1996.

Woodward, Bob, and Carl Bernstein. *All the President's Men*. New York: Simon & Schuster, 1974.

_____ . *The Final Days*. New York: Simon & Schuster, 1976.

Zelizer, Barbie. *Covering the Body: The Kennedy Assassination, the Media, and the Shaping of Collective Memory*. Chicago: University of Chicago Press, 1992.

INDEX

About the Author

LOUIS W. LIEBOVICH, Professor of Journalism and Media Studies at the University of Illinois, was a reporter for three newspapers in the 1970s, devoting most of his time to investigative reporting. He received his Ph.D. in mass communication from the University of Wisconsin in 1986. He writes articles and books on media history, particularly about the press and the presidency. This is his fourth book. Three others, published by Praeger, are: *The Press and the Origins of the Cold War, 1944–1947* (1988), *The Last Jew from Wegrow* (editor, 1991), and *Bylines in Despair: Herbert Hoover, the Great Depression, and the U.S. News Media* (1994).